THE PSYCHOLOGY
OF
RELIGION

THE PSYCHOLOGY
OF
RELIGION

by WAYNE E. OATES

WORD BOOKS, Publisher • Waco, Texas

This book is gratefully dedicated to the following students who were members of the class in the psychology of religion at the Southern Baptist Theological Seminary in the fall of 1972. They were my comrades in thought and study as we searched out the contents of this book together. I am honored to call them not only my students but more than that—my junior colleagues. Their names are as follows:

John Robert Amick
Robert G. Anderson, Jr.
Thomas Daniel Arnold
Kenneth Pershing Bentley
James Everett Chase
Ron Wayne Coker
Richard David Cowart
Vivian Virginia Davis
Henry Hampton Dunn
Jimmie Lee England
Harris Wayne Etheridge
Ronald Gene Ferguson
Russell Inman Gregory
Charles Franklin Hagan
Maurice Gene Hancock
Larry Douglas Hart
David Marlin Holley

James Little Jarrard
Robert Tillman Kendall
George Martin Klee
Danny Michael McCauley
Cherry A. Moore
Marvin Powell Nail
James Edward Norwood
Charles Avery Parker, Jr.
David Gaynor Parker
A. Ronald Richardson
Hilda Grace Scott
Michael Cecil Sigmon
Stephen Ray Skaggs
Jerry Don Smith
Randy Bryan Smith
Daryl James Tiller
Richard Derle Underwood
Thomas William Young, Jr.

CONTENTS

PREFACE

This book was developed in dialogue with students and is aimed to be a stimulus to conversation with other students. Student input has had much to do with the kind of thinking that I have developed in these pages.

I have sought to be objective in my presentation. Yet, I frankly admit, confess, and appreciate the Judaeo-Christian heritage of which I am a part and to which I am indebted. However, in taking such a stance, I hope that I have done so in such a way as to open conversation with people of other religions and with frank secularists who would refuse to be identified with any religion at all.

The psychological point of view here is not merely eclectic, but it does recognize the resources of many different schools of psychology. If one sought to categorize what is said here to my satisfaction, he would say that the attitude that prevails is a phenomenological one, and the method that persists is a developmental one. Yet this is not a stance taken to the exclusion of the hard-earned findings of experimental and behavioral psychologists. I would hope that a larger perspective than any of these holds the book together in a point of view. The Hebrew and Greek languages are at their bases structured, psychological points of view to those who look closely enough. This I have done at many points in the book. It is important to say so here. Yet a person does not have to be expert in these languages to follow the thought because careful translation of ideas is inconspicuously done.

I am indebted to Mrs. Wade Rowatt for her careful copy editing of this manuscript.

WAYNE E. OATES

Louisville, Kentucky

1

DEFINITIONS OF RELIGION

The word religion *will be used so often in the following pages that it will* be meaningless unless carefully defined. As one pulls down his dictionary and other authoritative sources and tries to pin down the meaning of this word, he is impressed by the vagueness, mixed feelings, and childish memories of people's religious backgrounds that characterize the mind of the average person. Stereotypes of certain religious people cloud the average person's perception when the word *religion* is used.

Furthermore, as one takes a psychological approach to defining religion, he sees that many concepts of psychology, especially those of personality theories, are really secular statements of older religious value systems. One might say that the contemporary educated person tends to think many religious thoughts, but he does so in the psychological idiom of today without necessarily being aware that these are religiously significant thoughts. My hypothesis is that the value systems of contemporary psychologists of personality are in fact secular statements of distinctly personal interpretations of religion. In the process of secularization, the institutional and transcendental aspects of religion have been removed, leaving the humanistic values of prophetic religion.

Furthermore, the psychology of religion is a concerted effort to bring these sacred and secular definitions of human life into dialogue with each other and to speak of God in both a sacred and a secular manner. The psychology of religion is an effort to identify the human experience of the divine, to identify and purge the distinctly idolatrous distinctions of religious experience, and to unmask the elements of human deceptiveness in what otherwise would seem to be lofty, transcendental religiosity. As such, the psychology of religion is a combined effort to appreciate the idea of the holy in human life and to keep the experiences of the religious consciousness down to earth.

15

In an effort to define religion, therefore, the first task is to clear away some misconceptions.

Some common misconceptions of religion arise from overclassifying it with one particular aspect of personality. For instance, religion is often overidentified with mind, reason, or emotion. Such pigeonholing of religion as a part of life leads to faulty thinking, vagueness of definition, and damaging practice. Religion and emotion are not coextensive terms. This distinction in itself is not clear without some plain examples.

Leuba, for instance, defined religion by dividing definitions current at the time of his writing into the intellectualistic, the voluntaristic, and the affectivistic. He himself defined religion as a "type of rational behavior." [1] However, the Hebrew conception of the totality of the being of persons, reinforced by contemporary scientific emphasis upon the wholeness of the person, makes Leuba's definition a historical museum piece.

In line with this overclassification, religious conversions are often rejected upon the value judgment that they are emotional experiences. A more precise example of confusion wrought by overclassifying religion with reason is found in discussions of mental illness. Pickett quotes St. Thomas Aquinas as saying:

> I answer that of actions performed by man, those only are properly called human which are proper to man as man. Now man is different from irrational animals in that he is the master of his actions. Wherefore those actions alone are properly called human of which man is the master. Now man is master of his actions through his reason and his will: whence also free will is defined as the faculty of will and reason. Therefore those actions are rightly called human which proceed from a deliberate will. And if any other actions are found in man, they may be called actions of a man but not properly human actions, since they are not proper to man as man.[2]

Such a hypothesis about religion assumes that when reason or mind departs, then the mentally sick person is something less than a person, something other than human. A common expression of this is that a person who is genuinely religious cannot be mentally ill. Somehow or other he is supposed to have lost his religion along with his mind. This is not what Pickett and St. Thomas necessarily mean to say, but it is exactly what the populace hear them say. Such a point of view does not have to be repeated more than once to prompt the treatment of mentally ill people as animals, such as Philip Pinel encountered at Bicêtre. (Pinel, it will be recalled, was an early psychiatrist in France who astounded his patients by releasing them from cages and chains in which they had

been bound by former superintendents of the hospital.) Mental patients
—people without reason—were caged and used for Sunday afternoon
amusements of persons who visited the place as if it were a zoo. The
Gadarene villagers accorded this kind of treatment to the demoniac.
They consigned him to the graveyard without the benefit of a funeral.
If his reason was gone, he was no more useful than the dead.

Such overclassification of religion with both reason or mind is also
reflected in the popular superstition that if a person is said to be mentally ill, necessarily he is not bright intellectually. The college counselor,
in talking with the family of a mentally sick student, will hear them say,
"Our son couldn't be mentally ill. He has made straight A's in all his
work up to this year!" The compulsive grade getter may very well be
considered mentally healthy and not be able to function competently
outside a school environment.

The concept of mind as being the total person has been challenged
by the theories of men like Kurt Lewin. He saw the intellectual or
cognitive aspect of personality as only one dimension of the dynamic
personality. Attitudes such as have been described are essentially value
judgments of persons rather than dependable and constructive descriptions of the nature of personality, according to Lewin.[3] Consequently,
from our perspective here, to overidentify religion with a personal desire
to glorify the intellectual or rational dimensions of human life as a
whole does little more than obscure rather than clarify the meaning of
persons and of religion.

Of course, overclassification of the nature of personality with mind
and reason is the obverse side of the rejection of the body as a legitimate
part of the personality and of the concerns of religion. This is alien to
the biblical conception of the wholeness of man. To be drawn into such
misconceptions results in the kind of confusion of which Goethe speaks
when he says:

> . . . none e'er comprehended
> How soul and body wedded are blended,
> Hold fast, as if defying separation
> Yet never cease their mutual irritation.[4]

Yet more than this, the director of religious education, the college
counselor, and the pastor see the results of such confused thinking in
counseling with students who perceive their basic bodily needs as evil, or
as without either moral or religious dimensions, or both.

The mutual irritation due to distorted teaching adds insult to injury
for the developing attitudes of persons, particularly in their preparation
for and participation in marriage. The rigid dichotomies of flesh and
spirit underlying many of the conflicts that prevent people from having
happy marriages are alien to the Hebrew mind, the prophetic witness,

and to great seers of history such as Browning. Therefore, the division and overclassification of personality or religion must be carefully rejected. In the spirit of Browning,

> Let us not always say,
> "Spite of this flesh today,
> I strove, made head, gained ground upon the whole!"

> As the bird wings and sings;
> Let us cry: "All good things
> Are ours, nor soul helps flesh more now, than flesh helps soul."

A BIBLICAL VIEW OF RELIGION

Many misconceptions of religion are outgrowths of distorted perceptions of human nature. Many of these distortions are challenged both by biblical understandings of the wholeness of man and recent holistic theories of personality espoused by psychologists. A review of some of these will clarify more accurately the meaning of religion.

Some of our distorted views of human nature grow out of Roman psychology. This psychology of human nature, for example, is embedded in the Latin language. The Latin word *persona* is a noun which is derived from a verb form *personare* which means "to sound through." The word has two usages in the Latin. The first meaning is "a mask," used by players in a drama to cover the whole head and to be changed to fit the character to be represented. The second meaning is "a personage, a character, a part" and is used to refer to the part, the role, or the character played by a person in the drama. This can be expanded a bit to refer to life itself as a drama, as did Shakespeare when he said that all the world is a stage and each of us is an actor. Thus, a secondary meaning is derived in which *persona* means the part or character which anyone plays in the world. This can be further developed in use to refer to any human being, and especially to his personage, or that certain standing that a person has by reason of his age, sex, or marital status among his fellows. This latter reference was particularly important in the Roman world in which the word *persona* was used to distinguish a freeborn citizen from a slave.

The Hebrews had no word for person. Nor did they have a word for body. The body was the person, and there was no differentiation between the physical and psychical, the natural and supernatural. In Hebrew thought, the *nephesh* is the inner aspect of the body, and the body is the outward form of the *nephesh*. "What happens to the body happens to the *nephesh*, so that even the mutilation of the dead body can be a terrible thing." [5] To read the Greek idea of the soul into the Hebrew word is a mistake because the word "describes the unity we call man" and may at times be used to mean life itself. *Nephesh* refers to "self," and "stands for personal pronouns—I, Thou, or He." [6]

Leb is another Hebrew word which, like *nephesh,* traps the elusive Hebrew understanding of that which the Western mind has come to call person. This word, usually translated "heart," is used frequently "to denote the personality as a whole on its inner side, the inner life or character." [7] *Nephesh* is the total person as a whole, and *leb* is its inner value and being. These are the two words native to the Hebrew understanding of the meaning of persons. When, therefore, the Bible uses the word *religion* in a positive sense, it is referring to the open, maskless experience of a person in relation to God in his inner life and character.

In Jesus' teachings the word *kardia* is used in the same sense that the Old Testament uses the Hebrew word *leb* for heart. The heart is the center of man's being, the source of the issues of life, and the core of man's spiritual motivation. In Jesus' teachings *psuche* and *pneuma* are used in companionate but not synonymous meanings. *Psuche* referred to the very life of the person which was more precious than anything else, that which it did not profit to gain everything and lose. *Pneuma* is a word which puts this in relation, not just to itself and its own preciousness, but to God, and was used to refer to the eternal, God-encountering dimension of man's total life-relationship. This relationship is the stuff of which authentic religion is made.

The Hebrews of the Old Testament did not have a word for the body but thought in terms of the whole body being exercised at any given and living moment through any given part of the body. However, in the New Testament, and particularly in the teachings of Paul, two words, *sarx* and *soma,* translated "flesh" and "body," capture the New Testament meaning of personality most completely. As Robinson says, these two words underscore the relational character of the religious dimensions of personality. In essence they

designate different aspects of the human relationship to God. *While sarx stands for man, in the solidarity of creation, in his distance from God, soma stands for man, in the solidarity of creation, as made for God.*[8]

Also, Rudolf Bultmann says that the word *soma* for "body" is the "most comprehensive term for the total person of man." He confesses with others that it is the "most complex," and understanding it is most difficult. But in his own definite way he says:

Man, his person as a whole, can be denoted by soma. . . . *Man is called soma in respect to his being able to make himself the object of his own action or to experience himself as the subject to whom something happens.* He can be called soma, that is, *as having a relationship to himself—as being able in a certain sense to distinguish himself from himself.* Or, more exactly, he is so called as that self from whom he, as subject, distinguishes himself, the self whom he can perceive as subjected to an occurrence that springs from a will other than his own. It is as such a self that man is called *soma*.[9]

Consequently, the rich, inner diversity of man's selfhood as a self in relationship with itself and in encounter with God emerges. The New Testament conception of personal religion presents this in a way which is missing in the monolithic concepts of the Old Testament and the segmented views of the Greek and Roman world.

Another Greek word *prosopon* used in the New Testament gives a rich and lucid meaning to person. This word is usually translated "face," or "countenance" in the literal sense, but it is used with several different connotations which reflect the essentially religious overtones of the meaning of personality. Its usage is quite akin to the Roman or Latin usage of *persona* with some significant additions. Four passages from the New Testament reflect the various shades of meaning with which the word is invested. In Matthew 6:16 Jesus refers to the Pharisees who disfigure their faces in fasting to be seen of men. He urges his disciples to be different. The face as a deceptive mask, hiding the real self, a pseudoself of appearances, reflects the rift that may come in personality between the apparent and the real self.

Anne Morrow Lindbergh gets at this dimension of duplicity between the apparent and the real self in her person when she writes:

> I find I am shedding hypocrisy in human relationships. What a rest that will be! The most exhausting thing in life, I have discovered, is being insincere. That is why so much of social life is exhausting; one is wearing a mask. I have shed my mask.[10]

Socrates expresses this clearly also in his prayer:

> O Lord, give me beauty in the inner soul
> And may the outward man and the inward man be at one!

In a second passage which uses *prosopon,* Paul describes his having refused to eat with the Gentiles (Gal. 2:11). Here religion worthy of acceptance is seen as the direct encounter of selves-in-relation to each other. The third passage refers to a sort of external religion in terms of the personage, role, or status of a person, just as does *persona* in the Latin. This is exemplified in 2 Corinthians 5:12 in which Paul talks about men priding themselves on the positions that they hold, the status they have achieved, and so on. Sincerity and inner integrity are missing. Finally, a fourth connotation is given to the word *prosopon* in Luke 9:51 in which the purposive nature of religion is symbolized in the fact that Jesus "set his face steadfastly to go to Jerusalem." Here the idea of purpose, goal, and intention is clearly marked out as an identifying dimension of religious faith.

In these four passages, which could be paralleled by other relevant passages, genuine religion may be defined in terms of the real self as over against the pseudoself; it is defined in terms of the dynamic interactions of an interpersonal nature in the betweenness situations of men, as Buber calls it; it is defined in terms of the purposive striving which characterizes a person's life; it is identified in terms of the role that men take in the drama of society.

Lexical definitions of religion, as such, are enlightening in the face of the discussions of the meaning of personality. The Latin language, in which the Roman psychology of man is embedded, also gives a definition of religion which aims at correcting the disjointedness of human nature. The mask and the total human being are separated. The behavior and the inner reality of man are at variance. Therefore, religion at its best pulls mankind together in inner peace and social concord. The word *religion* itself is a transliteration of the Latin word *religio* meaning to bind, to bind fast, or to fasten up. It is defined as reverence for God or the gods, or the fear of God. The word also carries with it a connotation of scrupulousness, anxiety to fulfill a covenant or an obligation. Furthermore, it refers to the objects of worship, veneration, and sacred feeling. The word is obviously related to another word, *religo,* which carries the meaning of chaining or fastening or holding back. This catches up two philosophical definitions which accent the ethical seriousness and the moral sensitivity to peril that usually go with religion.

Immanuel Kant defined religion as "the recognition of all our duties as divine commands." Also, Bergson related the religious character of man to his need to hold back his own intelligence from destroying him. Religion is the chaining of man's intelligence much as Prometheus was chained to the rock after having stolen the fire from heaven. Søren Kierkegaard says that we enter a certain kind of irreligion when we exchange our call to be prophets for our desire to be geniuses. Also, man's search for redemption began, according to the Hebrew faith, when he came to know good and evil. The common interpretation put on the binding quality of religion is that men are religious in a community of faith in which a tie of common worship binds their hearts together in the love of their God. The betweenness situation of the Greek is thus accented in the binding character of religion as seen through the Latin.

The word *religion* is not a major concept in the New Testament. The word which is translated "religion" is used very few times. There are two words for religion in the Greek. First, *threskeia* refers to the outward religious behavior of a person, such as in Acts 26:5. In Acts 26:5 Luke uses *threskeia* to refer to Judaism; and in James 1:27 the word is used in the positive sense to refer to the practical work of controlling one's speech and of caring for orphans and widows. Second, *sebomai* means the inner, personal act of the worship or fear-reverence of God. In Acts 16:14 Lydia is referred to as a worshiper of God, for example. Usually the word *religion* is rather foreign to the concerns of the New Testament.

The contemporary defensiveness about religion on the part of people who are involved in professional religious work was of little concern to the writers of the New Testament. Usually, as did the eighth-century (B.C.) prophets, they found themselves against what was ordinarily thought of as being religion in their day. This is not to taboo the use of the word *religion* today. Its meaning has been enriched with all the great gains of the Christian faith as a living religion. At the same time, this negative use of the term, native to the original prophetic attitude, still serves to remind the modern Christian of the difference between folk religion or primitive nature religion and the worship of the true and living God in Christ. However, the words for personal faith and religion are rich with positive meaning in the New Testament, as has already been seen.

PHILOSOPHICAL AND PSYCHOLOGICAL DEFINITIONS OF RELIGION

SUPREME VALUE

Henry Nelson Wieman and Regina Wieman, in their search for a "normative psychology of religion," built their definition of religion on the central importance of a supreme loyalty or value. They interpreted sin, conversion, and religious growth upon the never-ending assent of the Spirit of mankind toward the apex of values that are lastingly supreme.[11] Anton Boisen spoke of the nature of a person's spiritual struggle as the search for the approval of "those whose approval is most worthwhile." Paul Tillich defined religion and/or faith as the ultimate—as over against the penultimate—concern of a person. The demonic enters life when one attaches ultimate concern to a finite, penultimate object. Tillich called this the "absolutizing of the relative."

First, both personality and religion are seen as the highest value of mankind. As Goethe poetically states:

> Folk and serf and conqueror
> These concede in every age:
> The sons of earth find greatest joy
> In personality alone.[12]

Personality is perceived as being of supreme value then. As Allport defines religion,

A man's religion is the audacious bid he makes to bind himself to creation and to the Creator. It is his ultimate attempt to enlarge and to complete his own personality by finding the supreme context in which he rightly belongs.[13]

The supreme value of personality is in itself an expression of religious concern. This was the hallmark of the ethical teachings of Jesus. Jesus said: "The Sabbath is made for man and not man for the Sabbath." He reflected this in his treatment of people, in the way he manifested tenderness to those whose persons were facing destruction, and in the way he martialed his aggressions toward those who exploited human life and avoided their own selves in the process. They thought that they did God a service, that is, that they were religious.

This dimension of the supreme value of personality, and for that matter of life itself, comes to the surface of man's thoughts when the idea of suicide occurs to him. More primitive and unsophisticated individuals would express this insight in terms of a taboo. Uneducated persons might incorporate it into the familiar theological colloquialism that "all people who commit suicide are thereby sent to hell." Others may go so far as to say that this teaching is in the Bible, although it is not.

Even the most sophisticated cannot laugh away this feeling of ultimate responsibility for deciding to maintain or to end life. In fact, they may say that the main reason for the wrongfulness of suicide lies in the fact that there is a God who has created man and man has not created himself. To thus end this creation is to break the human bond and, hence, any bond with its Source. It is to attempt to be God, to think that one can dispose of his own destiny. Thus, the sense of ultimate value in human personality and human life pervades all these reactions.

UNIQUENESS OF INDIVIDUALITY

A second theme in philosophical and psychological definitions of religion and personality is that of the uniqueness of individuality of the person. Schleiermacher epitomizes this:

> For every man has in him all that another man has, but it is all differently determined; and the greatest similarity is only a diminishing or [relatively] vanishing difference.[14]

Cattell, on the other hand, defines personality as "that which enables us to predict what [man] will do in a given situation." [15] In other words, it is that pattern of dependable individuality which characterizes him. This helps his fellows to know him as an individual different from other people.

Just as personality is defined in terms of individuality, of the uniqueness of the person, so also is religion defined by Whitehead in terms of man's solitariness. He says that "religion is what the individual does with his own solitude." [16] He accents this by calling religion man's solitariness. This, Whitehead says, is symbolized by Prometheus on his rock, Mahomet brooding in the desert, Buddha under his tree, and the lonely Christ on his cross. Whereas this facet of Whitehead's thinking reflects his main thrust about mutuality in human life, and the isolated sentence does him injustice, nevertheless, this partial hearing of him has been picked up by arch individualists and used to denote the essence of religion. The remarkable diversity of American religious life may be the outworking of such individualism in the religious life, as such, and in the American culture as well. Heavy emphases upon a highly individual conversion, as well as the insistence of the nonconformists upon the communion with God through nature, arts, and personal meditation, give some empirical credence to this point of view. Berdyaev appreciates loneliness in religious living in a remarkably poignant way when he says:

> Only when man is alone . . . does he become aware of his personality, of his originality, of his singularity and uniqueness, of his distinctness from every one and everything else. A man may feel himself definitely more alone in the midst of his co-religionists than in the midst of men of totally different beliefs and persuasions.[17]

The English romantic poet, Lord George Gordon Byron, caught the quintessence of the religion of solitude and its dimensions in personality in his *Childe Harold's Pilgrimage:*

> There is pleasure in the pathless woods,
> There is rapture on the lonely shore,
> There is society where none intrudes,
> By the deep Sea, and music in its roar;
> I love not Man the less, but Nature more,
> From these our interviews, in which I steal
> From all I may be, or have been before,
> To mingle with the Universe, and feel
> What I can never express, yet cannot at all conceal.[18]

The fact still remains that the need to withdraw from the clattery external interferences into one's own inner communion with the Infinite articulates the religion of many people today and characterizes them as persons.

THE COMMUNAL DEFINITIONS

Conversely, the theme of individuality and solitude in the definitions of both personality and religion stands over against the third theme of the communal definition of both religion and personality. Berdyaev does not stop with individuality in his definition of religion, for instance. He sees it in tension with the need of man for relationship with his fellows and says that absolute solitude would be synonymous with hell and nonbeing.[19]

Religion implies a relationship; it may be defined as an attempt to overcome solitude, to release the Ego from its seclusion, to achieve community and intimacy. . . . But only God is capable of overcoming solitude.[20]

In the spirit of the New Testament aversion for identifying things of the spiritual life with what is commonly known as religion, Berdyaev continues the preceding quotation by saying:

Religion only implies a relationship, and, as such, can only be secondary and transitory. Transcendence and plenitude, as well as the purpose of existence, are only manifest in God. There is a tendency to overlook the fact that God is the primary consideration, that religion can prove an obstacle to man's communication with God.[21]

Certainly Harry Stack Sullivan would be among those psychotherapists who identify personality with man's need for relationship and say that personality *is* relationship. Apart from the interaction that goes on between man and man, personality does not exist. As Sullivan puts it, "People behave in interpersonal fields." [22] Roughly speaking, a whole grouping of contemporary psychologists of personality define a person in terms of the interactions of persons with each other.[23]

This accents a theme of interpretation of personality that needs separate identity: the individual's need for community. The basic conviction of certain psychologists is that personality becomes what it is by reason of the dynamic confrontation between persons. The contemporary philosopher who has drawn the attention of many different fields of inquiry today is Martin Buber. He, too, identifies personality with community. In his book, *Between Man and Man,* he says that

. . . modern collectivism is too often mistaken for community, but collectivity is not a binding but a bundling together: individuals packed together, armed and equipped in common, with only as much life from man to man as will inflame the marching step. But community . . . is the being no longer side by side *with* one another of a multitude of persons and this multitude, though it also moves towards one goal yet experiences . . . a dynamic facing of, . . . a flowing from *I* to *Thou.* . . . Bundled together, men march without *Thou* and without *I*.[24]

The whole discussion of personality and religion as individual over against community points to a basic polarity that exists between the individual and his community. Personality and religion are more often defined in terms of this reciprocity. Angyal chooses the term *biosphere* to cover these two forces in life itself. Within the biosphere is the organismic autonomy and the environmental heteronomy which are at one and the same time parts of each other. "Every process which is a resultant" of these two forces in relation to each other is part of the life process. These are really not antagonistic forces. They are "only degrees of ego proximity and ego distance. The degrees of ego proximity and ego distance are the symbolic expression of the gradient of autonomy and heteronomy." [25]

This is not unlike Schleiermacher's interpretation of life and personality as the "alternation between an 'abiding-in-self' (*Insichbleiben*) and a 'passing-beyond-self' (*Aussichheraustreten*) on the part of the subject." [26] In another place,[27] Schleiermacher says that the single and the particular are not possible except by means of a unity with God and community. The sum total of religion is the feeling of dependence upon the Absolutely Dependable.

T. S. Eliot poetically states the ever-existing tension of polarity between individuality and community in religion and personality when he says:

> What life have you if you have not life together?
> There is no life that is not in community,
> And no community not lived in praise of God.
> Even the anchorite who meditates alone,
> For whom the days and nights repeat the praise of God,
> Prays for the Church, the Body of Christ incarnate.[28]

ETHICAL DEFINITIONS

Definitions of religion and personality move in the direction of ethical absolutes at many points. Immanuel Kant, as one would expect, accentuates the ethical dimensions of personality and religion. As has already been noted, he defines religion as the interpretation of all duties as divine commands. In talking of personality, he says that everything in creation except personality "can be used by man as a means to an end; but man himself, the rational creature, is an end in himself. He is the subject of the moral law and is sacred by virtue of his individual freedom." [29] Furthermore, Berdyaev again says that personality "has an autonomous validity which prevents it from being converted into a means." [30] As Goethe has said, "with all its hundred thousand pranks, the World is one enormous Fool!" [31] The autonomous nature of personality is such as to make it always a subject rather than an object. It will not be fooled into being treated long as a thing!

This is the moving spirit of the writings of Martin Buber who focuses the religious quest and the quest for the meaning of personality together into a synoptic view. The I-Thou relationship is characterized by loving, encountering, and participating. The person is not an it but is either I or Thou in encounter. The moving dynamic of this encounter is love. As Berdyaev says, "Love transforms the Ego into a personality." [32] This is why Brunner makes the ethical distinction that the individual truly becomes a person by responsible love for others in community. "Individuality," he says, "is fulfillment of our creation as persons destined for community." [33]

Such a creative tension between the individual and the communal character of personality and religion, however, begins to give point, direction, and purpose to human life. This suggests the definitive statements about personality and religion. A consistent theme of the purposiveness of personality tends to separate philosophically oriented psychologists from the purely descriptive psychologists. Prescott Lecky gives the clearest statement of this point of view in his posthumously published book when he says:

> Personality is a concept of the organism, created by us as a means of assisting our understanding of psychological phenomena. Personality goal is the striving of the individual to maintain a unified organization. [34]

Gordon Allport, in the Terry Lectures of 1954, challenges his fellow psychologists to enlarge their horizons without sacrificing the gains they have made. He emphasizes the purposes of mankind that not only preserve life but make it meaningfully worth living. These purposes have a futurity to them and do not dwell merely on the past history of the individual. Personality is characterized in Allport's interpretative definition by an ongoing purposive growth which he calls "becoming." Religion to him represents the "final meanings achieved by unique personalities in diverse lands and times." [35]

More recently, Viktor Frankl has challenged the purely erotic and/or aggressive motivation of human personality and identified the will to meaning as the stuff of which human life is made. This parallels the thought of Paul Tillich in his concept of the basic, existential threats to human life—the threat of moral condemnation, the threat of meaninglessness, and the threat of annihilation or nonbeing. Survival to both Frankl and Tillich is more than bare biological survival. Human life is wasted without purpose, meaning, and creative impulses in existence. This kind of teaching has most recently taken hold in the human potential movement which has grown out of the "third force" psychology of Abraham Maslow. He says:

> The human being needs a framework of values, a philosophy of life, a religion or religion-surrogate to live by, in about the same sense that he needs sunlight, calcium, or love. . . . What man needs but doesn't have, he seeks for unceasingly, and he becomes dangerously ready to jump at *any* hope, good or bad. . . . We need a validated, usable system of human values that we can believe in and devote ourselves to (be willing to die for), because they are true rather than because we are exhorted "to believe and have faith." [36]

Maslow seems to have been searching for an empirically validated basis for living to the level of one's highest aspirations, being a productive and creative human being, and having a reliable basis for being a "hope-full" person. The phenomenon of hope becomes the enlargement of any vital definition of religion. Paul Pruyser speaks of this persuasively in his discussion of the dynamics of hoping. Following Gabriel Marcel, Pruyser says that *hoping* is a verb, a kind of action in the face of calamity.

> In order to hope, one must first have a sense of captivity, of being caught by the human condition. . . . The less life is felt as captivity, the less a person is susceptible to hoping. . . . If reality does not first give us reasons for despairing, it cannot give us grounds for hoping.[37]

Faith becomes religion when hoping is turned from a form of action in the face of tragedy to become a noun used to transmit an idea from one generation to another.

RELIGION AND THE KNOWN AND UNKNOWN

Gilbert Murray, in his book, *Five Stages of Religion,* has said that religion's basic concern is with the "uncharted regions" of the universe. The maps of the world are scientific expressions of the known. The mythologies and religions of man enable him to cope with the unknown, the uncharted regions. When he moves into these regions, he relies upon intuition, courage, adventure, and faith. His beliefs guide him when his knowledge thins out. Murray says that "all around us on every side there is an uncharted region, just fragments of the fringe of it explored, and those imperfectly; it is with this that religion deals" and that we deal with this region "directly, and by methods of emotion on sub-conscious apprehension." [38]

However valid Murray's perception may be, the point of view deals with only one side of the paradox of knowing and not knowing. Left as is, Murray's idea of religion would leave us with what Eric Rust calls "the God of the gaps." By this he means the inadequate view of religion as being a bridge over the gaps in man's knowledge. This would mean that the more one knows the less need one would have for religion. Some empirical evidence would suggest that as people move into the *mysterium-tremendum* of life, as Rudolph Otto put it, the more articulately religious they seem to become. A case in point is the burst of religious behavior on the part of both the astronauts and the populace during the flights to the moon. Yet this is counteracted by paradoxical data when one sees the decreasing amount of religious concern as well as public attention as the moon-walks become better known and more commonplace. Less religious affect is noticeable now that we know—or think we know—more.

Yet, to leave the matter here is to overlook the way in which the emotions of awe and gratitude take on a religious reference to God when the grandeur of man's knowledge appears at its zenith. We also tend to become religious in the presence of awful terror. An example is the near-phobia we feel about cancer. We can give thanks for the way in which antibiotics have helped us largely to overcome tuberculosis and pneumonia, two wicked killer diseases of the mid-thirties. Bousett, in an even older book than Murray's, on balance, has a much more adequate view of the relation of the known and unknown in the definition of religion. He says that religion at its best grows out of maintaining the paradox and bearing the tension of the paradox between the known and the unknown. Religion deteriorates when this tension is removed. For example, the tension between the law and grace can be removed by taking a given set of laws as knowns or by taking a doctrinal statement of salvation by faith and faith alone as a known. Either choice removes the tension and ambiguity between the two at the expense of the duality of the religious experience.

When one takes the tension between the known and unknown upon oneself and refuses to avoid it, then most arguments between science (knowledge) and religion (faith) begin to disappear. For example, one is no longer faced with the arbitrary choice of medicine as a known means of curing a disorder and faith as asking God—unaided by the knowns of science—to heal one's self or loved one. One can give thanks for the Salk vaccine, penicillin, and more recent psychotropic drugs and at the same time petition God to "let knowledge grow from more to more." Gratitude *and* petition, directed to God, are both religious sentiments. Therefore, the scientist peering through telescope or microscope can marvel at what is known as did Kepler when he said: "O God, these are thy thoughts I am thinking after thee!" The same scientist as religionist can have a kind of religious agnosticism similar to that in Psalm 139:1–6 (RSV):

> O Lord, thou hast searched me and known me!
> Thou knowest when I sit down and when I rise up;
>   thou discernest my thoughts from afar.
> Thou searchest out my path and my lying down,
>   and art acquainted with all my ways.
> Even before a word is on my tongue,
>   lo, O Lord, thou knowest it altogether.
> Thou dost beset me behind and before,
>   and layest thy hand upon me.
> Such knowledge is too wonderful for me;
>   it is high, I cannot attain it.

RELIGION AS COMMUNICATION WITH GOD

A final approach to the definition of religion focuses on communication with God. This has ordinarily been called prayer, yet the stereotypes of prayer keep us from thinking straight about communication with God. Lenski, in his book titled *The Religious Factor*, says that devotionalism or devoutness is the identifiable religious factor in human life. Kinsey and others made massive studies of sexual behavior of human beings. They sought to determine the relation of religion to sexual behavior. They discovered that the religious affiliation, participation in religious rituals, and so on were nongermane. However, the degree of devoutness at the personal level was statistically significant in the sexual behavior of persons. My premise in defining religion is that this devoutness is measurable in terms of the personal—verbal and nonverbal—communication the person or group carries on with God. Religion could be defined, then, as the responsible communion of an individual or group with God.

Yet, in conclusion, the very effort to define religion in explainable terms is to do so as Kant said—within the limits of human reason. These limits are severe. They omit the quality of ineffability which is inherent in anything worthy of the name of religion. As Korzybski said, we arrive in reality at that level of experience where we can only "point" at what we mean because what we seek to describe is indescribable. It is beyond the reach of words. This is true of meaningful communication with God. We know not how to pray as we ought, but the Spirit of God gives expression to these feelings too deep for words. These feelings are often called "needs," and from these needs grow the religious sentiments and structures of human life. What are these needs from which religion originates?

NOTES

1. James H. Leuba, *The Psychological Study of Religion: Its Origin, Its Function, Its Future* (New York: Macmillan, 1912), pp. 3–22, 339–61.

2. Thomas Aquinas, *Summa Theologica*, I–II, q. 1, a. 1, in *Opera Omnia* (33 vols., in 17 tomes, Parisiis: Apud Ludovicum Vives, 1871), vol. II, tome 1: "*Respondeo dicendum, quod actionum quae ab homine aguntur, illae solae proprie dicuntur humanae quae sunt proprie hominis, in quantum est.*" Colin R. Pickett, *Mental Affliction and Church Law* (Ottawa, Ontario: University of Ottawa Press, 1952).

3. Kurt Lewin, *A Dynamic Theory of Personality* (New York: McGraw-Hill, 1955), pp. 15, 16.

4. Johann Wolfgang von Goethe, *Faust*, part 2, act 2, sc. 2.

5. Eric C. Rust, *Nature and Man in Biblical Thought* (London: Lutterworth Press, 1953), p. 104.

6. Ibid., pp. 105, 102.

7. Ibid., p. 107.

8. John A. T. Robinson, *The Body: A Study in Pauline Theology* (Chicago: Henry Regnery, 1952), p. 31.

9. Rudolf Bultmann, *Theology of the New Testament* (New York: Charles Scribner's Sons, 1954), 1:192, 195–96. Used by permission.

10. Anne Morrow Lindbergh, *Gift from the Sea* (New York: Pantheon Books, 1955), p. 32.

11. Henry Nelson Wieman and Regina Wieman, *A Normative Psychology of Religion* (New York: Thomas Y. Crowell, 1935).

12. *West-Oestlicher Divan, Buch Suleika,* quoted by Gordon W. Allport, *Personality: A Psychological Interpretation* (New York: Henry Holt & Company, 1937), p. 32.

13. Gordon W. Allport, *The Individual and His Religion* (New York: Macmillan, 1950), p. 142.

14. Friedrich Schleiermacher, *The Christian Faith* (Edinburgh: T. & T. Clark, 1928), p. 47.

15. Raymond B. Cattell, *An Introduction to Personality Study* (London: Hutchinson House, 1950), p. 21.

16. Albert North Whitehead, *Religion in the Making* (New York: Macmillan, 1926), p. 16.

17. Nicolas Berdyaev, *Solitude and Society* (London: Centenary Press, 1938), pp. 68–69, 92.

18. From Canto the Fourth, "The Ocean," CLXXVII.

19. Berdyaev, *Solitude and Society,* p. 90.

20. Ibid., p. 91.

21. Ibid.

22. Harry Stack Sullivan, "The Study of Psychiatry," *Psychiatry* 10 (1947): 355–71.

23. Bernard Notcutt, *The Psychology of Personality* (London: Methuen and Co., 1953), p. 25.

24. Martin Buber, *Between Man and Man* (London: Routledge & Kegan Paul, 1947), pp. 31, 32, 33. Used by permission of The Macmillan Company, New York.

25. Andras Angyal, *Foundations for a Science of Personality* (New York: The Commonwealth Fund, 1941), p. 115.

26. Schleiermacher, *The Christian Faith,* p. 8.

27. Friedrich Schleiermacher, *Speeches on Religion: Its Cultured Despisers* (London: Kegan Paul, Trench, Trubner & Co., 1893), pp. 49–50.

28. T. S. Eliot, "Choruses from the Rock," *Collected Poems 1909–1935* (New York: Harcourt, Brace & Co., 1950), p. 188. Used by permission.

29. Immanuel Kant, "Kritik der praktischen Vernunft," *Gesammelte Schriften,* bk. 4 (Reimer-Verlag, 1908), p. 87.

30. Berdyaev, *Solitude and Society,* pp. 122–23.

31. Goethe, *Faust,* part 2, act 1, sc. 3.

32. Berdyaev, *Solitude and Society,* p. 89.

33. Emil Brunner, *Man in Revolt: A Christian Anthropology,* trans. Olive Wyon (Philadelphia: Westminster Press, 1947), p. 325.

34. Prescott Lecky, *Self-Consistency: A Theory of Personality* (New York: Island Press, 1945), p. 44.

35. Gordon W. Allport, *Becoming: Basic Considerations for a Psychology of Personality* (New Haven, Conn.: Yale University Press, 1955), p. 98.

36. Abraham Maslow, *Toward a Psychology of Being,* 2d ed. (New York: Van Nostrand-Reinhold, 1968), p. 206.

37. Paul Pruyser "On Phenomenology and the Dynamics of Hoping," *Journal for the Scientific Study of Religion* vol. 3, no. 1 (1963): 87, 92.

38. Gilbert Murray, *Four Stages of Greek Religion* (London: Oxford Press, 1925), p. 19.

QUESTIONS FOR FURTHER STUDY

1. Of the definitions of religion discussed in this chapter, which appeals to your experience in life most? Why?

2. Formulate your own definition of religion, and state your case for it from your consultation with the above footnotes and your own experience.

2

THE PHENOMENOLOGICAL APPROACH TO PSYCHOLOGY AND RELIGION

When a student faces the field of psychology in relation to his personal faith and the ecclesiastical institutions of his heritage, that student should ask: *"Which* psychology from among all the many types of psychology will serve as an anchor point for such a book as this?" Embedded in this question is the knowledge that there are many psychologies. The psychology we choose must include in its approach as a bare minimum the empirical realities of individual differences and social value systems. It must take seriously the reality of the religious experience and its meaning for the person as being important to him, regardless of what kind of assumption, biases, or painful memories the psychologist himself has about religious faith and religious institutions.

On the basis of these conclusions which I have reached, I have chosen one from the many types of psychology as a guiding approach for the whole book. Other types of psychology will be used and referred to from time to time, but this one kind of psychology will be the eyes through which the others will be seen. Experimental, developmental, psychoanalytic, and "third-force" psychologies will be referred to and appreciated. However, I have chosen *phenomenological* psychology as a base of integration for this book. I have done so because a phenomenological psychology (1) takes into consideration the unity of both consciousness and unconsciousness without overconcentration on either, (2) takes into consideration the value systems—for better or for worse—of individuals and groups without disparagement or denial of the reality of people's value systems, (3) takes into consideration the ways and means of changing persons' value systems without destroying them with threat and intimidation, and (4) provides a theologically applicable system of concepts which can be creatively used in the practical efforts of professionally trained ministers and religious workers.

WHAT IS PHENOMENOLOGICAL PSYCHOLOGY?

In the first place, phenomenological psychology has a history and philosophical background in pure phenomenology. Phenomenology, closely defined, is "a descriptive theory of transcendental pure consciousness. . . . It envelopes the whole world as *perceived* by a person as world meaning." [1] Its aim is to set aside previous habits of thought and start from the standpoint of everyday life, from the world as it confronts us. It is a "science of essential being." Although Husserl was a philosopher and not a psychologist, two of his methods of observing phenomena—or events—have been consciously used by psychologists.

BRACKETING

The first of these methods is what Husserl called "bracketing." As R. B. MacLeod says: "The phenomenologist begins his observation of phenomena by suspending his biases, by putting his implicit assumptions in brackets." Jerome Frank speaks of our value system, our self-concepts, our mythological (sacred or secular) as our assumptive world. MacLeod admits that it is "impossible to observe anything without bias, but there can be an attempt to identify bias and temporarily suspend it." [2] But, Husserl says, "We do not abandon the thesis we have adopted, we make no change in our conviction. . . . we set it, as it were, 'out of action,' we 'disconnect it,' 'bracket it.' " [3]

DISCIPLINED NAÏVETÉ

The second of these methods grows out of the first. Husserl calls it "disciplined naïveté," or, in my words, a mature childlikeness or humility as one brackets in his own standpoint, frame of reference, and set of values and deliberately attempts to identify bias and temporarily suspend it. This calls for an "apology for wonder" to come into relation to another person or group of persons with this kind of childlike eagerness to learn from them.

The phenomenological point of view, according to Seward Hiltner and Lowell Colston, has provided a basis for pastoral counseling. It has three merits: It takes seriously individual differences; it acknowledges the depth and complexity of the feeling responses of every human being; and it encourages the person to take initiative and consider his own feelings to the extent that is possible. [4] Whether one uses the case history method, the survey method, or the autobiographical method, as a student of religious experience, this phenomenological approach is an empathic search for what a person's experience means to him. This is a methodology more than it is an ideology, and as method the phenomenological approach is an effective psychological tool for exploring the inner *Eigenwelt* of individuals and groups.

BASIC ISSUES IN PHENOMENOLOGICAL
APPROACHES TO RELIGIOUS EXPERIENCE

The phenomenological approach to religious experience is especially important because the realm of religious experience is a realm of values, beliefs, intensely idiosyncratic behavior, and thought. Observing and describing these behaviors and thoughts awakens the biases, prejudices, and beliefs of the observer. The need for a disciplined empathy and suspended judgment is doubled in the observation of the religious life. Combs and Snygg in their book, *Individual Behavior,* identify the basic issues of a phenomenological approach to human behavior. They are as follows: [5]

First, the factor of *threat* is a focal issue. When an individual or group is faced with a new set of values, one that is strange to them and alien to the inner world view of the individual or group, defenses are set up in the face of such threats. Resistance to change is mobilized. Attempts to maintain the consistency of self-organizations are part of this resistance. What are some ways of describing this organized selfhood?

Second, the individual or group experiences or perceives the world as a *phenomenal field*. The phenomenal field of an individual or group is the person's or group's entire universe. The behavior of an individual or group is determined by this perceptual or phenomenal field at the instant of decision. The behavior is what seems best to the individual or group at a given instant. Past and future blend into an instantaneous action of the moment.

Furthermore, the individual's life or phenomenal field has a more specific focus in what Combs and Snygg call the "phenomenal self." This is what we ordinarily mean when we use the word *I* to describe our personal being. We may associate things, values, groups, and persons with this I. We are likely to say, *"I* am parked on Third Street," thereby extending our I to include our automobile. Husbands and wives who tenderly love each other over many years tend to think of the other's being as their own and vice versa. Hence, separation is painful, especially when the separation is final in death. This basic I is the phenomenal self.

Finally, the phenomenal field, focused in the phenomenal self, has relatively durable or lasting dimensions. The phenomenal self has both transient and lasting characteristics. The *self-concept* of a person consists of those more durable aspects of the phenomenal self. Those things that "remain," to use a biblical term, are the core of one's being, the self-concept. One can arrive at these by finishing the following sentence in as many as a dozen different ways: "I have always been the kind of person who . . ."

These core conceptions of one's own being are the ones most easily threatened and which resist change. The genius of the phenomenological method is to become acquainted with, to understand empathically, a person at the core of his being by bracketing in one's own self-concept inasmuch as is possible.

COMMUNICATION AND CHANGE AGENTS

One of the motives of persons who study the psychology of religion is to make changes in themselves and other people. They are, therefore, "change agents." As change agents they are acted upon by and act upon other persons. This ranges all the way from the use of preaching, teaching, and counseling with persons to social action efforts to change people's attitudes and self-concepts about bad housing, credit buying and loan exploitation, racial prejudice, war, and the right to die when life has no longer any real substance or meaning. The changes that are effected are a part of the growth of the self, in the event of improvement and maturation, and the deterioration of the self, in the event that the changes are destructive. Whether changes are an improvement or a deterioration of the self is a matter of value judgment in itself. Even the values attached to such changes will fluctuate with the passage of time. What looks like a tragic change today may, ten years later, reveal itself as the best thing that ever happened to a person. What looked like one giant step forward to perfection three years ago may today reveal itself to be the impulsive blundering of blind people who did not know what they were doing.

In either event, the person who is a change agent relates to a person who needs to change but does not know it or wants to change and needs help in the process. They have two disparate but overlapping phenomenal fields. Their private worlds interact with each other. Communication is the trunkline of power to change or be changed. The process of communication is acquiring a greater mutual understanding of each other's phenomenal fields. Learning is the widening of our phenomenal field. When this occurs, threat is lowered, and the self becomes more open, teachable, and eager for change and growth. It takes place on the basis of mutuality, for communication takes place best when two persons or a leader and a group of persons either have something in common or work at reducing the element of threat between them long enough and hard enough to develop and discover something they do have in common. Communication is essentially the process of acquiring a greater mutual understanding of each other's perceived universe, or phenomenal field. This calls for a two-way pattern of acceptance. Acceptance of another does not necessarily mean agreement with another, but it does mean that we understand another in terms that cause the other to feel that we indeed and in fact do understand.

Yet even this kind of self-emptying understanding is threatening to people who have never experienced such an encounter before. They are likely to suspect it as being phony or unreal, or to take it as an occasion for becoming dependent and infantile to test out whether it is so. They may refuse to accept it at face value because it calls for an expression of gratitude and they themselves—in their self-concept—are trying to prove that they are self-sufficient and need help from no one. Hence, the very act of seeking to understand and learn the internal frame of reference of a person may pose a threat to the sense of privacy, personal territory, and individual identity of another person. In other words, love itself can be a threat, whether it is examined or unexamined love.

Inherent within the assumptions of such an empathic view of psychology are several questions that need to be answered here. The first question is: Does not the assumption of an inner self, a self-concept, simply restate the Platonic view of a separate soul and deny the importance of observable behavior as a more scientific and experimentally verifiable psychology? My answer is that if one has a Platonic view of life then the soul could be interpreted this way. However, the biblical view of the soul is overshadowed by Platonic translations. The biblical view interprets the human being as a total being. Having a soul as a possession is inaccurate thinking. Being a living soul, soul meaning "life," is a more accurate way of expressing it. A person's life is more important than gaining the whole world. Therefore, I am not posing a little man in a box caged on the inside of the body of a person. Rather, behavior is an expression of the total life, but its interpretation must take into consideration the meaning it has to the behaver. For example, a mental patient scratches his eyes out. He is a very religious person and knows his Bible well. A minister leaps to the conclusion that this man is being severely tempted to do something sexually wrong. The scriptural reference to sexual lust as a cause for "plucking one's eye out" comes immediately into mind. This is an external, outsider's interpretation, that is, the other person's phenomenal field. A doctor interviewing the patient sought the patient's own phenomenal field for an interpretation. The patient revealed to him that he had a terrible fear that he would kill someone; he was so full of anger. Therefore, he made himself blind so that he could not as easily kill someone else. Whether this meaning or perception occurred before or after the act of blinding himself, at the moment this is the patient's own individual perception of his field of events. His very telling about it is behavior, verbal behavior. At the moment of blinding himself, he did what at the time seemed to be the better of two bad alternatives.

If one supposes that he could have talked with this patient before he destroyed his eyesight, and if one proposes to change this behavior, then he must establish a relationship to the patient that is free enough of threat for the patient to tell him how he, the patient, sees himself from within. Otherwise, the anger that threatens to overwhelm him will continue to be misinterpreted.

Another question arises: Whose values as to what is best are to be followed, those of the psychologist, psychiatrist, or pastor or those of the patient? This question poses a false dichotomy because it assumes that the professional person or the patient—one or the other—is absolutely right and the other is absolutely wrong. The phenomenological approach is not a "value monologue" such as this. To the contrary, a threat-free dialogue can form an amalgam of the two "value orientations" and both change some, arriving at a third possibility different from either of them. This process of subtle and factual change is described by Douglas Steere in his book, *On Listening to Another*.

Have you ever sat with a friend when in the course of an easy and pleasant conversation the talk took a new turn and you both listened avidly to the other and to something that was emerging in your visit? You found yourselves saying things that astonished you and finally you stopped talking and there was an immense naturalness about the long silent pause that followed. In that silent interval you were possessed by what you had discovered together. If this has happened to you, you know that when you come up out of such an experience, there is a memory of rapture and a feeling in the heart of having touched holy ground.

Have you ever been writing a letter when your capacity to listen to the other and to his situation suddenly comes into focus and all you have been saying or meant to say is swept up into something infinitely more important? You have listened and you have been listened to and you have heard, even though a complete recasting of what you had set down before is now exacted of you.

Have you ever talked with someone who listened with such utter abandon to what you were trying to tell him that you were yourself made clearer in what you were trying to express by the very quality of his listening? Have you ever found this listening changing what you started out to tell and moving it over into quite a different channel? Perhaps you had begun to speak of the loveless character of your own religious group, of how little they cared for each other, and at bottom, how little concerned they were for what happened to each. In the course of telling this, although your listening companion had scarcely spoken a word, it may be that little by little it began to dawn upon you that you were describing not so much the situation of your religious group as the condition of your own heart. Now you began to see what was required of you, and you found yourself reduced to silence. You may have begun by describing your own inner agonies which had been mounting up until they finally blotted out all hope. You had meant to complain bitterly against a fate that had pressed you to such a state of desperation. You had meant to collect a litre or two of sympathy. But as you talked, and as your friend listened with that perfect understanding love which gave you his complete attention, the true state of things dawned upon you and you no longer needed sympathy or a towel for your tears. Painful as the insight was, you now saw things from another perspective and you stopped talking. You no longer needed to talk, or if you did continue, it was now on another theme and level.

Perhaps you had sought out a friend to confess something you could no longer keep in the solitary confinement of your own heart. You were not sure you would have the courage to admit how low you had fallen and you began in evasively safe regions, not sure either of yourself or of your friend. But the utter and easy attentiveness, the free and open listening of your friend lifted the latch on the gate and it swung open noiselessly and effortlessly, and all that you had held back tumbled out. Now it was out and now it was over and you had died a little death, but in the patient eyes of the friend which you scarcely dared to lift your own to look into, you discovered that you were still in the land of the living.[6]

A final question can well be asked about the phenomenological approach to religious experience: How can one be sure that his observation of the other person's perceptions and behaviors is objectively accurate or that his observations are not really things that the observer wants to see? The answer is that one cannot be absolutely sure, but a great measure of objectivity can be achieved. Also, much room must be allowed for the effects that the very act of observing and being observed has upon the behavior another person expresses. Consequently, religious behavior research must take into account the maxim that all observation of persons particularly is *participant observation*. By this I mean that the observer participates in the process of the life of the observed at one and the same time. As long as one is observing inanimate phenomena or, to a less extent plant and animal life, one's range of objectivity is wider although not perfect. Human beings respond humanly to being observed, and the responses themselves are a form of change taking place between them and their fellow human beings as change agents. This interaction view of observation is not original with me but has been technically defined by Harry Stack Sullivan and is a common assumption of people who are not engaged in academic competition with each other.[7] The myth of pure objectivity is a cherished possession of academicians in almost every classroom discipline. However, for our purposes here, we are in need of a kind of psychology of human existence that does not make a fetish of such a myth.

SOME RELIGIOUS MEANINGS OF A PHENOMENOLOGICAL PSYCHOLOGY

When one stands in the presence of the innumerable expressions of religious behavior evident in the world today, he has two choices. One can erect heavy defenses for his own particular biases as a religious person and defend them polemically. There is a place for this approach in high-level debate and market-place propaganda. One can also take a non-defensive, open approach that acknowledges his own biases but seeks to learn from the religious concerns of others. I am proposing the latter mind set. This is why a phenomenological kind of psychology seems to offer the widest range of possibilities for the exploration of forms of the religious life which may be very foreign to those of either myself as an author or of you as my reader. When taken in the context of the Judaeo-Christian tradition, the perceptually oriented psychology suggested here has several distinctly religious meanings.

First, it comes to terms with the basic fear of change and the feeling of personal threat many people experience when met with the opinions, ideas, and behavior of people who are the change agents of life. No matter how well-intentioned or pure a person's motives are in getting to know, serve, and change another person, the person values his own known ways of being. The resistance one can meet is not to be underestimated. To perceive the other person as a flat plane of behavior that can be changed with adequate reward or punishment is to overlook the complexity of human motivation and to deal with more superficial and obvious kinds of behavior. The self-concept of a person undergoes revision in direct proportion to the alleviation of threat to the consistency, maintenance, and survival of the self as it is. To suggest change is to suggest an *ex*change of the new for the old, the unknown for the known, and this provokes fear. In the New Testament sense, the perfection of love involves the "casting out" of fear. Fear comes from punishment, and it also comes from the necessity to change the known for the unknown.

At the same time one insists, therefore, upon more than a purely external behavioral view of the human relationship of change agents to those whose behavior they would modify, this point of view in no way is calculated to negate, disparage, or nullify the hard empirical data of experimental and/or behavioral psychologists. It is to say, however, that behaviorism and phenomenology are not mutually exclusive but can be creatively complementary hypotheses unless one wants to be a special pleader for one or the other hypothesis. Ideological imperialism is not restricted to religious propagandists; the many fields of psychology can as easily fall into the same trap. This I want to avoid as much as possible in this book.

Second, a phenomenological methodology—not propaganda—is an operational expression of the principle of incarnation. It is a kenotic—or self-emptying—approach. The person who *is* the change agent renounces his own prerogative by reason of rank, office, or point of view. This enables him to see for a time the inner world view and perspective of the other person. The other person instead of being an It to be manipulated, managed, and controlled becomes a Thou to whom to be related, to be understood, and to be known. Inherent in the psychological question of how a person can empathize with another and still be a different self in one's own right is a theological question. The early church fathers wrestled with this in their attempts to express the Christian doctrine of the incarnation. They concluded that the Christ became as fully human as we are in order that we might become Christlike as he was. Yet at the same time they maintained that he remained as truly divine as if he had not become human.

Eastern religions solve the problem by saying that both the self of the one person and the self of the other person are caught up and absorbed into a selfless, transcendent state together.[8] The Christian direction of sharpening and intensifying the sense of personal identity is a more distinctly Western, Occidental resolution of this dilemma. The Buddhist and/or Hindu movement seems to be that of transcending, blending, and distilling away any sense of selfhood into a singular awareness of the Infinite or the All. The student, however, who has been steeped in Western culture moves on the assumptions of the Western Christian tradition whether he perceives himself as a committed Christian or not. Such students are keenly concerned about maintaining a separate sense of selfhood, identity, and personal territory. They may develop the capacity for empathy and learn the disciplines of commitment to understanding another person's point of view in lieu of their own. As they do so, they move on the principle of incarnation that is explicitly articulate in Christian teachings. The hypotheses of the phenomenological psychologists seem to me at least to be secular statements of the working principle of incarnation. However, to say this is in no way to put words in their mouths. Rather it is to develop lines of continuity between the Western Christian teachings and contemporary psychology.

The final distinctly religious meaning of the phenomenological approach to psychology is its implicit doctrine of mankind, as such. The implication is that the person is an active agent in his own right. In addition to being heavily conditioned and programmed by other people, the individual actively and uniquely responds to this conditioning and programming in his own particular way. In other words, people do make decisions that are their own. These decisions may have accumulated in directions that alienate, estrange, and separate the person from those other persons who have been a part of his making as a person. This person, therefore, stands afar off; he is a "stranger" in Albert Camus's sense of the word. Movements of others to overcome those barriers may be interpreted as a threat which creates more alienation, estrangement, and separation.

As we move through the varieties of religious experience discussed in the rest of this book, the way in which religion itself can be used as a way of maintaining alienation, estrangement, and separation or of increasing understanding, empathy, and community will become increasingly obvious. All the while, the basic issues raised by the phenomenological approach to psychology will be raised again and again. At many points, they will seem inoperable and invalid. At others, they will seem a valid and useful set of presuppositions. In either event, the issues raised will be the important ones to discuss, regardless of the conclusion the reader may reach.

NOTES

1. Edmund Husserl, *Ideas: General Introduction to Pure Phenomenology* (New York: Collier Books, 1962), pp. 427–28.

2. R. B. MacLeod, "Phenomenology: A Challenge to Experimental Psychology," *Behaviorism and Phenomenology*, ed. T. W. Mann (Chicago: University of Chicago Press, 1964), p. 54.

3. Husserl, *Ideas*, p. 98.

4. Seward Hiltner and Lowell Colston, *The Context of Pastoral Counseling* (New York: Abingdon, 1961), pp. 45–46.

5. Arthur Combs and Donald Snygg, *Individual Behavior*, rev. ed. (New York: Harper and Row, 1959).

6. Douglas Steere, *On Listening to Another* (New York: Harper and Bros., 1955), pp. 1–2.

7. Harry Stack Sullivan, *The Interpersonal Theory of Psychiatry* (New York: W. W. Norton, 1953), p. 368.

8. Wayne Oates, *Christ and Selfhood* (New York: Association Press, 1961).

QUESTIONS FOR FURTHER STUDY

1. What are the ways in which people characteristically respond to threat, according to Combs and Snygg in chapter 8 of the revised edition of *Individual Behavior?*

2. Relate the phenomenological approach of Combs and Snygg to the existential psychology of Rollo May and others in May's book, *Existence.*

3. From a theological point of view, to what extent can the theology of Paul Tillich be correlated with their kind of psychology?

4. From a psychological point of view, study the work of B. F. Skinner in his books *Science and Behavior* and *Beyond Freedom and Dignity* and pose his arguments against such an approach as that of Combs and Snygg.

3

THE PSYCHOLOGICAL ROOTS
OF RELIGION

A tree is known by its fruits, but the fruits are directly nourished by the roots. Earl Loomis, a psychoanalyst, says that we admire the beauty of roses but overlook their dependence upon lowly ingredients of the beauty such as manure! The pietistic religionist loves to play Eric Berne's game "Greenhouse" and admire from a distance the flower and fruit of religious conversion, ecclesiastical achievement, and so on. The psychologist of religion takes a closer look at the root and nourishment of the plant and does not just admire the beauty of the flower and enjoy the fruit. The practical, optimal result of this closer and more critical look is to provide basic data for reproducing healthy religion in persons and for offsetting the blights and diseases that assail religious growth. At this point, psychology of religion and pastoral care join forces, the first becoming the conceptual basis for adequate care and cure of souls.

Furthermore, a close study of the psychological origins of religion provides the student with a broad and deep appreciation of what psychologists since the late 1800s have actually said about religion. The teaching and learning of psychology at both the undergraduate and graduate level is plagued with the broad assertions of this, that, or the other psychologist about religion. The primary sources of, for example, Freud or Skinner are rarely examined closely but quoted in general. Consequently, students are likely to overgeneralize about what psychology says about religion and miss the wide variety of conceptions of religion and its origins in the lives of persons to be found in the total field of psychology.

CONCEPTIONS OF THE ORIGINS OF RELIGION

Considerable overlapping of emphasis makes any discussion of conceptions of the sources of religious concern in man a blending spectrum

43

of interpretations. Sharp lines of demarcation are both impossible and misleading. The different emphases must be seen together to be appreciated, understood, and evaluated properly.

RELIGION AS AN INSTINCT

The most obvious point to begin the discussion of theories of the origin of religion is with those persons who, like Morris Jastrow, at the turn of the century frankly regarded religion as an instinct of man:

> The certainty that the religious instinct is, so far as the evidence goes, innate in man, suffices as a starting point for a satisfactory classification. . . . the definite assumption of a religious instinct in man forms part of almost every definition of religion proposed since the appearance of Schleiermacher's discourses.[1]

Jastrow not only takes this position himself, but he also imputes it to everyone else! This point of view is not explicitly taken by Rudolf Otto,[2] but the upshot of his contribution points toward a separate "category" or "faculty" for religion. He comes very nearly to positing a "nonrational category" as a fourth estate of personality in relation to the tripartite faculty psychology which Kant mediated to us.

Göte Bergsten, a more recent writer, steeped in the pastoral literature which has grown out of psychotherapeutic approaches to man's emotional needs, says that "it is not necessary to deny that religious needs may be innate because one discards the idea of a religious instinct." When he speaks of "a religious tendency," he means an innate religious sensitivity. This tendency may be "aroused by something spiritually objective," or it may "remain latent; a mere potentiality sleeping in the inmost being of men."[3]

One would raise the question as to whether or not the instinct explanation of religious origin is not a restatement of the older Calvinistic doctrine of predestination and election. If religion is an instinct, it certainly does not manifest itself significantly in some people, only in the elect and the concerned. John Calvin stated it in this fashion:

> The covenant of life not being equally preached to all, and among those to whom it is preached not always finding the same reception, this diversity discovers the wonderful depth of the Divine judgment. Nor is it to be doubted that this variety also follows, subject to the decision of God's eternal election . . . salvation is freely offered to some, and others are prevented from attaining it.[4]

Apparently, discussions of basic theological issues such as this are not shut off completely by the advent of the scientific era. Rather, the context for the discussion is shifted from the categories of revealed theology to those of an empirical science such as biology, psychology, or physics. The basic issues remain; the areas of investigation are narrowed as they were in Schleiermacher's system, and the terminology undergoes much change.

This concern with the instinctive sources of religious concern is a late nineteenth- and early twentieth-century concern. It has not yet been reformulated in the psychological concerns of the 1970s. However, the raw materials for a resurgence of this pattern of thinking are at hand. The psychiatric experimentation in the 1950s with severing the nerve connections of the prefrontal lobe with the rest of the brain raised real questions as to whether the prefrontal lobe was the biological base for distinctly moral, aesthetic, and even religious concerns. An occasional person has been observed who was either genetically or congenitally determined to be born without a prefrontal lobe. These persons, according to Ackerly, are mechanical, anxiety free, and unconcerned with the so-called higher reaches of human interest in aesthetics, values, and faith. The question arises: Is religious concern so located in man's biochemical organism? Furthermore, questions about the moral and religious life are reopened by the recent discoveries about the coding of human genetics in the nucleic circle (deoxyribonucleic acid—DNA) of which the genes are composed and which is the chemical bearer of hereditary characteristics. The capacity of scientists to rearrange these characteristics and control the form which life takes provokes one to ask what effects such rearrangements will have on the moral and religious development of such a prefabricated human being.

Furthermore, the scientific probing of the possibility of the artificial production of human life independent of the egg and sperm of woman and man further tantalizes the imagination. We are still intrigued by our not-so-science-fiction interests in a different kind or order of intelligence possibly to be found on other planets. The explorations of extrasensory perception invariably raise the question as to whether this kind of perception is a special religious intuition, impulse, or instinct. Finally, the experimentation with drug-induced religious experience by reputable persons such as Walter Houston Clark and Houston Smith causes one to wonder whether there is not a native religious consciousness underneath our highly constricted secular thought processes.

Many of these topics will be discussed in detail later in this book, but they need at this point to be related to the earlier questions of this century about the native origins of mankind's religious concern.

RELIGION AS A BY-PRODUCT OF DEVELOPMENT

A second group of thinkers perceive religion as arising, not from any one instinct, but as being derived from the organization, integration, direction, and refinement of the impulses. They see it as a by-product of the inherent demand for growth and development of a person's life. Edwin D. Starbuck, one of the pioneers in the psychology of religion, puts this point of view as follows:

> It should constantly be borne in mind that religion has not been nourished from a single root, but that, on the contrary, it has many sources. Among the facts in the preceding chapters there are evidences that other deep-rooted instincts besides that of sex have been operative in religious development. Out of the instinct of self-preservation and the desire for fulness of life in the physiological plane, there seems to have arisen, by progressive refinement and irradiation, the religious impulse toward spiritual self-enlargement. . . . The process of religious development has consisted in arousing discharges from (instincts and lower nervous centres) through the higher psychic centres and in working them into a higher synthesis.[5]

Starbuck and his contemporary G. Stanley Hall saw conversion, for example, as a distinctly adolescent phenomenon as youths experienced the storm and stress of this era. More recently, Gordon Allport made the somewhat categorical statement that a person cannot conceptualize or experience the thought of God adequately until past puberty. In other words, religion, from this point of view, is a derivative of human development. The "higher synthesis" to which Starbuck refers reflects a definite evaluational approach to levels of integration, leaving room for much ethical consideration. More pessimistic interpreters might say that from this point of view religion is nothing but an epiphenomenon of human development. More optimistic interpreters could reject such reductivism and say that religious dimensions of personality begin to appear when the individual reflects upon the direction and meaning of his development, his pilgrimage of growth. Where is it all going, and where is he in the web of social relationships in which his growing takes place?

Starbuck's point of view can be found also in Coe, Ames, and others and has made an enduring contribution to religious education. No interpreter of the religious life, since these men, can safely do his work without taking seriously the processes of growth and development. Gardner Murphy says that the human personality begins to cogitate upon the nature of the totality of the self in relation to others. In this process the interpreter of the religious dimensions of personality asks the same question Murphy asks:

> Should the student of personality . . . postulate a nonempirical entity distinct both from the organism and from its perceptual responses to the forms and symbols which are called self? [6]

Murphy would say no to this question, but at the same time he later confesses that the difficulty of personality theory "seems to be not with our research or our definitions as to personality, but with plain fogginess as to the nature of man." [7] Whether we like his answers or not, we must say that he is asking some basic questions that are essentially religious in nature. As he has meditated upon and described the process of differentiation, growth, and experience through which the self becomes the self, he stands on the same fog bank with many others and asks, "What is man?" Starbuck answers by saying that man is a growing, developing, seeking personality. He becomes religious as he works all his impulses into a higher synthesis. His religion is derived from the maturing necessities and the chosen directions of his growth.

Furthermore, it was Sigmund Freud who detailed a view of religion as originating in the infantile surge toward and regression from maturity. Operating upon some of the same developmental assumptions as did Starbuck and others, Freud and others arrived at different conclusions. Freud said that religion represents a childish stage of human development—both individual and social—which man needs to outgrow. Religion is an illusion, the composite of the childlike hopes of man, he would say. Freud puts it in this way:

> When the child grows up and finds that he is destined to remain a child forever, and that he can never do without protection against unknown and mighty powers, he invests these with the traits of the father-figure; he creates for himself the gods, of whom he is afraid, whom he seeks to propitiate, and to whom he nevertheless entrusts the task of protecting him. Thus the longing-for-the-father explanation is identical with the other, the need for protection against the consequences of human weakness; the child's defensive reaction to his helplessness gives the characteristic features to the adult's reaction to his own sense of helplessness, i.e., the formation of religion.[8]

When Freud fixed his attention upon the physical origin of religious ideas, then he concluded that "they are illusions," by which he meant the "fulfilments of the oldest, strongest, and most insistent wishes of mankind," and that the strength of religion lies in "the strength of these wishes." [9]

Freud had other very important aspects to his theory of religion. These ideas concerning his theory of illusion are only part of his conceptions. However, these are the ones on which he made his reputation concerning religion. Freud also gave a more positive view of the function of religion in personality development. It is especially applicable to the late adolescent and delayed adolescent in today's culture. In his own words, Freud says:

> Apart from . . . pathological phenomena, it may be said that in the present case religion achieved all the aims for the sake of which it is included in the education of the individual. It put a restraint upon his sexual tendencies by

offering them a sublimation and safe mooring; it lowered the importance of
his family relationships, and thus protected him from the threat of isolation
by giving him access to the great community of mankind.[10]

Religion, then, normally is built upon four great human needs: (1) the
need for ethical control and sublimation, (2) the need for reducing the
importance of parents and siblings, (3) the need for protection from
isolation, and (4) the need to become a part of the community of
mankind.

J. C. Flugel, a later psychoanalyst, is right when he says that Christianity is "pre-eminently a son and brother religion rather than a father
religion. One leaves father and mother, follows Christ and becomes
related to the larger community of Mankind. This religion may just as
easily be a form of rebellion as a means of control." Prophetic religion
tends to be a rebel religion, not a conformity religion.[11]

Even later psychologists relate the origin and growth of religion to the
process of development. For example, Gordon Allport says that "to
feel oneself meaningfully linked to the Whole of Being is not possible
before puberty." He says that psychologists have studied the earlier
years more than they have adolescence and adulthood and therefore their
estimates of religion have been biased by such theories as "familism,
dependence, authority, wishful thinking, and magical practice." [12] Consequently, much is yet to be discovered as to the sources of religious sentiments in the farthest reaches of human adulthood.

RELIGION AS REVERENCE FOR LIFE

Albert Schweitzer identifies religion with the reverence for life and
the will-to-live. He says that *veneratio vitae,* reverence for life, is the
"most direct and at the same time the profoundest achievement of my
will-to-live" and that "ethics, too, are nothing but reverence for life." [13]
Our religious world view, according to Schweitzer, would then arise from
being grasped by the will-to-live, which is the ground of all being. As he
puts it, "world-view is a product of life-view, not vice versa." [14] Religion
originates in the active will-to-live and one's theology is an after-reflection
of this.

Very akin to this kind of thinking is the point of view of William
Ernest Hocking, who feels that religion starts when man begins to value
life as life. He does not give in to the assumption that religion springs
from curiosity or to any lesser thing than the deep-going desire, as deep
as the will-to-live itself.

Religion is to be understood as a product and manifesto of human desire;
and that of no secondary or acquired desire such as curiosity, but of deep-
going desire, deep as the will-to-live itself. . . . If we should venture to name
this deep-set desire which we call religious it might be represented as the ulti-

mate demand for self-preservation: it is man's leap, as individual and as species, for eternal life in some form, in presence of an awakened fear of fate.[15]

Such a spirit is obvious in the experience of Fyodor Dostoevsky, who was condemned to death by the firing squad. He had no way out of the death sentence. He was led out to be shot. Just as he was to be killed—the soldiers with their guns loaded, shouldered, and cocked to fire—the emperor issued a reprieve. Dostoevsky, commenting later in his book, *The Idiot,* says:

> What an eternity! What if I did not die. All eternity would be mine. Oh, then I would change every minute into a century; I would not lose a single one; I would keep track of all my instincts, and would not spend any of them lightly.[16]

This is something of the deep sense of urgency that gripped the fellowship of the early church when they knew that at any moment they, like their Master, could be hauled before the tribunal and killed. Also, their firm belief in the imminent return of the Lord made life itself very precious and very religious. The will-to-live was heightened. To it they must be true. As Schweitzer puts it:

> The highest knowledge, then, is the knowing that I must be true to the will-to-live. . . . The essential nature of the will-to-live is determination to live itself to the full. It carries within it the impulse to realise itself in the highest possible perfection. In the flowering tree, in the strange forms of the medusa, in the blade of grass, in the crystal; everywhere it strives to reach the perfection with which it is endowed. In everything that exists there is at work an imaginative force, which is determined by ideals. In us, beings who can move about freely and are capable of pre-considered, purposive working, the impulse to perfection is given in such a way that we aim at raising to their highest material and spiritual value both ourselves and every existing thing which is open to our influence.
>
> How this striving originated within us, and how it is developed, we do not know, but it is given with our existence. We must act upon it, if we would not be faithful to the mysterious well-to-live which is within us.[17]

However, the Christian faith would probe deeply the believer's conception of life itself. The pantheist can reverence life for its own sake. The bereaved person who has lost his nearest of kin can reverence life so dearly that he will despair of his own life at the loss of his loved one. The apostle Paul was aware that life itself could be a separating power in the relationship to God and was persuaded that "neither life nor death" could separate him from the love of God in Christ. The injunction that the saving of life can be accomplished only through the loss of life has been interpreted ascetically. On the other hand, this same command of Christ cuts through the ethical confusion that can arise out of the idolatry of a time-bound, finite, restricted understanding of the meaning of what life is.

RELIGION AS AN ENCOUNTER WITH THE INFINITE

The very effort to define life reminds man of the infinite nature of that which he is seeking to define. Some, like Gilbert Murray, trace the religious dimensions of man's personality to his encounter with the infinite. Murray says that

> . . . religion essentially deals with the uncharted region of human experience. A large part of human life has been thoroughly surveyed and explored; we understand the causes at work; and we are not bewildered by the problems. That is the domain of positive knowledge. But all round us on every side there is an uncharted region, just fragments of the fringe of it explored, and those imperfectly; it is with this that religion deals.[18]

Also, Max Muller, rejecting the idea that religion arises from a separate faculty or theistic instinct, insists that religion emerges from a sense of the infinite:

> One of the essential elements of all religious knowledge is the admission of beings which can neither be apprehended by sense nor comprehended by reason. Sense and reason, therefore in the ordinary acceptation of these terms, would not be sufficient to account for the facts before us. If then, we openly admit a third function of our consciousness for the apprehension of what is infinite, that function need not be more mysterious than those of sense and reason.[19]

In the same context Muller says that although each religion has its own peculiar growth, "the seed from which they spring is everywhere the same. That seed is the perception of the infinite." [20] He says that although the fragments of our finite knowledge may cover this sense of the infinite, it is always there. He urges that we dig deep enough and promises that we will find this seed, buried, supplying the life to the fibers of all true faith.

Pascal, the seventeenth-century mathematician and physicist, who Martin Buber says "became homeless in infinity," [21] stimulated religious feeling in his readers by appealing to their awareness of the infinite:

> Returning to himself, let man consider what he is in comparison with all existence; let him regard himself as lost in this remote corner of nature; and from the little cell in which he finds himself lodged, I mean the universe, let him estimate at their true value, the earth, kingdoms, cities, and himself. What is man in the Infinite? [22]

RELIGION AS MAN'S ENCOUNTER WITH FINITUDE

Man's contemplation of the infinite thrusts him into a painful awareness of his own finitude. As Hocking again says, "Religion is a reaction to our finite situation. . . . This reaction seems to be, at its heart, as instinctive as a start or a shudder." [23] This is that state of helplessness of which Freud spoke and with which he himself struggled. As Schleiermacher contemplated the nature of religion, he was impressed with the feeling of dependence which to him was universally apparent among men. He said that "in the midst of finitude to be one with the Infinite and in every moment to be eternal is the immortality of religion." This comes from having encountered one's ultimate dependency. He says that "the feeling of absolute dependence [is] a coexistence of God in the self. Consciousness, the totality of being from which all determination of self-consciousness proceeds, is comprehended under the feeling of dependence." In another place he says that "to feel oneself absolutely dependent and to be conscious of being in relation to God are one and the same thing." [24]

Rudolf Otto expressed the theme of finitude as a source of the religious dimension of personality in his idea of the creatureliness of man. He saw religion historically and psychologically as arising from the feeling of awe, fear, dread, attraction, and fascination in the presence of the numinous, *mysterium-tremendum*. Such numinous experience enriches reason and gives heart to morality. It eludes or transcends comprehension in rational or ethical terms and is essentially ineffable.

Paul Tillich, in his definition of man's religious dimension in terms of his ultimate concerns, thrusts this concern over against the backdrop of man's finitude. Man tries to "grasp the infinite with the categories of finitude, the really real with the categories of experience, and . . . it necessarily fails." [25] Tillich feels that the concept of finitude is central to the understanding of God, "for it is the finitude of being which drives us to the question of God." [26] Religious experience roots in this handling of finitude. As Tillich points out, man realizes his finitude through the experience of time (having to die), space (fear of losing one's place in life or not having a place in life), causality (being dependent on something or someone else), and substance (the fear of losing one's self, one's identity).[27] As he defines it, finitude is "the possibility of losing one's ontological structure and, with it, one's self." [28]

In fact, the experience of sin, as an encounter with man's own finitude, may be considered as "holding out on the possibilities of losing one's self." The elevation of the self against God, rejecting one's own humanity willfully, represents man's pride. Revelational theology has usually considered the fact of original sin as more than just finitude or man's desire to be infinite. Man's first disobedience to God arose when he willfully rebelled against God by erecting himself as God. This is what Freud, in describing neurotics, called a "childish feeling of omnipotence."

THE INTERPERSONAL SOURCES OF RELIGION

Man soon learns that he is not only finite as an individual; he also lives among a people of finitude, a people of sinfulness. The social scientists have been quick to form theories of the origin of religion. Kinship-covenant approaches to religion have been articulated by certain theologians. For instance, Pederson aptly states this in his penetrating study of the religious life of Israel:

> When we look at the soul, we always see a community rising behind it. What it is, it is by virtue of others. It has sprung up from a family which has filled it with its contents and from which it can never grow away. The family forms the narrowest community in which it lives. But wherever it works, it must live in community because it is its nature to communicate itself to others, to share its blessings with them. [29]

W. Robertson Smith, in interpreting the religion of the Old Testament particularly, was impressed by the way in which Semitic religion was rooted in the solidarity of the community. So marked and obvious was this solidarity in the Old Testament that H. Wheeler Robinson has called it "corporate personality," affirming that the sense of the community preceded the awareness of individuals. Smith says forcefully:

> From the earliest times religion, as distinguished from magic and sorcery, addresses itself to kindred and friendly beings, who may indeed be angry with their people at times, but are always placable except to the enemies of their worshippers or to renegade members of the community. It is not in vague fear of unknown powers but with a loving reverence for known Gods who are knit to the worshippers by strong bonds of kinship, that religion, in the only sense of the word, begins.[30]

Here the idea of a covenant-making God, so inseparable from a Hebrew-Christian view of religion, enters with full force, for the covenant was always made with an individual with a people in mind. Sin was interpreted as a breaking of that covenant, as a disruption of a relationship to God and his people.

Emile Durkheim, at the same time he did much special pleading for sociology as a separate science, set forth an essentially communal or kinship theory of the origin of religion. He pointed out that "nearly all the great social institutions have been born in religion" and that "if religion has given birth to all that is essential in society, it is because the ideal of society is the soul of religion." [31] In so many words, he says that the *"sui generis* out of which religious experience is made is society." [32]

Sigmund Freud gave a much more profound conception of religious origins than his illusionistic conception. Drawing heavily upon the writings of W. Robertson Smith, he set forth a distinctly social psychology of religious myth in his book, *Totem and Taboo*. He followed Charles Darwin and assumed that men originally lived in comparatively small groups or hordes. (The word *horde* in Freud's vocabulary means an organized group of limited size and not the large mass which it connotes in English.) The jealousy among the younger brothers of the oldest and strongest clan or horde leader inhibited sexual promiscuity of the men with women. The brothers rose up and killed the leader, and the father clan was replaced by the brother clan. Religion, therefore, arose out of the need to handle the sense of guilt, shame, and remorse which the brothers felt for having killed the leader. The leader's image was transformed from that of a threatening enemy to that of a forgiving friend. Morality, although based on the necessities of society, nevertheless has a deeper rootage in the need for atonement for the sense of guilt the clan bears for having destroyed their leader.

The religious meal, or the totem feast in primitive religion, as Freud described it, is that occasion in which "the clansmen acquire sanctity by consuming the totem: they reinforce their identification with it and with one another." [33] Thus, their hostility has taken the form of repentance; their rejection has become adoration. They receive the communal meal as a symbol of forgiveness. They take into themselves the likeness of their dead leader who now lives again through them. In speaking in another place of the Christian community, Freud said that "the tie which unites each individual with Christ is also the cause of the tie which unites them with one another." This tie of love, which was formerly competition, has now directed its hostility outward toward unbelievers.

> Fundamentally indeed every religion is . . . a religion of love for all those whom it embraces; while cruelty and intolerance toward those who do not belong to it are natural to every religion.[34]

Another Jew, Martin Buber, interprets religion in interpersonal terms. He observes children's "instinct to make everything into a Thou, to give relation to the universe," even to the point of carrying on conversation with a simmering kettle. This universal need for encounter with a Thou is the fertile source of religious concern. Religion is found in community, but not just any kind of community, says Buber. "The community is built up out of living mutual relation, but the builder is the living effective Centre." [35] Buber comes very near to making the need for a Thou into a separate entity, but to draw this conclusion is to miss his inherent mysticism. In a word, the need to be in touch, for tenderness, to be in creative relationship with an other and the Other, is the source of the spiritual dimensions of personality.

RELIGION AND MAN'S INDIVIDUALITY AND UNIQUENESS

Those who emphasize the interpersonal origins of religion represent both sides of man's struggle for individuality and uniqueness as the ambivalent aspect of the religious dimensions of personality. This is what Buber calls the "separated I," [36] or the "unique one." [37]

Yet man could not be an individual except in relation to a community. Out of the deep tragedy of his own life, Søren Kierkegaard demarcated the struggle to become a self as the pilgrimage of the religious person. He correlated man's despair with the ambiguities involved in becoming a self. Even if one succeeded in becoming a self, he would fall into despair for having done so! [38] Becoming a self before God is a lonely experience in which one exists "before God" and feels the awfulness of the eternal qualitative difference between him and God.

The existential struggle of man to discover who he is and to identify himself in relation to the basic anxieties of his humanity is also highlighted by Paul Tillich when he calls this process of becoming a self before God "the courage to be." [39]

Gordon Allport defines the developed religious sentiment in terms of a "comprehensive attitude whose function is to relate the individual meaningfully to the whole of being." [40] Although Allport rejects any simple, one-cause explanation of religious origins and says that mature religion is a "rich pudding, smooth and simple in its blend, but intricate in its ingredients," he emphasizes repeatedly the "ultimate individuality of the religious sentiment." [41] He perceives the major task of psychology in relation to religion to be increasing man's self-knowledge. Increased self-knowledge will enable man to "bind himself wholesomely and wisely to the process of creation." [42]

The science of psychology has emphasized the varieties of religious experience, the importance of the individual in religion, and the diversity of religious truths with an undergirding commitment to the uniqueness of each life, that which separates it from every other life.[43] In the same context he says that each life has a necessary, separate, unique patterning different from that of every other life.

This insistence upon the uniqueness of man as an individual necessarily points man's religious quest in the direction of the discovery and realization of his individuality. God has made himself known in his creation of the individual by setting him apart from the rest of creation in some particular ways. Thus he has stamped his own image on the person as surely as he gave him fingerprints, a tone of voice, and many other visible and audible evidences of uniqueness. Man's religion is realized in his discovery and creative demonstration of his individuality. However, Buber would consider such insistence upon the uniqueness of man to be an artificial understanding of man's true nature. He says that "individuality neither shares in nor obtains any reality" and that "individuality in differentiating itself from others is rendered remote from true being." [44]

LEADERSHIP AND THE ORIGIN OF RELIGION

When an individual begins to separate himself from the community and to assert his uniqueness, the fact still remains that he cannot do so in isolation from the community. He must either reject the community of which he is a part or draw it after him as its leader. In this sense Buber is right when he says that "no man is pure individuality." [45] On the other hand, a community inveterately develops some kind of leadership. As Aristotle and Homer both pointed out, even the gods on Olympus had to have a king.[46] Therefore, the religious dimension of personality is closely associated with man's need for leadership. Aristotle's *Politics* bears a direct relationship to his interpretation of the spiritual life of man as emerging from his search for a First Cause, an Unmoved Mover, as an ultimate source of authority and responsibility.

When we turn to the Hebrew-Christian tradition, only a casual glance is needed to see the intense preoccupation of religious people with the demand for a king in the Old Testament story. As the spiritual kingdom was built, leaders such as Abraham, Isaac, Jacob, Moses, Samuel, David, and Solomon supplied the meaningful motifs of the spiritual strivings of the people. The communal disintegration of the Exile was accompanied by the leadership of the prophets and the emergence of the Messianic hope, the hope for a delivering leader upon whose shoulders would rest the "government of the people."

The divine right of kings, as it has emerged from time to time historically, is forcefully relevant to the leadership theory of the origin of religion. The corruption of this so-called divine right of kings has appeared regularly in dictatorships when, from Alexander the Great to Hitler, despotic rulers have sooner or later either deified themselves or been deified by their subjects. In psychotic manifestations of religious concern, the extreme delusions of grandeur in which the patient is persuaded that he is God, Christ, or the father of God further reflect the curious elision of the need for individuality and the need to be a king.

The conflictual division among religious groups cannot be totally explained in terms of the struggle for leadership and the need of the group for a leader. Yet, obviously this is a large component, for instance, in the fragmentation of Protestantism today. The emerging goal of both the mature person and the healthy religion at this point is the balanced handling of the problems of authority and responsibility. We can point to similar secularized struggles for authority and leadership in conflicts in the field of psychology. The leadership of this or that psychologist becomes a determinative factor in interpretation of personality and therapy!

This could be one of the reasons for Sigmund Freud's intense fascination with Darwin's theory of the primal horde and his leader. Freud himself was the leader of a community which expressed well-nigh religious devotion for him. He felt keenly the rivalry of his near contemporaries and apparently feared their destructive criticisms. The divisions within Freudianism have been surpassed only by those within Protestantism.

RELIGION AND THE UNITY OF MAN'S BEING

Obviously, the struggle to achieve individuality is linked with the leadership need of man. This is rooted in the need of a community to symbolize itself. Such pressures within man are not always in harmony with each other. The unity of his selfhood is constantly under threat from this and other conflicts that assail his being. Therefore, some efforts to explain the origins of the religious dimensions of personality suggest that man's need to maintain the unity of his being is a fertile source of religious concern.

Aristotle said that there are three souls of man—the nutritive, the sensitive, and the rational—but he threw his whole weight against the idea that these were separate souls. Rather, he chose to use the term *soul* to apply to the cohesive reality in man's essential nature. He said that if there were a force which held the soul together it would be more fitting to call that force soul than the parts which were supposed to be souls.[47] Furthermore, this unitive need of man is reflected in the Genesis account of the creation, that man and woman are, in some sense or other, partial beings without each other. The twain become one flesh. This henosis is, as Derrick Sherwin Bailey has pointed out, the ontological basis of the sexual relationship.[48] Also, this unitive striving of mankind, according to A. R. Johnson, is the most distinctive characteristic of Hebrew interpretations of personality.

> This recognition of the mental activity of the Israelites as predominantly synthetic, the awareness of totality, is important. It is, perhaps, hardly too much to say that it is the "Open Sesame" which unlocks the Hebrew language and reveals the riches of the Israelite mind.[49]

The Hebrew conception of the resurrection of the body, made most articulate in primitive Christianity, further represents the depths of the religious dimensions of man's need to maintain the unity of his being.

Prescott Lecky developed a theory of personality and motivation which provides a personality-model counterpart for this kind of interpretation of the source of religious concern. He calls his point of view "self-consistency." He says that as long as man is alive

> . . . he must be thought of as a unit in himself, a system which operates as a whole. . . . One source of motivation only, the necessity to maintain the unity of the system, must serve as the universal dynamic principle. . . . We assume a constant striving for unity.[50]

Gordon Allport, in an imaginative dialogue between a student and his professor of psychology, explores the meaning of religion as a quest for unity in the disorder of life. The essential intent of the religious consciousness is to fulfill life's highest potentialities. Allport concludes that the Christian philosophy that motivates the self to strive for comprehensive and unified goals is conducive to mental health.[51]

Of course, E. B. Tylor's theory of animism, which explains the origin of religion in man's belief in spirits, is a sort of "reverse twist" of the need of man for the unity of his being. Man, according to Tylor, developed his religious life from his experiential encounter with spiritual separations within his being. He first sensed these separations within himself in sleep, dreams, visions, ecstasies, and the deliria of illness. Then he saw the departure of the "spirit" from his fellows when they died. Ancestor worship, nature worship, totemism, polytheism, and the like built rapidly upon this encounter of spirits and man's attempts to stay in touch with the "better part" of himself.[52]

Contemporary experience in counseling reflects the almost panicky fear people have of going to pieces, and the way they exhort themselves and each other to pull themselves together. The fear of mental illness has become the modern counterpart of the fear of hell in the Edwardian period of American revivalism. In fact, it may be called a secularization of the doctrine of hell in which the main fear is what Tillich has called "the threat of destruction" and "the threat of nonbeing." The nameless anxiety, which Tillich calls "basic" anxiety, causes man to ask what the basic meaning of his life is. He becomes ultimately concerned in terms of his encounter of the abyss of meaningless, shattered and scattered selflessness.

Comprehensive approaches to medicine, commonly known as psychosomatic medicine, point up the segmentation of selfhood that occurs when the spiritual dilemma of a patient is converted into physical symptoms and/or when emotional tensions actually produce lesions in the tissue structure. The "healing team" approach to the needs of the whole patient, combining the resources of medicine, religion, education, social work, and so on reflects the sensitivity of the helping professions to man's need to achieve and maintain the unity of his being. Hence, the religious dimensions of personality become all the more obvious in man's need for the coherence of his being, particularly in light of the Hebrew understanding of the oneness of man's person.

MAN'S CONTRADICTORINESS AND THE RELIGIOUS DIMENSIONS OF PERSONALITY

However, man is essentially a contradictory being, especially as we see him in his unredeemed war with himself. Spiritual concern which arises out of the essential contradictions in man is a deeper insight into religious origins. For example, Henri Bergson would contend that no single element of religious concern manifests itself in an "unadulterated state" but comes amalgamated with others. He sees the religious order emerging creatively from tension between man's intelligence on the one hand and the natural desire to preserve the life and balance of man on the other hand. As a result of this tension, Bergson says, *"Looked at from this first point of view, religion is a defensive reaction of nature against the dissolvent power of intelligence."* [53] The thought behind this seems to be that in man's intelligence is the power to destroy himself. Religion becomes a form of control of this power. On the other hand, man's intelligence gives him the capacity to perceive his own finitude, his inevitable death. Therefore, Bergson says, *"Looked at from this second standpoint, religion is a defensive reaction of nature against the representation, by intelligence, of the inevitability of death."* [54]

The creation story identifies man's fall and subsequent need for salvation with his rebellious and uncontrollable desire to be "like God, knowing good and evil." The upshot of the tension between natural self-preservation and intelligence, according to Bergson, is what he calls "static religion," which "when it stands alone, attaches man to life, and consequently the individual to society, by telling him tales on a par with those with which we lull children to sleep." [55] But the thesis of the nature-intelligence antithesis gives rise to another polarity, the tension between intelligence in its finite setting and the larger, mystical striving of man. "We know," says Bergson, "that all around intelligence there lingers still a fringe of intuition, vague and evanescent." [56] This conflict between man's finitude and his mystical power to touch the "transcendent cause of all things" gives rise to a second kind of religion, the only kind worthy of the name, dynamic religion. This kind of religion is rare, but "in the innermost being of most men (there is) the whisper of an echo" in it.[57]

A more profound understanding of the contradictoriness of personality as a source of religious concern is that of Anton T. Boisen. According to Boisen in his book, *Religion in Crisis and Custom*,[58] the great periods of spiritual creativity occurred when individuals and groups were under severe stress and in great crises. He takes the Great Depression as an example and, through the use of social surveys, correlates the emergence of many smaller religious groups of Pentecostals with the crisis of economic privation. As these spontaneous religious awakenings occur and begin to consolidate their gains, they develop customs, rituals, and institutions for defining and transmitting their heritage. Here the pull between institutional and intensely personal or charismatic religious expressions becomes apparent.

Boisen also correlated severe mental illnesses with "reactions to a sense of personal failure" in personal crisis situations in the lives of mental patients whom he studied. He evaluated the prognosis of the patient in terms of the nature and direction of "concern" in the patient. The tension between traditional and personal religious loyalties and between the need for individual freedom and the approval of "those whose approval the patient considered most worthwhile" was the spawning ground for both great religious ideas and distorted mental pathologies. The critical situation could go either way: toward the benign solutions of an effective religious expression of the deepest within the patient or toward the more malignant concealment and defense of the real person.[59]

Andras Angyal, in his "theoretical model" of personality, points out the polarity that exists between the homonomous trends and the autonomous trends within the biosphere, or the total person. Whereas he says that "religion contains many elements" and these "have very different origins and character," nevertheless, he accents the homonomous features of religion and identifies them as man's need to "share in a meaningful cosmic order." [60] He sets these homonomous trends over against the absolute necessity, however, for autonomous achievement in the creative artist, the saint, the hero. He even suggests a religious, artistic, and social typology on the basis of the predominance of one or the other of these trends in the given individual. The whole of man is expressed in the paradoxical tension of these trends.

The Christian doctrine of man has always, when stated in keeping with its biblical and historical sources, been more concerned with the origin of man himself than with the origin of religion. Man is a creature, made in the image of his Creator. This origin, as man, puts him into inescapable dialogue with his Creator. Subsequent to his creation, man affirmed his own freedom through negation of and rebellion against his Creator. Man was thrust into a life of conflict with himself, of covetousness in relation to his fellows, and of unreality in his estrangement from God. Hence, as Emil Brunner says, "The Christian doctrine of man . . . takes this conflict seriously, and does not try to explain it away or neutralize it in any direction." [61] The contradictoriness of man's need for individuality and community, for affirmation of release from his finitude, and his fearful attempts to control and yet have use of his intelligence—all this reflects the essential ambiguity of man's existence. The anxiety thus created is the precondition of distorted and sinful behavior which in turn burdens man with a load of guilt. His need for forgiveness, reconciliation, and restoration becomes the precondition of his return to God by faith through Christ, which is the essence of Christian experience.

AN OVERVIEW OF RELIGIOUS ORIGINS

This discussion began with the conception of religion as arising from a special instinct and has progressed to the point of considering the creation and the fall of man. The movement toward the integration and wholeness of personality away from atomistic conceptions of this or that part of a person as the source of religious concern has been another discernible movement. The earlier theorists reduced both personality and religion to a simple, one-factor phenomenon. The more recent thinkers in the field, such as Allport, Angyal, and others, see both religion and personality as complex, comprehensive expressions of life itself, moving toward wholeness and consistency of organization. Allport declares:

> For if the religious sentiment were of uniform composition, marked by a single phenomenal core, then our task of psychological analysis would be straightforward; but . . . this simplicist . . . approach is not acceptable . . . and our attack must be pluralistic and varied. [62]

Religion, Allport says, "is a white light in personality which, though luminous and simple, is in reality multicolored in composition." [63] Therefore, what we have is a spectroscopic analysis in the description above of the various attempts to identify the source of religion in personality. Each one of the interpretations blends into all the others when we push it far enough.

It needs to be repeated: Allport's approach represents a definite shift in the modes of scientific thinking in the twentieth century as compared with nineteenth-century scientific theory. The simple causation approach to science in which A causes B, especially in the case of human actions, is really a psychologizing of natural processes for teaching purposes only. This is what Felix Mainx calls an "inadmissible" turning of "ideas into natural objects." We can do this only so long as "we isolate partial causes from the event and do not take fully into account, or do not fully know, the constellations of conditions given in the system itself." [64]

In the same vein of thought, H. A. Overstreet says that the most important change "in respect to causality that science has introduced into our contemporary thinking is to turn the age-old 'linear' conception into a 'field' conception. As in a field of force, everything is both cause and effect." [65] He goes even further to say that "what is the cause . . . is one of those monocausal—and really nonsensical questions that no disciplined mind now asks." [66]

Therefore, when we apply this kind of energetic, field, interaction conception of causation to the origins of religious concern in human personality, the reduction of religion to this or that one-cause explanation is as naïve in the field of science as it appears to the disciplined theologian. The reductivist, as well as his logic, is outmoded! When, therefore, we hear someone say that "religion is nothing but . . . ," regardless of what he reduces it to, we can conclude that he is either a professor who has quit studying or a sophomoric thinker whose teachers have kept him in the dark!

The earlier phenomenologists of religion did a great deal of special pleading for this or that branch of science, usually their own specialty. Leuba made a strong case for making theology "a branch of psychology." Durkheim identified religion with society, and naturally the study of religion would for him become a branch of sociology. More recently Erich Fromm has made a deep impression upon theologians, but the impression he tends to leave is that religion should be a branch of psychoanalysis. This is certainly the impression left by ministers who insist upon psychoanalysis for every minister. In such approaches the one-cause theory of religion is shifted into a panacea theory of religion or a one-cure theory of a given science. Thus, specializations in the field of science, especially in the area of the helping professions, tend in either theory to have their beginning in a marked rebellion against religion followed by later efforts to encompass religion in their developing specialty. Such segmented thinking also grows out of scientific thinking which has been outmoded by a more comprehensive understanding of the unity of the fields of science. Competitive special pleading for this or that science has led to a semantic morass which hinders the intracommunication of the scientists themselves. Little wonder is it that the scientific interpretations of religion have been characterized by this same segmentation.

However, more recent scientific activity reflects a comprehensive interpretation of life. It rejects partial explanations of human personality by special pleaders for this or that budding profession. A holistic, communicative, and cooperative approach to human personality is emerging. Professions are seeking to find themselves, not only in relation to themselves, but also in relation to each other. Multidisciplinary approaches are being developed in hospitals and educational institutions. More and more, the religious dimensions of the personal needs of individuals and groups are being provided for by trained chaplains in hospitals, for instance. All this activity and thought emerges from comprehensive rather than segmental approaches to human personality.

Therefore, the reader who started this chapter seeking for a one-cause explanation of why people are religious is deflected toward a more profound understanding of religious concern. He sees religious concern emerging in human personality at every point the theorists say it does, but it does not just emerge at any one of them. He sees religious concern as the permeating meaning and the set direction of the total personality as that person lays his whole life upon a given course considered ultimate and unconditional for him. This becomes God for him. The Christian would say, "Take heed that it is not an idol!" The theological task in relation to the psychological evaluation of religion as a phenomenon is to introduce the science of the nature of God in order to separate the false gods from the true God. The distortions of human life, studied so carefully by the psychologist, in turn become empirical descriptions of man in contradiction, revolt, and estrangement; in other words, man in sin.

The discerning student of Henry Nelson Wieman's account of values would be prone to read his value-judgment conception of religion into what has just been said. However, this is not what is intended. Here again the ambidextrous meanings of the concept of religion itself can be underscored. The neoorthodox understanding of the Christian faith has contributed much toward correcting the homocentric kind of theology that measures truth in terms of its value to man, unreconstructed and unredeemed. They have emphasized man's distressing need for redemption. Likewise, they have emphasized a conception of the science of theology which balances the empiricism of such approaches with a deductive kind of science based upon both biblical and historical revelation. However, great care needs to be exerted, in shifting from one of these approaches to the other, that they are historically understandable only when seen as critical correctives of each other and not in isolation from each other.

This leads to the most profound understanding of the origin of religion: We look in vain when we search for the source of religion purely and solely in terms of man's need for religion. The argument from appetite can go to seed in this way. The theologian pushes the issue more ultimately by asking the question as to the nature, character, and intention of God. It needs to be said again that on matters of fact, particularly those which elucidate the functional processes of human life as it is lived, nothing will do but empirical observation. This observation must be existential as well as scientific. Any statements in the name of faith pretending to explain and elucidate these processes which are not at the same time ready to do the work of examining, observing, validating, and testing of hypotheses are certainly misguided. However, the function of faith in relation to psychology is to give clues, to value presuppositions, and to insist that questions be asked because of their importance and not because of the methods by which they may be studied.

Therefore, the question as to the nature, character, and purposes of God must be asked in any discussion of the origins of religions. The Christian revelation of God in Jesus Christ both raises and answers the question in such a way that the fellowship of discussion, inquiry, and personal encounter is stimulated and sustained rather than shut off and stifled to death. Psychologists of religion have too long lived compartmentalized lives in the name of a false kind of scientific allegiance which avoids asking distinctly theological questions about the results of their surveys, questionnaires, case histories, or autobiographies. Nor can we ask these questions in such a way as to shut off discussion, in an *ex cathedra* fashion, so to speak. The interaction between psychology and religion has been first a soliloquy of religion and then one of psychology. A deep reciprocity of methodology such as has been suggested here should make an active dialogue of the relationship.

NOTES

1. Morris Jastrow, *The Study of Religion* (New York: Charles Scribner's Sons, 1902), pp. 100–1, 153.
2. Rudolf Otto, *The Idea of the Holy: An Inquiry into the Non-Rational Factor in the Idea of the Divine and Its Relation to the Rational*, 2d ed., trans. John Harvey (London: Oxford University Press, 1950).
3. Göte Bergsten. *Pastoral Psychology* (New York: Macmillan, 1951), pp. 106–7.
4. John Calvin, *Institutes of the Christian Religion*, trans. John Allen (Philadelphia: Presbyterian Board of Publication, 1909), bk. 3, vol. 3, p. 140.
5. Edwin D. Starbuck, *The Psychology of Religion: An Empirical Study of the Growth of Religious Consciousness* (New York: Charles Scribner's Sons, 1900), p. 403.
6. Gardner Murphy, *Personality: A Biosocial Approach to Origins and Structure* (New York: Harper & Bros., 1947), pp. 490–91.
7. Ibid., p. 52.
8. Sigmund Freud, *The Future of an Illusion* (London: Hogarth Press, 1943), p. 42.
9. Ibid., p. 52.
10. Sigmund Freud, "An Infantile Neurosis," 1918, *The Complete Psychological Works of Sigmund Freud* 17 (1958): 114–15.
11. J. C. Flugel, *Man, Moral and Society* (New York: International Press, 1945), pp. 272–73.
12. Gordon Allport, *Becoming*, pp. 94–95.
13. Albert Schweitzer, *Civilization and Ethics* (London: A. & C. Black, 1929), pp. xiii–xiv. American edition copyrighted by Macmillan, New York, under the title, *The Philosophy of Civilization*.
14. Ibid.
15. William Ernest Hocking, *The Meaning of God in Human Experience: A Philosophic Study of Religion* (New Haven, Conn.: Yale University Press, 1922), pp. 49–50. Used by permission.
16. Fyodor Dostoevsky, *The Idiot* (New York: Brentano's, 1887).
17. Albert Schweitzer, "Civilizations and Ethics," *The Philosophy of Civilization*, trans. Campion (New York: Macmillan, 1929). Used by permission.
18. Gilbert Murray, *Five Stages of Greek Religion* (Boston: Beacon Press, 1925). Used by permission.
19. Max Muller, *Lectures on the Origin and Growth of Religion* (London: Longmans, Green and Co., 1968), pp. 20, 21, 24.
20. Ibid., p. 48.
21. Martin Buber, *Between Man and Man*, p. 132.
22. Blaise Pascal, *Pensées* (New York: Modern Library, 1941), p. 42.
23. Hocking, *Meaning of God in Human Experience*, p. 50.
24. Friedrich Schleiermacher, *The Christian Faith*, pp. 126, 17.
25. Paul Tillich, *Systematic Theology* (Chicago: University of Chicago Press, 1952) 1: 82.
26. Ibid., p. 166.
27. Ibid., pp. 192–97.
28. Ibid., p. 201.

29. Johannes Pederson, *Israel: Its Life and Culture* (London: Geoffrey Cumberlege, 1940) 1–2: 263. Used by permission of Oxford University Press, London, in conjunction with Branner of Korchs Forlag of Copenhagen.

30. W. Robertson Smith, *Lectures on the Religion of the Semites* (London: A. & C. Black, 1894), p. 55.

31. Emile Durkheim, *The Elementary Forms of the Religious Life* (London: G. Allen and Unwin, 1915), p. 419.

32. Ibid., p. 418.

33. Sigmund Freud, *Complete Psychological Works*, trans. James Strachey (London: Hogarth Press, 1955) 13: 419.

34. _____. *Group Psychology and the Analysis of the Ego* (London: Hogarth Press, 1948), pp. 43, 51.

35. Martin Buber, *I and Thou* (Edinburgh: T. & T. Clark, 1937), p. 45.

36. Ibid., p. 65.

37. Martin Buber, *Between Man and Man*, pp. 40 ff.

38. Søren Kierkegaard, *The Sickness unto Death* (Princeton, N.J.: Princeton University Press, 1941).

39. Paul Tillich, *The Courage to Be* (New Haven, Conn.: Yale University Press, 1952).

40. Gordon W. Allport, *Becoming*, p. 94.

41. Allport, *The Individual and His Religion*, pp. 8, 11, 26.

42. Ibid., p. 98.

43. Gordon W. Allport, *Personality: A Psychological Interpretation* (New York: Henry Holt & Co., 1937), p. 558.

44. Buber, *Between Man and Man*, pp. 40 ff.

45. Ibid., p. 65.

46. Aristotle *Politics* 1

47. Aristotle *De Anima* 1. 5. 411

48. Derrick Sherwin Bailey, *The Mystery of Love and Marriage* (New York: Harper & Bros., 1952), pp. 43 ff.

49. A. R. Johnson, *The Vitality of the Individual in the Thought of Ancient Israel* (Cardiff: University of Wales Press, 1949), pp. 7–8.

50. Lecky, *Self-Consistency*, pp. 80–81.

51. Gordon W. Allport, "The Roots of Religion," *Pastoral Psychology* (May 1954): 13–24.

52. E. B. Tylor, *Primitive Culture: Researches into the Development of Mythology, Philosophy, Religion, Language, Art and Custom* (New York: Henry Holt & Co., 1969) 1: 428 ff.

53. Henri Bergson, *The Two Sources of Morality and Religion* (New York: Doubleday, 1954), p. 129. Italics author's.

54. Ibid., p. 122.

55. Ibid., p. 131.

56. Ibid., p. 211.

57. Ibid., p. 212.

58. Anton T. Boisen, *Religion in Crisis and Custom* (New York: Harper & Bros., 1955).

59. _____, *The Exploration of the Inner World* (New York: Harper & Bros., 1952).

60. Andras Angyal, *Foundations for a Science of Personality*, p. 178.

61. Emil Brunner, *Man in Revolt: A Christian Anthropology*, trans. Olive Wyon (Philadelphia: Westminster Press, 1947), p. 83.

62. Allport, *The Individual and His Religion*, p. 4.

63. Ibid., p. 9.

64. Felix Mainx, "Foundations of Biology," *International Encyclopedia of United Science* (Chicago: University of Chicago Press, 1955), vol. 1, pt. 2, pp. 641–42.

65. H. A. Overstreet, *The Great Enterprise* (New York: W. W. Norton & Co., 1952), p. 167.

66. Ibid.

QUESTIONS FOR FURTHER STUDY

1. Is this discussion of the origins or psychological roots of religion one which is alive today, or was it characteristic of the late 1800s and early 1900s?

2 As you examine the history of your own religious group, would you say that it originated primarily from psychological forces in life or from sociological forces in life?

3. Read Freud's book *The Future of an Illusion* and Allport's book *The Individual and His Religion*. Compare and contrast them.

4

THE PSYCHOLOGY
OF RELIGIOUS DEVELOPMENT

The methodology and point of view of the psychologist of religion tends to stand or fall on the assumption of process in human life and religious experience. Even the now of life has a beginning, midpoint, and end! This assumption dates back to Heraclitus who perceived the universe as being in flux. He said: "All things flow. You cannot step twice into the same river; for fresh waters are flowing in upon you." [1] Heraclitus felt that the multiple changes of human life and the universe moved progressively through strife between opposing forces and felt that this tension was "the father of all and the king of all." [2] Heraclitus also believed in a dependable law of change and growth to which he gave the name *logos*. Everything changes, but the way in which everything changes remains constant. This is the logos. Here we find an early intuition of the fact of lawful process in human experience.

When we look into the New Testament, we find that the parables of Jesus are filled with insights into the dynamic, developmental nature of Christian experience. Probably the parable of the sower (Matt. 13: 1–9; Mark 4:1–9; Luke 8:4–8) gives the most concrete recognition to the importance of rootage and growth. The seed of the gospel does not even take root in some lives. In others, it has no depth of soil. Other seeds fall upon thorns and are choked out as the thorns grow up. Still others fall on good soil and bring forth good fruit. Apparently one of the secrets of the kingdom of heaven is the awareness of rootage, growth, and fruitage. It takes a person with ears that can hear to hear such a truth as this.

The fourth Gospel, at the same time it sets forth the fact of the new birth into the kingdom of God, also relates faith in Christ to "the power to become the sons of God" (John 3:1–14; 1:12–13). Furthermore, as will be seen later in the discussion on maturity as one of the spiritual goals of man's becoming, the apostle Paul, in his discussion of Christian love, persistently relates it to growth in the spiritual life. The whole atmosphere of the Hebrew-Christian conception of God and man is imbued with a conscious awareness of the developmental character of the relationship between the people of God and the covenant-making Father-God. A poignantly beautiful example of this is found in Hosea's words: "When Israel was a child, then I loved him, and called my son out of Egypt. . . . I taught Ephraim also to go, taking them by their arms; but they knew not that I healed them. I drew them with cords of a man, with bands of love: and I was to them as they that take off the yoke on their jaws, and I laid meat unto them" (Hos. 11:1, 3–4).

Just as this figure of speech gathers up the parental concern of God for the growth of the spiritual abilities of his children, so also do the words of Isaiah accept a distinctly maternal symbol of the developing relationship between God and man: "Shall I bring to the birth, and not cause to bring forth? said the Lord: shall I cause to bring forth, and shut the womb? saith thy God. Rejoice ye with Jerusalem, and be glad with her, all ye that love her: rejoice for joy with her, all ye that mourn for her: That ye may suck, and be satisfied with the breasts of her consolations; that ye may milk out, and be delighted with the abundance of her glory. For thus saith the Lord, Behold, I will extend peace to her like a river, and the glory of the Gentiles like a flowing stream: then shall ye suck, ye shall be borne upon her sides, and be dandled upon her knees. As one whom his mother comforteth, so will I comfort you; and ye shall be comforted in Jerusalem" (Isa. 66:9–13).

Here, in these two passages, are found symbolic references to two of the great developmental tasks of human life, walking and feeding.

AUGUSTINE

The Christian theologian who saw the human person most steadily and completely in terms of the total, unfolding life process of the spiritual pilgrimage of man was Augustine. He had the courage to see and record the process of human development in all its religious dimensions in his own autobiographical study, *The Confessions*. Augustine delved into the depths of his own being, but *The Confessions* are not a soliloquy. They are a dialogue between Augustine and God. Furthermore, *The Confessions* represent the autobiographical approach to the understanding of the intimacies of religious experience. He uses the technique of reminiscence to call "to mind his past," "reviewing the very bitterness of his remembrance," that he may "deepen his fellowship with God." As he pushes his remembrance to the uttermost, Augustine gives a thoroughgoing developmental understanding of his own religious experience. He moved from that time when he was "torn apiecemeal, turned from the one good God, lost among the multiplicity of things" [3] to the time in which he could with unity of heart and being worship God and live securely among men. One of the basic contributions, it seems to me, that Augustine made to the understanding of the religious dimensions of personality becomes apparent in his shift from the static nondevelopmental point of view of the Neoplatonists and Manichaeans to the dynamic, developmental, and depth point of view of the Hebrew-Christian view of life.

BERNARD OF CLAIRVAUX

Another distinctly theological contribution to the understanding of the development of personality was written by Bernard of Clairvaux in A.D. 1126. In his treatise, *On the Love of God*,[4] Clairvaux delineates four progressive degrees of life. The first level of love is that degree "whereby a man loves himself for his own sake." The natural desires of man are "at the service of the author of nature." The second stage or degree of love is that in which a person "now loves God, then, but still for a while for his own sake and not for himself." This is the love of God for what God can do for one. "From the occasion of frequent necessities God must be approached by man with constant appeals," and his petitions become a way of expressing his love to God. He loves God for his own sake and not for the sake of God himself. The third stage in the development of the spiritual life of love, according to Bernard, is that in which man loves God, not for his own necessity, but loves God for God's sake: "He . . . gives praise to the Lord, not for that He is good to him, but for that He is good, he truly loveth God for Himself and not for his own sake. . . . This is the third degree of love by which God is now loved for His very self." [5]

Yet, says Bernard, "there is even a fourth stage of maturing love. This is the stage in which man loves himself for the sake of God, and does not even love himself except for the sake of God." However, even at this stage of maturity, love is not perfected because the perfection of love does not belong even to those who are blessed before the resurrection. Bernard takes into consideration the fact that finitude and humanity are always characterized by an incompleteness of the power to love. Whereas Bernard does not give any elaborate and detailed outline of the development of personality, he has taken seriously the fact of growth and development in the dynamic character of Christian love. As we shall see later, the Christian concept of perfection and the psychological concept of maturity are both discussed in the context of love whether one consults the New Testament concept of agape or the contemporary psychological literature on maturity.

JOHN BUNYAN (1628–88)

The English preacher and author, Bunyan, with quaint but uncanny precision depicted the long and arduous pilgrimage of development within the spiritual life of a Christian. Bunyan, in his book, *Grace Abounding,* wrote an autobiographical account of his own spiritual pilgrimage. He delved, as did Augustine, into the depths of his own being through the process of recall and remembrance until he encountered a meaningful pattern of God's providential dealings with him in the course of his own development. His increasing awareness that he was in face-to-face encounter with God brought him into a more acute knowledge of his own selfhood. This knowledge took the form of a confessional experience concerning the whole direction, meaning, and purpose of his life. He said that he was as one bound who felt himself shut up into the judgment to come, that the grace and love and mercy of God abounded to him as the testing and maturing temptations went from one stage of intensity to another. When he reached the point that the Lord Jesus Christ enabled him to break out of his loneliness into a "longing for the company of some of God's people," he said, "I could scarce lie in my bed for joy and peace and triumph through Christ."

Bunyan's remarkable life story describes his religious experience in terms of his life history and personal development. This same motif is followed in his description of the Christian life, *Pilgrim's Progress.* His book outlines the ten stages of the Christian's pilgrimage from the City of Destruction to the Celestial City. The Christian life is portrayed, not as a static realization of a transactional type of salvation, but as a jagged, uneven, yet forward-moving development from one level of spiritual achievement to another through temptation. Spurts of progress are often met by doldrums of despair, indifference, and vanity. Bunyan, himself, describes this in his own reaction to the Bible. He says that sometimes he sees "more in a line of the Bible than I could well tell how to stand under." He says also that another time "the whole Bible hath been to me as a dry stick, or rather, my heart hath been so dead and dry unto it that I could not conceive the least dram of refreshment, though I have looked it all over." [6] M. Esther Harding, in her book, *Journey into Self,*[7] introduces analytical psychological concepts alongside Bunyan's magnificent allegory. She, an analyst, feels that Bunyan reveals useful case material for the psychological study of the inner life of man.

SØREN KIERKEGAARD

Probably the most detailed discussion of the development of personality from a religious point of view is given by Søren Kierkegaard, who was born in 1813 and who died at a relatively early age in 1855. Kierkegaard perceived himself as a psychologist of the Christian life. He saw life as being rooted in values and valuation. He used the term *stages of life* in the same sense that we use the term *ways of life.*

The stages of life's way which he identified do not represent inevitable, evolutionary phases of personality development. The idea of a continuous process of development is actually irrelevant and inapplicable to Kierkegaard. Rather, the stages on life's way are qualitatively different ways of life. A personality in transition cannot, by a mere process of reflection, move from one to the other. Nor can he merely trust to time that he will grow inevitably from one to another. The change from one sphere to the other, says David F. Swenson,

> is never necessary but always contingent; if it presents itself as possible, it also presents itself as possible of nonrealization. Whenever the transition from one stage to another does take place, it always comes to pass through a 'leap of faith' and requires divine assistance through a true, creative act of God within the framework of a pre-existent creation.[8]

Granting this, that it is impossible to reach one stage from another by mere development, it can be said that in the thought of Kierkegaard the stages on life's way have a positive relationship to each other. They are successive steps on the way toward a more nearly perfect and richer life. However, they cannot be realized without the leap of faith and the creativity of God.

Kierkegaard lists three stages of life—the aesthetic, the ethical, and the religious. The aesthetic stage is that of pleasure. "Only an immediate relationship concerns aesthetics."[9] The person who lives the aesthetic way of life avoids the necessity, yea, is not aware of the necessity, of making decisions and choosing between alternatives. "He rushes down into the manifold of life, . . . he dashes himself against a solid dam."[10] The aesthetic way of life is essentially a sensual way of life, embodying the satisfactions of the senses. The main threat to the aesthetician is boredom. The aesthetic man lives neither in hope nor in recollection, and the threat of the future and the impingement of the past jeopardize the tranquillity and charm of the moment.

The second stage on life's way is the ethical stage. This phase of life is characterized by the primacy of duty. For the ethical man "the chief thing is, not whether one can count on one's fingers how many duties one has, but that a man has once felt the intensity of duty in such a way that the consciousness of it is for him that assurance of the eternal validity of his being."[11] Furthermore, the ethical stage is characterized by an acute awareness of time and the necessity of decision. Not to make a decision is to make a decision! The ethical man comes into collision with sin as a fact which he is quite incapable of assimilating. The ethical man fulfills himself in this encounter with sin which in turn demands a "dialectical leap and appeals to the transcendency of the religious."[12]

The third stage or way of life, according to Kierkegaard, is the religious stage. Here, the ethical situation confronting man becomes an issue, not merely of what is right and wrong, but of existing as a self before God. The consciousness of being "before God" comes somewhat preliminary to the transition from the ethical to the religious stage. As Kierkegaard says in his book, *The Sickness unto Death,* the measure for the self always is the way in which in the religious stage of existence man becomes aware of "the eternal qualitative difference between him and God." Self-consciousness, in the sense of being a self before God, and God-consciousness are coterminous in the religious stage. Man falls into despair as he becomes a self before God. He may despair, in a pseudo-fashion, in not willing to become a self. Or, in the third place, he may despair at having willed to become a self and having succeeded. In the latter phase of despair he may become a self not before God but over against God.

But religion is essentially a passive relationship to the divine, accompanied by suffering and a sense of guilt. This kind of religion Kierkegaard calls Religion A. He distinguishes it from Religion B which is a transcendent experience of religion. The individual's eternal destiny is threatened; the sense of guilt is transformed into a sense of sin. The continuity between the actual self and the ideal self, the temporal self and the eternal self, is broken. The self is made free from the law of God by the simple confession of the fact that it is unable to comply with the demands. The totally invalidated personality recognizes itself to be so, and God manifests himself as love in time outside the individual in an intimate personal encounter of acceptance.

Two salient features characterize the Kierkegaardian conception of stages. First, he gives a depth and qualitative understanding of the movement of the self as it actualizes its potentialities, thereby rejecting a purely temporal conception of the development of personality. In the second place, he gives a vertical as well as horizontal interpretation of the relationships involved in the achievement of selfhood. He interprets the self in relationship to God as well as in its dialogic relationship to itself and to its community.

HORACE BUSHNELL

Another theologian who dealt with the problem of personality development and religious experience was Horace Bushnell (1802–76). In 1860 he wrote his book, *Christian Nurture,* which was reprinted in June, 1953, by the Yale University Press. This book is a prophetic document in the field of the development of personality in much the same way that the writings of Walter Rauschenbusch were prophetic in the field of social relationships. Contrary to much popular opinion, Bushnell assumed the corruption of human nature but felt that it was wisest to undertake the remedy of the corruption at once in the very earliest stages of human life. He felt that it was never too early for good to be communicated and that the spirit of truth need not wait for the child's ability intellectually to understand before it began to operate. He likened the development of a child to the parable of Jesus in which he said that the kingdom of heaven is as a grain of mustard seed. In an essay written in 1844, as early as that, he proposed a constructive alternative to the spiritually sterile revivalism which waited until a person was an adult and then sought to convert him to Christianity. The essence of this essay is as follows:

> We hold that children are, in a sense, included in the faith of their parents, partakers with them in their covenant, and brought into a peculiar relation to God, in virtue of it. On this ground they receive a common field of faith with them, in their baptism; and God on his part, contemplates, in the right, the fact that they are to grow up as Christians, or spiritually renewed persons. As to the precise time or manner in which they are to receive the germ of holy principles, nothing is affirmed. Only it is understood that God includes their infant age in the worn book of parental culture, and pledges himself to them and their parents, in such a way, as to offer the presumption, that they may grow up in love with all goodness, and remember no definite time when they became subjects of Christian principle. Christian education then is to conform to this view, and nothing is to be called Christian education which does not.[13]

Bushnell felt that the overemphasis upon conversion of adults, which implied the free moral agency and personal responsibility of children, was a subtle way of parents absolving themselves from the responsibility for the moral and religious character of their children. He concentrated, therefore, on the organic unity of the family, seeing it as a body of interpersonal relationships exerting power over character which is more than just influence. Because this power is both unconscious and un- designed, children are spiritually transformed or, as the case may be, malformed through the personal holiness, or lack of holiness, of parents in relation to their children. Bushnell believed that qualities of educa- tion, habit, feeling, and character have a tendency always to grow in a family and by long continuance can become thoroughly inbred in this stock. He affirmed not only the inheritance of original sin but also the transmission of righteousness.

Through such teachings as these, Bushnell laid the theological ground- work for an intense development, in the fields of the psychology of religion and religious education, of nurture approaches to religious ex- perience. Although he dealt with the problems of parent-child relation- ships, theologically and cross-sectionally, he nevertheless opened the way for later religious educators to work out highly refined schemes of the development of personality and other religious consciousness. We turn now to evaluate some of these.

HALL, STARBUCK, JAMES, AND SHERRILL

The twentieth century marks a vast amount of vital activity among the psychologists of religion. The monumental studies of G. Stanley Hall on adolescence set the empirical framework for questionnaire analysis done by E. D. Starbuck and others. The major contribution of these works seems to be that of identifying conversion as a typically adolescent phenomenon and interpreting religious experience in terms of this particular state of personality development. An overall emphasis is apparent, particularly in the work of E. D. Starbuck, which insists that religious experience is an intensification of the process of maturation. For instance, a teen-ager goes through a normal process of storm and stress, doubt and rebellion. The experience of guilt also emerges. Under religious influences the teen-ager undergoes a rapid growth process which telescopes and intensifies these encounters in his developing selfhood.

William James, in his classical book, *The Varieties of Religious Experience,* also interprets conversion in terms of a dynamic growth process. He identifies it as that process, gradual or sudden, whereby a person who has been consciously inferior, divided, and unhappy becomes consciously superior, unified, and happy by reason of his firmer grasp upon spiritual realities. He inserts the time factor in his definition of conversion by saying that it may be "gradual or sudden."

But probably the most comprehensive synthesizer of all the foregoing insights, as well as those which will follow in the contributions of contemporary developmental psychologists and psychotherapists, is the late Lewis J. Sherrill of Union Theological Seminary. In his book, *The Struggle of the Soul,*[14] Sherrill identifies the religious life as a pilgrimage in which the merging, dynamic self of an individual is called out of one stage of development into another by faith. He is challenged to move out, not knowing where he goes, and not shrink back and thereby "lose his soul," to use a concept from Hebrews. Using biblical concepts and elevated poetic imagery, Sherrill discusses the growth of the human person in infancy, childhood, adolescence, adulthood, and later maturity. He points out that this developmental process may, according to the spiritual meaning that is attached to it, be to the individual a saga, a treadmill, or a pilgrimage. He draws heavily on the New Testament, especially the Book of Hebrews, to identify the larger spiritual context of the faith pilgrimage of the individual in the Christian community.

THE DEVELOPMENTAL INSIGHTS OF THE PSYCHOLOGISTS OF PERSONALITY AND PSYCHOTHERAPISTS

GESELL AND HIS ASSOCIATES

As we turn from the distinctly theological and more or less prescientific conceptualizations of the psychology of religious development to more empirical and scientific data, the first major contribution we need to consider is that of Arnold Gesell, Francis Ilg, and Louise Ames. These research persons are interested primarily in the description of child behavior. Working with a highly selected group of children, they have carefully observed the behavior of their test group from infancy through adolescence. They have recorded their findings in four monumental studies: *The Infant and Child in the Culture of Today*,[15] *The First Five Years of Life: The Pre-School Years*,[16] *The Child from Five to Ten*,[17] and *Youth: The Years from Ten to Sixteen*.[18] These works describe the growth gradients of children in a series of stages or degrees of maturity by which the child progresses toward a higher level of behavior. However, these books seek only to present the frames of reference which can "be used to locate the stage of maturity which a child has reached in any given field of behavior." [19] Whereas these books present primarily a description of what behavior is like at different stages, Francis Ilg and Louise Ames have written another book entitled *Child Behavior*[20] which not only tells how behavior develops, but also gives specific advice on what to do about the many child behavior problems that appear at different developmental stages in the life of the growing individual.

In Gesell's conception of the development of personality, there are seven stages: (1) the embryo stage, 0–8 weeks; (2) fetus, 8–40 weeks; (3) infancy, birth to two years of age; (4) preschool, 2–5 years of age; (5) childhood, 5–12 years of age; (6) adolescence, 12–20 or 24 years of age; (7) adulthood. It is important to note that the chronology or rapidity of appearance of these different stages is not nearly so important as the order of their appearances. Gesell and his associates worked out "behavior profiles" for each six-month period after two and each week period before two. They described the process of growth as a paradoxical mixture of creation and conservation. Each achieved stage is consolidated and conserved into the creation of new growth at the next stage. The achieved results of a given stage are the grounds upon which the individual stands in order to grow into the next.

Gesell and his associates make a great deal of the fact of individuality in children. Individuality of a child appears in the growth pattern whereby he temperamentally handles his own stage of development as it appears. They emphasize the importance of not standardizing and stereotyping behavior responses of children but seeking to understand the individuality of a given child.

One of the most important factors in the Gesell studies is their working hypothesis that the stages of growth are not evenly related to each other. There is a jagged rhythm of growth. There will be a spurt of growth and activity, a time of breaking out and vigorous expansion, a time of inwardized-outwardized, troubled, and confused behavior, and a time of rounded, balanced, smooth, and consolidated behavior. Ilg and Ames outline this in a rhythm of the typical growth of children: [21]

2 years	5 years	10 years	Smooth, consolidated
2 ½	5 ½–6	11	Breaking up
3	6 ½	12	Rounded, balanced
3 ½	7	13	Inwardized
4	8	14	Vigorous, expansive
4 ½	9	15	Inwardized-outwardized, troubled "neurotic"
5	10	16	Smooth, consolidated

Two specific notes need to be made here as to the distinctly religious dimensions of the development of personality as the schemata have been set forth by Gesell and his associates. First, parents tend to interpret the behavior of children as being good or bad in terms of the spurts of growth and the periods of quiescent consolidation. Growth is considered to be times of difficulty, badness, and unmanageableness. Great moral and spiritual trepidations fill the hearts of parents during these times. On the other hand, the times of quiescence and consolidation are likely to be identified with goodness, virtue, and perfection in behavior. But the wisdom of growth is deeper than the wisdom of mothers and fathers who yearn for one good night's sleep or for a little peace and quiet in the house!

The second observation that needs to be made is that Gesell and his associates have taken seriously the expected and typical, religious, ethical, and philosophical attitudes of a child at each stage along the developmental cycle at which an individual child may be found. Each of the behavior profiles as recorded in these studies has a descriptive section on what parents, teachers, and pastors may expect in terms of religious ideation coming from the child at a given age level. Such problems as death and deity, time and space, belief and magic, and Santa Claus are discussed in detail.

Some specific objections have been raised by the use of Gesell's research to the exclusion of other types of information and insight. One of them is that these facts which he presents are relatively misleading unless they are set within the context of an understanding relationship on the part of the parent. To use a figure of speech, they are like the words of a song without the music. The interpersonal relationship supplies this added dimension. Also, Margaret Mead, in her book, *Male and Female*, without naming Gesell at all, gives a fairly specific criticism of his methodology. She says:

We . . . find it important to re-emphasize the fact that whatever the adults say, or feel, or repress, the child does have a body . . . the child is not only a *tabula rasa*, but a vigorous, maturing organism with modes of behavior appropriate to its own age and strength. But it is not a maturing organism in a glass box, or in a consulting room. The artificialities of the world-lit cubicle in which a child can be photographed from six angles are useful ways of getting an abstract picture of the behavior pattern the child has developed as it grows up among other human beings. The other human beings may be subtracted for the moment, and the child viewed as a developing organism pushing its way towards adulthood, but in the whole of human experience this never happens.[22]

PSYCHOANALYSIS AND PERSONALITY DEVELOPMENT

Probably the most influential theory of personality development in contemporary life is the psychoanalytic concepts set forth originally by Sigmund Freud and developed in larger detail by Karl Abraham. The psychoanalytic conception of personality is based on several postulates which must be understood as integral to the point of view. The first postulate is the theory of narcissism, or the attachment of the undifferentiated powers of life known as the libido to the self itself. Cathexis is the second postulate which means that the libido is attached to an object, ordinarily a meaningful person in one's life. The third postulate is regression, which means the resistance of the organism to a forward movement into life through the transfer of the libido to a loved person other than the self.

Regression more usually means the need of the organism to return to the totally parasitic, irresponsible, and completely cared-for life of the intrauterine existence of the individual. This happens particularly when the organism is subjected to undue stress. The fourth postulate is that of fixation. This means the arresting of libidinal development at an immature level of growth, resulting in a fixed pattern of reaction to life at a given point.

The stages of development according to Freud and Abraham are as follows: (1) the dependent, or oral, stage of development which is usually associated with feeding and weaning; (2) the aggressive, or anal, stage of development which is usually associated with toilet training, bowel and bladder control, and the need for cleanliness and order; (3) the genital, or the oedipal, stage of development, which is characterized by activated needs for identification with the parent of the same sex and competition with the parent of the same sex for the warmth and tenderness of the parent of the opposite sex; (4) the latency stage, which is characterized by intense intellectual activity, closeness to the same sex, development of gangs; (5) puberty, or genital maturity, which is characterized by the development of the reproductive capacities at the biological level and the choice of a person of the opposite sex as a mate at the psychosocial level.

Karl Abraham, in his selected papers on psychoanalysis,[23] correlates these stages of personality development with what he calls character formation. He develops a typology of personality, particularly as it appears in neurotic persons, on the basis of each one of these different stages of personality development. A more highly detailed psychoanalytic personality typology based on these stages of development is described in Leon Saul's book, *Emotional Maturity*.[24] Probably the most widely read and clearly written statement of these stages has been worded by O. Spurgeon English and G. H. J. Pearson in their book, *The Emotional Problems of Living*.[25]

As one reads these books, beginning with Freud, he sees a movement from the poetic insight of Freud to a carefully detailed and almost fixed developmental determinism in a book like that of English and Pearson. One of the basic criticisms of this conception of personality development is that personality itself is seen almost purely in terms of the longitudinal, early childhood skills development of the person. The vocational strivings of the individual are reduced to these explanations. Room for cultural and class variations in the various experiences of feeding, toilet training, and masculine and feminine role taking is squeezed out in the narrow confines of this fixed theory. Some of the larger issues in parent-child relationship, such as basic acceptance and rejection, are overlooked in preoccupation with these biological functions.

OTTO RANK

One of Freud's students, Otto Rank, raised serious questions about the long-term nature of classical psychoanalytic treatment. He observed that life has a traumatic beginning in birth. The individual is thrust out of the womb and expected to begin the trek toward independence. This anxiety-stamping trauma, Rank felt, sets the pattern for all later problems and a motif for therapy. He saw treatment of personality problems as a sort of "mid-wifery" in the new birth of the spirit of the person. Definite ends were set for the treatment and the person approached, the end being, as it were, the death of an old way of life. The therapist then held out the hope of the birth of a new life. The actual similarity of his point of view to the Apostle Paul's conception of regeneration is specifically identified by Rank in his book, *Beyond Psychology*.

JOHN BOWLBY

The trauma of birth is a common experience of all persons, but Bowlby and his associates observe more recently that the basic capacity for commitment is taken from many persons when their attachment to their mother is disrupted very early in life. The child who has had a reasonably secure relationship with his mother and is parted from her will react in a three-phase pattern of *protest, despair,* and *detachment.* "After a series of upsets at losing several mother figures," a child in time will "act as if neither mothering nor contact with humans has much significance for him." He will gradually commit himself less and less to succeeding figures and in time will stop altogether attaching himself to anyone. He will become increasingly self-centered and, instead of directing his desires and feeling toward people, will become preoccupied with material things such as sweets, toys, and food.[26] Although Bowlby makes no specific application of his concepts to religious experience, the psychologist of religion immediately notes his reference to the child's loss of the capacity to commit himself. Kenniston's studies of the uncommittedness of a group of college students for whom it is a way of life to be uncommitted are supporting data for the hypothesis that these patterns, established early in life due to shattered trust and broken attachments, are in effect hamperings of the religious capacity of the person to give himself to God, cause, community, or marriage.

ERIK ERIKSON

The work of Erik Erikson is built on the assumption of not just one or two crises, but on a series of eight great crises from infancy to old age. Each of these crises is actually a crisis of faith and ethical responsibility. He details these crises in his book, *Identity and the Life Cycle,* and relates these to the development of the ethical and spiritual life of a person in his book, *Insight and Responsibility.*

The crisis of infancy is between trust v. mistrust, and the ethical value is hope. Concerning the religious significance of this, he says:

But since we have already embarked on general observations, a word must be said about one cultural and traditional institution which is deeply related to the matter of trust, namely, religion.

It is not the psychologist's job to decide whether religion should or should not be confessed and practiced in particular words and rituals. Rather the psychological observer must ask whether or not in any area under observation religion and tradition are living psychological forces creating the kind of faith and conviction which permeates a parent's personality and thus reinforces the child's basic trust in the world's trustworthiness. The psychopathologist cannot avoid observing that there are millions of people who cannot really afford to be without religion, and whose pride in not having it is that much whistling in the dark. On the other hand, there are millions who seem to derive faith from other than religious dogmas, that is, from fellowship, productive work, social action, scientific pursuit, and artistic creation. And again, there are millions who profess faith, yet in practice mistrust both life and man. With all of these in mind, it seems worth while to speculate on the fact that religion through the centuries has served to restore a sense of trust at regular intervals in the form of faith while giving tangible form to a sense of evil which it promises to ban. All religions have in common the periodical childlike surrender to a Provider or providers who dispense earthly fortune as well as spiritual health; the demonstration of one's smallness and dependence through the medium of reduced posture and humble gesture; the admission in prayer and song of misdeeds, of misthoughts, and of evil intentions; the admission of inner division and the consequent appeal for inner unification by divine guidance; the need for clearer self-delineation and self-restriction; and finally, the insight that individual trust must become a common faith, individual mistrust a commonly formulated evil, while the individual's need for restoration must become part of the ritual practice of many, and must become a sign of trustworthiness in the community.

Whosoever says he has religion must derive a faith from it which is transmitted to infants in the form of basic trust; whosoever claims that he does not need religion must derive such basic faith from elsewhere.[27]

The element of hope that is generated in infancy is defined by Erikson as "the endearing belief in the attainability of fervent wishes in spite of the dark urges and rages which mark the beginning of existence." [28]

On the basis of this hope is built the second great crisis of emotional and ethical development. In early childhood, the stress of life is drawn upon the tension between autonomy and doubt or shame. The development of will, commonly spoken of as "will power," is the ethical strength generated at this stage. Erikson defines will as *"the unbroken determination to exercise free choice as well as restraint, in spite of the experience of shame and doubt in infancy."* [29]

The third stage of development is the play age, and the developing person either develops initiative or recoils into guilt. Purpose is the ethical strength or virtue of this age of play. *"Purpose . . . is the courage to invisage and pursue valued goals uninhibited by the defeat of infantile fantasies, by guilt and by the foiling fear of punishment."* [30]

The fourth stage of growth is the school age, in which the pattern of life follows either that of industry or that of inferiority. The work identity of the person is laid here. Competence becomes the strength of character developed or blunted here. *"Competence . . . is the free exercise of dexterity in the completion of tasks, unimpaired by infantile inferiority."* [31] This is the basis for interpersonal cooperation and implements tools and skills.

Adolescence follows the play age, and the struggle for a clear focus of identity as over against the confusion of one's identity as a leader, as a sexual being, and as believer in an ideology becomes what someone has called the "battleground of character." The particular quality of life that ideally should emerge with and from adolescence is fidelity. Erikson defines fidelity as *"the ability to sustain loyalties freely pledged in spite of the inevitable contradictions of value systems."* [32] Erikson says that fidelity is "the cornerstone of identity." This is reminiscent of the research of Bowlby on the impairment of the capacity for commitment due to repeated breakage in attachment in the earlier years. This is especially important for the psychology of religious experience, the kind of experience that calls for dedication and commitment. From a classical theological point of view, this has been called "sanctification" or "consecration."

The sixth stage of maturation in Erikson's schedule of the development of personal strengths is young adulthood and the crisis is drawn between intimacy and isolation. Of course, the capacity to be intimate with another human being or group of human beings is built upon the virtues of competence and fidelity. Out of this blend grows the virtue of young adulthood, the virtue of mature love. *Love . . . is mutuality of devotion forever subduing the antagonisms inherent in divided function.*[33] Overcoming ambivalence between such divided functions as love and hate, individuality and communion, leadership and comradeship is a work of love.

The seventh stage of growth is adulthood. The adult faces the choice between generativity and self-absorption. As he does so the virtue of care emerges. *"Care is the widening concern for what has been generated by love, necessity, or accident; it overcomes the ambivalence adhering to irreversible obligation."* [34] A person loves his works, ideas, and children, but to care for them is to "stay by" them through thick and thin because one's obligation is perceived as irreversible. This is the issue in sustaining one's commitment to a religious vocation in the face of severe disillusionment, caring for one's grown sons and daughters even when they adopt different life styles from one's own, and continuing to believe in God when adversity comes.

The final stage of life is maturity, which comes at different ages for different people. The crisis faced by the older person is between integrity and disgust or despair. The cardinal virtue of the later years of life is wisdom, which Erikson defines as a *"detached concern with life itself, in the face of death itself."* [35] The recent concern of pastoral psychologists and physicians with the issues of death and dying focus on the importance of the virtue of wisdom as growing out of facing matters of life and death. Of course, the young who have to go to war come to terms with life and death much earlier.

HARRY STACK SULLIVAN

Harry Stack Sullivan has done much to offset some of the basic fallacies of these too rigid conceptions of the development of personality. At the same time, the basic values of classical psychoanalysis are retained. Sullivan, instead of using a libido concept, used the much more commonly understood concept of experience, by which he meant an "undifferentiated life striving at birth" which begins to differentiate into several different "modes of experience." These modes are threefold in terms of the speech history of the individual:

1. The prototaxic mode of experience, which occurs before speech develops and encompasses the nonverbal experience of the individual.

2. The parataxic mode of experience, which refers to experience characterized by symbols used in a private or autistic way, such as an infant's babbling, or a mental patient's delusional conversation.

3. The syntaxic mode of experience, which refers to a person's ability to

communicate to another through the use of language and other types of symbolic expression.

Sullivan, on the basis of this fundamental emphasis upon communication, goes on to outline the stages in the development of personality:

> Infancy extends from a few minutes after birth to the appearance of articulate speech, however uncommunicative or meaningless. Childhood extends from the appearance of the ability to utter articulate sounds of or pertaining to speech, to the appearance of the need for playmates—that is, companions, co-operative beings of approximately one's own status in all sorts of respects. This ushers in the juvenile era, which extends through most of the grammar-school years to the eruption, due to maturation, of a need for an intimate relation with another person of comparable status. This in turn, ushers in the era that we call preadolescence, an exceedingly important but chronologically rather brief period that ordinarily ends with the eruption of genital sexuality and puberty, but psychologically or psychiatrically ends with the movement of strong interests from a person of one's own sex to a person of the other sex. These phenomena mark the beginning of adolescence, which in this culture (it varies, however, from culture to culture) continues until one has patterned some type of performance which satisfies one's lust, one's genital drives. Such patterning ushers in late adolescence, which in turn continues as an era of personality until any partially developed aspects of personality fall into their proper relationship to their time partition; and one is able, at adulthood, to establish relationships of love for some other person, in which relationship the other person is as significant, or nearly as significant, as one's self. This really highly developed intimacy with another is not the principal business of life, but is, perhaps, the principal source of satisfactions in life; and one goes on developing in depth of interest or in scope of interest, or in both depth and scope, from that time until unhappy retrogressive changes in the organism lead to old age.[36]

The spiritual dimensions of Harry Stack Sullivan's developmental conceptions are great enough to capture the imagination of the serious theologian who will take the time to master Sullivan's insights. For instance, Sullivan shifts the emphasis from a biological determinism of personality development and makes the experience of communication and a search for meaningful community central in the distinctive development of the human being. The negative counterpart of community and communication is isolation and loneliness. Sullivan gives a penetrating understanding of the intensity of loneliness in the lives of spiritually isolated people. The alienation of a person from whose whole approval he considers most worthwhile, from the nourishing associations of those who should love him and affirm his worth, makes of him an alien, a stranger, and a pilgrim on the earth. The overcoming of this barrier by a love that knows no barrier characterizes man's redemption.

Furthermore, Sullivan's understanding of the development of personality gives the religious educator and the theologian insight into the approximate meaning of theological truth to the growing person. Sullivan enables us to beam our message of reconciliation and redemption to the growing person at the level of every day's quietest needs.

The infant receives the atmosphere of worship through touch and tone, through being held and handled securely, firmly, and gently.

The child learns the religious dimensions of life through his mastery of the words of the religious community, the names of religious places, persons, things, smells, and sounds, colors, and lights.

In the juvenile era, religion becomes meaningful in terms of the child's relationship to his playmates. Being a Baptist is not nearly so important to him as being able to play on schedule with his Catholic neighbor friend. He prefers the church where his playmates go. Religion is spelled out to him in terms of the other children of his age throughout the world. This is a wonderful time to teach him the how and why of the lives of children of other races, other religions, and other social differences.

In the preadolescent phase of personality development, religious experience becomes meaningful to the growing person in terms of the close intimate relationship he has with one friend. This is the "chumship" stage. He is more likely to be influenced profoundly by that person of his own sex and comparable status to whom he would rather be near than to anyone else he knows. This "Jonathan and David" knitting of the soul together provides the child with an inner serenity with people his own age that becomes the ground upon which he stands as he moves out to people of the opposite sex. The uncanny experiences of religious awesomeness and wonder of the earlier years of life are overcome at this stage with a growing understanding of the friendship and closeness of God and Christ.

Adolescence is characterized by the revelatory power of the encounter between the different sexes. Religious experience becomes the quest for the freedom of the surging powers of creativity in sex, coupled with the questioning of one's ability to control the unleashed powers of life. The conflictual storm and stress of this period raises many ethical questions producing high idealism and corresponding discouragement in the adolescent period.

Late adolescence is that era of personality development in its religious dimensions in which the vocational, marital, and philosophical portions of the individual's existence are brought into reconciliation with each other pointed toward the one-term goals of life. This is the era of consolidation. Here religious experience becomes a systematizing and ordering of life. Family rituals become extremely important at this stage of development.

Finally, adulthood represents the religious encounter of bondage and freedom: the bondage of older immaturities that hinder one from establishing relationships of attention, considerateness, and care for other persons; the freedom to let oneself go in abandon and devotion without the hindrances of fear. Here it is that "perfect love casts out fear."

ROBERT J. HAVIGHURST AND DEVELOPMENTAL TASKS

Another comprehensive and flexible conception of human development is that of Robert J. Havighurst. He calls the things a person must learn, if he is to be judged and to judge himself to be a reasonably happy and successful person, "developmental tasks." In a sense human development is a vocation, a calling, and the different encounters with the demands of maturity are tasks. Havighurst defines these as follows:

> A developmental task is a task which arises at or about a certain period in the life of the individual, successful achievement of which leads to his happiness and to success with later tasks, while failure leads to unhappiness in the individual, disapproval by the society, and difficulty with later tasks.[37]

These developmental tasks of the individual are presented to him when he faces the new demands and expectations from society around him upon his having received new physical and psychological powers through the normal process of growth. For instance, when a child's legs grow larger and stronger and he is enabled to walk, the society expects this task of him. Furthermore, these developmental tasks arise also from the cultural pressure of society. For instance, learning to read is a part of the culture, and societal pressures tend to demand this of the individual. More than this, Havighurst points out that the "personal values and aspirations of the individual, which are part of his personality, or self, . . . increasingly [are] a force in [their] own right in the subsequent development of the individual." [38]

Whenever a developmental task is presented to an individual, he is open to the educational efforts of his community. As Havighurst puts it, "when the body is ripe, and society requires, and the self is ready to achieve a certain task, the teachable moment has come." [39] These "teachable moments" are the "fullness of time" for the learning of a given skill for living, purpose of life, adjustment to reality, and discovery of a richer selfhood.

One of the fuller aspects of Havighurst's point of view is its emphasis upon the total life span of an individual from birth through childhood into maturity and even into old age. It is not biased in the direction of the purely infantile aspects of personality development. Likewise, Havighurst's concern is fundamentally educational as well as therapeutic. He sets himself to deal with the broad range of the guidance as well as the more narrow range of the treatment of people. IIis point of view, therefore, is a larger context into which to place some of the findings of research persons who have drawn most of their insights from the study of neurotic or even more seriously ill persons.

ARNOLD VAN GENNEP

The French anthropologist, Arnold Van Gennep, has given a communal understanding of the way a community, religious or secular, tends to develop *rites of passage* or rituals to enable individuals to interpret, decide, and make the move from one stage in life to another. He identifies three kinds of rituals—the rites of separation, the rites of transition, and the rites of reunion or reincorporation. For example, the Bar Mitzvah of a Jewish child moves him into adulthood. The engagement of a couple is a rite of separation. The wedding and honeymoon are a combined rite of transition, and various rites such as the dedication of a home would be rites of reunion. The religious community, through its ordinances, customs, and habitual ways of doing things, consciously participates in the movement of persons from one stage to another. The sacraments of the Catholic and Anglican churches tend to parallel many of the stages of development detailed by psychologists and psychotherapists. More recently secular rituals such as the driver's license, owning one's first car, buying a home, selling out or breaking up housekeeping, retirement, hospitalization, and going to a nursing home—though not interpreted by the religious community—have begun to take precedence over sacraments, ordinances, and other religious rites. Without the community of faith, persons go unsupported through these great events in their lives.[40]

SOME THEOLOGICAL IMPLICATIONS OF RELIGIOUS DEVELOPMENT

A synoptic view of the preceding theological and scientific analyses of the processes of psychological, ethical, and religious development reflects several important theological implications.

THE INSEPARABILITY OF REDEMPTION FROM DEVELOPMENT

In both the classical theological interpretations of the spiritual pilgrimage of man and the scientific conceptions of the personality development of man, the redemption of man from sin and the emergence of a free self in man, respectively, are inseparably tied up with a struggle of the soul in the process of time and becoming. When one draws upon the categories of revelational theology, he thinks in terms of regeneration and sanctification, whereby the Christian is born into a new life and brought to the fullness of the stature of Christ. In secular conceptions of the development of personality, brought out more recently in scientific pursuits, the teleological striving of individuals toward maturity is pictured through the process of growth. Therefore, the use of the method of correlation will reveal that the scientific conception of maturity today is in a sense a secularization of the religious conception of perfection and eschatology.

THE DEVELOPMENTAL CHARACTER OF A DYNAMIC ETHIC

John Bunyan saw that the spiritual life and growth of the Christian is not a smooth and easy path. To him it had many jagged turnings in the way. Likewise, Gesell, in his highly detailed descriptive psychology of personality development, underlines the fact that growth and development are not smoothly accomplished. They are filled with many spurts and jags. The overall patterning of behavior is more important than the immediate lag or doldrum of outward growth. Likewise, the very darkest and foreboding developmental task may not only be threatening as a task but also promising as a "teachable moment."

Furthermore, the qualitative evaluation of a given kind of behavior changes from stage to stage in human development. For instance, homosexual thoughts and activities may be qualitatively and ethically different thoughts and activities in the life of a person at the age of ten or eleven from what the same acts or thoughts would be at the age of thirty-five or forty. Likewise, the ethical life of an individual is gauged meaningfully in terms of the added difficulty of ethical living which unsolved developmental tasks create in the life of a person who, nevertheless, is facing newer tasks every day. For the psychologist of religious experience who attends to the confessional needs of parishioners before God in prayer, this insight into the meaning of temptation, as such, becomes an indispensable one for effective pastoral care and counseling. The person who has mastered, for instance, Havighurst's conception of developmental tasks and teachable moments has an unusually deepened appreciation of the weight of some of the burdens that people carry.

THEORIES OF DEVELOPMENT AND DRAMAS OF REDEMPTION

Contemporary psychologists and psychotherapists have evolved varied theories of development as has been seen in the foregoing descriptions. Within the temporal confines of the life of man these research people have given detailed analyses of both the vicissitudes and the potentialities of man. The more they chart the developmental process of man's becoming a self, the more they encounter the necessity of evaluating the ultimate goals of man's being. This is why, apparently, psychologists of personality are becoming more and more concerned with the broader aspects of culture and personality. Likewise, it is why religious concern becomes apparent as a man's explorations in personality development mature. Gordon Allport and Erich Fromm are cases in point.

Just at this stage the theologians themselves have made a basic contribution to a psychological understanding of the development of personality. The apostle Paul, St. Augustine, Bernard of Clairvaux, Søren Kierkegaard, and John Bunyan, themselves, encompassed many of the realities of the development of personality in the dramas of spiritual redemption which have been reviewed above. However, they are unique in their contributions at several points: First, they had the courage to interpret spiritual development in terms of their own personal autobiographies. (Interestingly enough, Sigmund Freud did this himself in his book, *The Interpretation of Dreams*.) They developed symbolic or mythological patterns for conceptualizing the spiritual pilgrimage of man. At one important point, though, these theologians transcend the conceptions of the developmental psychologists. They seek the ultimate goal and not merely the proximate goal of man's becoming. Another way of stating it is that they interpret the spiritual pilgrimage of man in terms of his essential nature and his infinite destiny as well as in terms of his obvious nature (which can be observed) and his finite destiny.

This pinpoints the essential contribution that theologians have made to the understanding of the development of personality. Søren Kierkegaard, in his conception of the stages on life's way, repudiates the idea that personality development is automatic progress and that if left alone and given proper conditions a personality will inevitably develop. Although this idea is not set forth in any great dogmatic way by the developmental psychologists, nevertheless, it is a tacit assumption that can be all too easily drawn from what they say. Kierkegaard, to the contrary, saw the stages on life's way as essentially valuational stages. He saw personality development as occurring through radical transformation when a person, through faith, encounters God and thereby is enabled to take the leap from one stage to another through an activated decision to grow.

When we have taken into account and given full credence to all the nourishing factors in personality development, we still come face to face with the quiet reality that we are not quite able to avoid: Man decides upon faith whether or not it is better for him to grow or to remain as he is! This is a decisive evaluation in the presence of any developmental task. Such a decision arises from his inmost depths and is made basically upon the transcendent ultimacy or the handy expediency in the measure of reality the person grasps. When, therefore, we say that a person is in touch with reality, the theologian immediately goes to work to evaluate the kind of reality with which he may be in touch. Is it a proximate or an ultimate concern that fosters his growth?

PERSONALITY DEVELOPMENT AND CHRISTIAN ESCHATOLOGY

Focusing the proximate concerns of man with his ultimate is a major problem in personality development of both the individual and the group. The proximate concerns of man are always in tension with his ultimate concerns, whether he knows it or not. This tension in personality is essentially an eschatological tension. Biblical theology, as such, grapples with the meaning of this tension between the temporal and the ultimate for the perfection of the saints, the edification of the Body of Christ, and the consummation of the Christian community at the set end of the age.

John Marsh discusses the whole problem in light of the meanings of *chronos* (measured time, duration) and *kairos* (time of opportunity and fulfillment). He very aptly says that "biblical conception of time is not that of evaluation or progress, or even of chronological succession." In biblical realism *kairos* is at bottom a time of promise (prophetic and historical) and fulfillment, and essentially "history consists of times bringing opportunities, the basic time and the decisive opportunity being that of the coming of Jesus Christ." [41]

Personality development in such an understanding of time and growth would not be the result of the mere passage of time or of inevitable progress. Rather, growth hinges upon decisions made at given redemptive moments in life. Personality is conditioned but not determined by circumstances and chronological age. The self is the accrued results of its faith responses to the decisive grace of God revealed in opportune moments of life. Eternal life breaks through in the *kairos,* involving man in anxious confrontation of the necessities of his finitude and the free possibilities of God's grace. These are decisive moments, proximately in man's hands by reason of the response of faith, but ultimately in God's hands. Oscar Cullmann defines *kairos* thus:

> Kairos in secular usage is the moment in time which is especially favorable for an undertaking; . . . it is the fixed day, which, in modern jargon, for example, is called D day. . . . The New Testament usage with reference to redemptive history is the same. Here, however, it is not human deliberations but a divine decision that makes this or that date a kairos, a point of time that has a special place in the execution of God's plan for salvation. Because the realization of the divine plan of salvation is bound to such points of kairoi chosen by God, therefore it is a redemptive history.[42]

This conception of time reasserts the difference between mere chronological maturity and spiritual maturity. Kierkegaard was being faithful to the biblical realism of time when he interpreted movement from one stage of life to another as a decisive change of "ways of life," not as the automatic growth of a plant if given enough time and the right conditions. Decision, which he called a leap of faith, was necessary for growth.

Apart from this understanding, personality development becomes simply a process of adjustment to the least common denominator of the meaningless process of history into which we are born. The creative breakthrough in a decisive moment of time of the promises of another age is not possible. All that now is directly results from what has been.

Contemporary conceptions of personality development have in too many instances (although most certainly not in all instances) been posited upon the scientific optimism characteristic of the age of enlightenment. Man's tension between the proximate and ultimate concerns of life has been settled in terms of a proximate understanding of reality. Thus reality has been defined in commonsense terms. Consequently, the struggle of the soul to respond to the decisive breakthrough of the ultimate concerns of an individual about his existence are relegated to a realm known as fantasy or illusion. The research of Boisen reflects the chaotic, undisciplined, and pride-ridden concern of psychotic patients as to the ultimate end of their existence as well as that of the world as a whole.

My whole point here is that Christian eschatology (which may be defined as the study of the relation of the ultimate destiny of the universe to the ordering of the proximate situation of man in society) is reciprocally related to our understanding of personality development. Our eschatology shapes the goals of our personal strivings, whether we know it or not. These goals, in turn, specifically determine our interpretation of the developmental pilgrimage of the individual personality. These two ideas are so rarely seen as being in relation to each other that I hesitate to mention them together lest I fail utterly to communicate what I mean. However, I draw much comfort from the writing of Ray Petry who has said that the eschatological, cataclysmic conception of life is held to have no rapport with the more developmental conception. The "cataclysm of the Gospels and the more developmental conception of modern times are held to be in necessary conflict. Yet, there may be evolution and growth within cataclysm; and cataclysm may take place within process." [43] Often lost in the semantic confusion of today is the direct connection which Jesus made in his parables between the growth and cataclysm in God's redemption of man and society. The "fullness of time" of the coming of the Kingdom, on the one hand, and the expectant growth necessary for that *kairos,* on the other, were held in balance with each other.

Stages of personality development and the communication of religious reality are related. One of the greatest truths that has come to us through the developmental study of personality is that religion is communicated differently at different stages of the development of a person. Religious concern manifests itself with different meanings at different levels of spiritual growth, as Bushnell intuitively discerned long before our time. The ultimate reality of God is mediated through the proximate relationships of parent to child. The whole religious quest consists of opening the doors of childhood to the incursions of the Eternal. When a damaging human relationship closes in upon a growing child, the shutter of his soul may be closed to the light of God. At length the picture of God that he gets is a distorted one, but on the other hand, an open relationship of parent to child can more and more turn the child away from the parent himself to a direct relationship to God. One of the contributions that theologians have made to our understanding of the development of personality is that God himself is capable of breaking through some of the distortions of interpersonal relationships and establishing direct encounter with the person himself. God encounters a person through other redemptive personalities or communities around the individual. The mystic and the contemplative religious person clings rather tenaciously to the quiet conviction that God may reveal himself directly to the individual apart from other types of interpersonal relationships. To say that God usually manifests himself to a growing person through his significant field of interpersonal relationships is a very different thing from saying that God *cannot* manifest himself in any other way!

Great theological battles have been fought back and forth over the terrain on which developmental psychologists are working today. The same basic issues, for instance of Pelagianism and Augustinianism, have tended to emerge again in the controversial discussions of contemporary psychologists of personality. Controversies emerge in a distinctly secular semantic framework and seem to be new problems to those who have either remained uninformed about historical theology or have rejected these categories as representatives of a kind of authority which they could not tolerate. Nevertheless, the same basic issues remain, and in a sense religious concern goes on, although it has been pushed underground.

NOTES

1. John Burnette, trans., "Fragment 91–b," *Early Greek Philosophy* (London: A. & C. Black, 1930), pp. 133 ff.

2. Ibid., "Fragment 44."

3. E. P. Pusey, trans., *The Confessions of St. Augustine* (Mt. Vernon, N.Y.: Peter Pauper Press, 1838), p. 28.

4. Edmund G. Gardner, ed. and trans., *The Book of St. Bernard on the Love of God* (New York: E. P. Dutton, 1915), p. 97.

5. Ibid.

6. John Bunyan, *Grace Abounding*, tercentenary ed. (Grand Rapids, Mich.: Zondervan, 1948), pp. 103–4, 128.

7. M. Esther Harding, *Journey into Self* (New York: Longmans, Green & Co., 1956).

8. David Swenson, *Something about Kierkegaard*, rev. ed. (Minneapolis: Augsburg, 1945), pp. 162–63.

9. Søren Kierkegaard, *Stages on Life's Way,* trans. Walter Lowie (Princeton, N.J.: Princeton University Press, 1945), p. 413.

10. _____, *Either-Or,* trans. David Swenson and Lillian Swenson (Princeton, N.J.: Princeton University Press, 1949) 1: 83.

11. Ibid., 2: 223.

12. Regis Jolivet, *Introduction to Kierkegaard,* trans. W. H. Barber (London: Frederick Muller, 1950), p. 140.

13. Horace Bushnell, "The Kingdom of Heaven As a Grain of Mustard Seed," *The New Englander* (October 1844) 2:600–19, quoted in H. Shelton Smith, *Changing Conceptions of Original Sin: A Study in American Theology Since 1750* (New York: Charles Scribner's Sons, 1955), p. 142.

14. Lewis J. Sherrill, *The Struggle of the Soul* (New York: Macmillan, 1951).

15. Arnold Gesell, Francis Ilg, and Louise Ames, *The Infant and Child in the Culture of Today* (New York: Harper & Bros., 1944).

16. _____, *The First Five Years of Life: The Pre-School Years* (New York: Harper & Bros., 1940).

17. _____, *The Child from Five to Ten* (New York: Harper & Bros., 1946).

18. _____, *Youth: The Years from Ten to Sixteen* (New York: Harper & Bros., 1956).

19. _____, *Infant and Child,* p. 26.

20. Francis Ilg and Louise Ames, *Child Behavior* (New York: Harper & Bros., 1955).

21. Ibid., p. 14.

22. Margaret Mead, *Male and Female: A Study of the Sexes in a Changing World* (New York: William Morrow, 1949), p. 145. Used by permission.

23. Karl Abraham, *Selected Papers,* trans. Douglas Bryan and Alix Strachey (London: Hogarth Press, 1948), pp. 370 ff.

24. Leon Saul, *Emotional Maturity* (Philadelphia: J. B. Lippincott, 1947).

25. O. Spurgeon English and G. H. J. Pearson, *Emotional Problems of Living: Avoiding the Neurotic Pattern,* rev. and enl. ed. (New York: W. W. Norton, 1955).

26. John Bowlby, *Attachment and Loss* (New York: Basic Books, 1969), 1: 28.

27. Erik Erikson, *Identity in the Life Cycle* (New York: International University Press, 1959), pp. 64–65.

28. _____, *Insight and Responsibility* (New York: W. W. Norton, 1964), p. 118.

29. Ibid., p. 119.

30. Ibid., p. 122.

31. Ibid., p. 124.

32. Ibid., p. 125.

33. Ibid., p. 129.

34. Ibid., p. 131.

35. Ibid., p. 133.

36. Harry Stack Sullivan, *The Interpersonal Theory of Psychiatry,* ed. Helen Swick Perry and Mary Ladd Gawel (New York: W. W. Norton, 1953), pp. 33–34. Used by permission.

37. Robert J. Havighurst, *Human Development and Education* (New York: Longmans, Green & Co., 1953), p. 2.

38. Ibid., p. 4.

39. Ibid., p. 5.

40. Arnold Van Gennep, *The Rites of Passage* (Chicago: University of Chicago Press, 1960).

41. John Marsh, "Time," *A Theological Word Book of the Bible,* ed. Alan Richardson (New York: Macmillan, 1952), p. 263.

42. Oscar Cullman, *Christ and Time* (Philadelphia: Westminster 1950). Used by permission.

43. Ray Petry, *Christian Eschatology and Social Thought* (New York: Abingdon, 1956), p. 44.

QUESTIONS FOR FURTHER STUDY

1. Choose one of the devotional books—Augustine's *Confessions,* Bernard's *On the Love of God,* or Bunyan's *Grace Abounding.* Compare your religious experience with the author's.

2. Choose one of the psychologists, such as Gesell, Sullivan, Erikson, or Havighurst. Consult their primary works listed in the notes for this chapter. Compare your own emotional and spiritual development to their system.

3. What does the idea of development have to say about the nature of conversion?

4. Compare any one of the prescientific explorers of personal growth with any one of the scientific explorers.

5

CONVERSION: SACRED AND SECULAR

Conversion is not a uniquely religious experience, although it may be. Conversion is not limited to any one religion, although one form of religion may make more of the phenomenon as a religious experience than another form does. However, no one seems to deny that conversion, in whatever form it takes, is a profound psychological experience with far-reaching social and interpersonal effects when indeed it is profound. From the beginning of its efforts as a scientific study of religious experience, the psychology of religion has, as a discipline, been concerned with conversion. Conversion is an observable, behavioral phenomenon. It can be spoken of in both a sacred and a secular manner. In fact, the experience is being less and less referred to in a sacred manner. This is true even in the literature of the psychology of religion because of the more distinctly secular ways of speaking of the experience. Therefore, one of the things the reader will want to look for, hopefully, as these pages are being read, is the way in which this potentially religious experience is referred to in increasingly secular manners. To begin this study, we need to get some of the definitions of conversion clearly in mind.

What Is Conversion?

Conversion, strictly defined, is a noun referring to the act of being converted in any sense from one position or conviction to another, from one party or form of religion to another, from one group affiliation to another. More often than not, in the psychology of religion, the word *conversion* is used to refer to an abrupt change toward an enthusiastic religious attitude, with the highly emotional features being conspicuously evident, whether they are lasting or not.

In the biblical accounts of the New Testament, conversion as a noun is used only once, and that is in Acts 15:3 which refers to the "conversion of the Gentiles." The word is used as a verb to refer to the act of turning away from God, as it is in Galatians 4:9, but it is ordinarily used in speaking of man's turning to God, as in Acts 9:35 and 15:19. Regularly, the verb for turning, *epistrephein,* means to reverse one's direction in life, to change one's devotion or loyalty, or to repent or rethink one's way of life as one lives before and in relation to God. The words for *turning* are often associated with the words *repent* and *believe.* One turns from darkness to light (Acts 26:18), from idols to God (1 Thess. 1:9), from vain things to a living God (Acts 14:15). When one turns to the Lord, the veil is removed, says Paul in 2 Corinthians 3:16. To be converted is an inward but objective change in man in that he confronts and comes to terms with God. Conversion is not a ritual, an outward deed, or a purely subjective experience inasmuch as God is working in the processes of man's life to will and to do his good work. It leads to an observable new way of life, but this is the result of a spiritual transformation and fresh identification with God in Christ.[1]

The biblical teachings concerning conversion are descriptions of encounters with oneself in relation to God all along life's way. They are never associated with any particular ritual, but are distinctly personal changes of direction because of significant revelations of one's self and of God. Such would be the spirit of William James in his 1901–02 Gifford Lectures on Human Nature. As a professor of psychology at Harvard, he became the best-known and most-quoted psychologist of religion of our times. In his lectures, later published as a book, he says of religion in general:

> I prefer to ignore the institutional branch [of religion] entirely, to say nothing of the ecclesiastical organization, to consider as little as possible the systematic theology and the ideas about the gods themselves, and to confine myself as far as I can to personal religion pure and simple.[2]

Against the backdrop of a previous chapter on the divided self, James begins a chapter on conversion with the following classical definition:

> To be converted, to be regenerated, to receive grace, to experience religion, to gain an assurance, are so many phrases which denote the process, gradual or sudden, by which a self hitherto divided, and consciously wrong, inferior and unhappy, becomes consciously right, superior and happy, in consequence of its firmer hold upon religious realities. This is at least what conversion signifies in general terms, whether or not we believe that a direct divine operation is needed to bring such a moral change about.[3]

Inherent in this definition are several assumptions about conversion that have become "standard operating assumptions" of the field of psychology of religion since James idelibly stamped it with his influence.

First, a variety of terms is used by different persons to describe conversion, depending upon their own ideological persuasion. Some of these terms are distinctly theological and refer to divine intervention. Others are more psychological and attempt empirical descriptions of human behavior, as such. To James they are "so many phrases" to describe a common phenomenon.

Second, a self-psychology of personality is used as a working hypothesis of human nature. This self is capable of being divided and being united. The concepts of self-psychology are inherently a value-oriented psychology. Values are the basis of conflict. The self is not to be thought of in terms of selfishness or unselfishness, but much in the sense that the Revised Standard Version translates the words *life* or *man* from the words such as *psyche* and *soma*. The self refers to a person-as-a-whole or "being," as in human "being." The later self-psychologists such as Freud, Jung, Adler, Rank, Sullivan, Horney, Fromm, Angyal, Lecky, Rogers, Maslow, Snygg, and Combs gave more elaborate views of the self. An excellent symposium of many of these views is to be found in Clark Moustakas's, *The Self*.[4] However, in principle and content, these assumptions are implicit or explicit in the definition of conversion by James, as well as in his chapter, "The Divided Self." If one will disentangle his conception of the soul from Platonic theories of its separateness from the body, and if one will lean hard on the unity of the person as a whole in Hebrew psychology, then one can say that the self in twentieth-century psychologies of personality is a near-equivalent for the word *soul* without some of its Platonic and religious propaganda connotations.

Third, another built-in presupposition of James's definition of conversion is *conflict within the self*. This conception falls into step with Pauline and Augustinian religious experience and theology. Paul said: "What I would, that I do not; but what I hate, that I do." In his confessions, Augustine said: "I said within myself: 'Come, let it be done now,' and as I said it, I was on the point of resolve. I all but did it, yet I did not do it."[5] James says of Augustine: "Augustine's psychological genius has given an account of the trouble of having a divided self which has never been surpassed."[6] I would amend his words "having a divided self" to "*being* a divided self," because the words James uses infer, to me at least, that we *have* a self, when in reality we are—existentially—a self-as-a-whole. Platonic assumptions lurk in James's wording. The issue in any event, however, is that of conflict between the self that I am and the self I want to become, the life that is and the better life that can be. The resolution of this conflict is the essence of the conversion experience. In this view, if there is no conflict, there is not likely to be any conversion.

James presupposes that conversion may or may not be the result of "direct divine operation." Thereby he established the intention to speak of conversion in either supernatural or humanistic terms. James opens the way for a creative tension between psychology as a behavioral science and religion as a distinctly theological endeavor. When one settles this tension on one side or another, he becomes either a psychologist or a theologian, but not a psychologist of religion. To create an antiphony between behavioral science and "theological dynamics," to use Seward Hiltner's phrase, is the task of the psychologist of religion. When the creative tension is rejected in behalf of the firm certainties of a psychological system or a theological dogma, however valuable these are, then the boundary situation remains untouched and unexplored.

Fifth, James perceives conversion as a *process* related to time. It is a "process, gradual or sudden." We are keenly aware of this issue in the churches of the Great Awakening which were founded on the presuppositions of the reality of conversion as the primary, valid index to religious certitude before God. We are prone to assume that the more sudden or gradual a conversion is the more valid, religiously or psychologically, it is. We are likely to impute the "miraculous intervention of God" to the more sudden conversion and to describe the more gradual conversion to religious nurture and correct psychological development. In both instances, we are likely to have a distorted perception. The commitment of the psychological approach is to see the process of development in both the gradual and the sudden conversion. In either event, the element of process-in-time is there.

For these five bases of a psychological approach to religion, inherent in his definition of conversion, we are permanently indebted to William James. Hence, his definition of conversion has become somewhat normative for a working hypothesis of conversion. The task that is at hand now is to describe more recent approaches to the nature of conversion since James's pioneering work. These varying perspectives are not necessarily contradictory but tend to be mutually complementary of each other.

Perspectives of Conversion

CONVERSION AS THE RAPIDATION OF GROWTH

By rapidation we mean that a given process in human life and development is sped up by intervention from without. By placing plants in a hothouse and controlling the weather, nutriment, and care, plants grow and produce faster. By placing a person in an engineering program of education, the assumption is that he can become an engineer in ten years whereas it would take a lifetime by the apprentice-direct experience of working one's way up from a sweeper in an engineering company to the position of chief engineer. Rapidation as applied to conversion would mean, by analogy, that the experience of conversion hastens, steps up, intensifies, normal growth.

The earliest proponents of this interpretation were G. Stanley Hall and Edward D. Starbuck. Starbuck stated the point of view as follows:

> Theology takes the adolescent tendencies and builds upon them; it sees that the essential thing in adolescent growth is bringing a person out of childhood into the new life of maturity and personal insight. It accordingly brings those means to bear which will intensify the normal tendencies. It shortens up the period of duration of storm and stress. . . . [The essential distinction appears to be that] conversion intensifies but shortens the period by bringing the person to a definite crisis.[7]

Starbuck overidentified conversion with adolescence, probably because his sample of people were adolescents. However, the studies of Jung and Erikson have supplied data for correcting this overidentification. Carl G. Jung points out that the heavier crises of faith, often resulting in psychological illness, occur after the age of thirty-five. As a result, his primary concern was with the failure of meaning in adult lives, not the origins of neurosis in childhood trauma.

The developmental hypotheses of Erikson also suggest that other times of storm and stress are even more intense than those of adolescence, such as the search for intimacy in the face of loneliness in young adulthood, the crises between generativity and self-absorption in adulthood, and the struggle between integrity and despair in later maturity. Each of these times is a time of conflict for a divided self that needs unification in order to grow. The growth of the self toward love, care, and wisdom, to use Erikson's "schedule of human virtues," may be slow or rapid. Are these not times calling for conversion? Could not conversion shorten the process of maturity by bringing a person to a definite crisis? I think it could; but if so, one would need a dynamic rather than a static view of conversion. Conversion would have to be seen as an ongoing process that occurs more than once, although the initial occurrence would be the time after which—before God—a person would never be the same again by reason of an initial, conscious covenant of faith in God.

Another assumption in Starbuck's concept of conversion as the rapidation of growth is that he seems to assume that conversion always results in growth toward maturity and *never* in regression to an infantile state. James distinguished between "the religion of sick souls" and the "religion of healthymindedness," giving a prelude to what we now know as the psychopathology of religion. This field has collected data to demonstrate that conversion does not always shorten the process of growth but also may rapidate an already-in-progress regression of the person to a more infantile state.

The rapidation view of conversion must be challenged at this easy assumption that all rapidation is forward in its movement toward greater growth and maturity. More recent authors have observed that rapidation may be backward or regressive. Leon Salzman, for example, describes religious conversions as being of two kinds: (1) the progressive or maturational type, and (2) the regressive or psychopathological type. The first results in "the positive fulfillment of one's powers with self-awareness, concern for others, and oneness with the world." It is a conjunctive, anxiety-relieving, integrating conversion that matures the person. The second kind of conversion may either "precipitate or be a part of the psychotic process." The latter kind of conversion is marked by exaggerated irrationality and intensity of beliefs and results in a high percentage of backsliding of converts. It regularly includes contempt, hatred, intolerance, compulsive proselytizing, and the need for martyrdom and punishment for beliefs.[8]

CONVERSION AS THE UNIFICATION OF A DIVIDED SELF

As has already been suggested in the discussion of James's definition of conversion, the unification of the divided self is an optimum result of conversion. The division of the self should not be mistaken as a pathological phenomenon such as is superficially and popularly referred to as a split personality or schizophrenia. Schizophrenia more technically refers to a break with reality, withdrawal of one's affections from real to fantasied objects, and so on. The *dissociated* personality comes much more near to describing the divided self. A more intensive treatment of the religious life of both the schizophrenic person and the dissociated person will be found in a later chapter on psychopathology and religion. The focus of this chapter, however, is upon the dimensions of the self in persons who have no clinically definable mental illness in the strict medical use of those terms. These persons are caught between the poles of several dilemmas that pull them in different directions.

The first dilemma of the divided self is a *dilemma of loyalties*. The average person between the ages of eighteen and twenty-five is caught between loyalty to the way he has been brought up and the way of life of close friends and associates his own age. He has a loyalty to his parents and a loyalty to his peers. A nineteen-year-old girl, for example, has a war of independence going on with her mother at the same time the majority of her associates are smoking marijuana, going to marijuana festivals, and getting arrested by the police. She has a strong and positive devotion to her father, a negative attitude toward her mother, and a desire to help her friends who are in prison and in mental hospitals because of selling and/or using drugs such as LSD, hashish, and heroin. The beginning of her discovery of peace within her conflicting loyalties will be what Horace Bushnell called "the expulsive power of a new affection." Here the power of a new relationship magnetically relocates "the habitual center of personal energies" and creates a higher thesis for the polar tension between her parental loyalty and peer-group loyalty. This can be the emergence of a new leader in her life, such as a pastoral counselor, a teacher, or an older friend. It can be the discovery of a new cause, such as a vocational interest. It can be the persuasion to accept a new set of beliefs embodied in a new peer group. In any one or all three events, she is recentered on a new affection that overcomes the conflict.

The second dilemma of the divided self is the *dilemma of authority*. Erikson calls this the leadership polarization. The conflictual self is at war over the authority of parents, wife or husband, employer and institution. Much of the religious conflict expressed by persons is at its roots a conflict over what they were taught by their parents. A self can be deeply divided over the ways in which parental religious teachings have both become a part of the self and at the same time are rejected by the self. The need to be dependent upon parents is at war with the call to be independent of them. Leaving father and mother and following one's religious leader is a pitched battle within the self. Leaving father and mother to be married may be a way to escape from the authority of parents. Once the escape is effected the mate becomes of no more use, which may issue in divorce or chronic resentment of the authority of marriage as an institution.

Again, the ways in which husbands and wives dominate each other and strive for power in the home is another source of conflict over authority. The resolution of this conflict in a shared recognition of the authority of God is a new basis of humility and a possible sparking of the conversion of a whole family as result.

The conflict between the authority of God and one's own authority is the inner core of the conflict over authority. As Nietzsche is reported to have said: "There is no God! If there were, how could *I* not be he!" This struggle is called *hybris* or self-elevation. The psychoanalysts called it primary narcissism. The central thrust of healthy conversion is to sensitize persons to their finitude, to enable them to accept their humanity, and to cause them to prophesy concerning the grace of God but to be aware that they do so "in part" at the same time.

The third dilemma of the divided self is *conflict over freedom and restriction*. The late Andras Angyal called this the tension between the autonomous and homonomous needs of a person.[9] This conflict comes to focus most vividly in the collision of the freedom impulses of a person with the strictures of institutional religion. This conflict issued in the conversion of Martin Luther to a kind of freedom—later called Lutheranism—from Catholicism. This dynamic change has been portrayed by Erikson in his *Young Man Luther*. Before Luther, the conversion of Augustine was from a loose kind of limitless freedom of a rather wild life to the ordered disciplines of Catholicism. Similarly, John Henry Newman was "converted" from Anglicanism to Catholicism. Yet it was John Bunyan who was imprisoned for preaching without the legal permission of the Church of England. Today, one sees people from the free church tradition of Baptists, Quakers, and so on being converted to the more binding ritual and liturgy of the Episcopal church and the devout Catholic priest being converted to less ordered and structured expressions of faith such as Quakerism, as was Gregory Zillboorg, the psychoanalyst.

The divided self is nebulous and vague until one sees it in terms of these dilemmas of loyalty and authority and of freedom and structure. Until one gets such specifics in mind, the thought of a divided self is just another cause for free-floating anxiety, circular thinking, and re-unification. However, such specifics have a way of at least marking out the battlegrounds of conflictual selves and locating the arenas that call for responsible decision. Responsible decision is integral to thoroughgoing conversion, yet these decisions must have the strong meat of specific relationship, of the self-as-a-whole to itself, to others, to institutions, and to God. Without these specifics the new birth in conversion may turn out to be a pseudocyesis, that is, an imaginary birth rather than a real one. All of the premonitory symptoms of a real birth will be there, but as Socrates says, it will upon delivery be a wind-birth.

CONVERSION AS A CHANGE OF DIRECTION

Conversion in its New Testament sense, as well as words used in the Old Testament for the experience of transforming encounters with God, literally means a change of direction, a "wheeling about," a U-turn in life. In the life of the Apostle Peter, for example, there were many such turnings, and the Lord Jesus Christ told him that he would "turn again" after his, Jesus', death. Then he was to strengthen his brethren and enable them to do likewise (Luke 22:31).

This conception of conversion is the most easily communicated of all the conceptions mentioned in this discussion. The reason, in my opinion, for this ease of communication is that it encompasses *both* the decision of a person to change his direction *and* the participation of God in the revelation of *which* direction to take. The experience may be gradual or sudden, dramatic or undramatic, or even unnoticeable by others. Yet the event takes place.

A vivid description of the turning of the spirit of man from bondage to freedom, from darkness to light, from the clutch of necessity to the risks of freedom, is found not only in biblical accounts but also in Plato's *Republic:*

And now, I said, let me show in a figure how far our nature is enlightened or unenlightened:—Behold! human being living in an underground den, which has a mouth open towards the light and reaching all along the den; here they have been from their childhood, and have their legs and necks chained so that they can not move, and can only see before them, being prevented by the chains from turning round their heads. Above and behind them a fire is blazing at a distance, and between the fires and the prisoners there is a raised way; and you will see, if you look, a low wall built along the way, like the screen which marionette players have in front of them, over which they show the puppets.

I see.

And do you see, I said, men passing along the wall carrying all sorts of vessels, and statues and figures of animals made of wood and stone and various materials, which appear over the wall? Some of them are talking, others silent.

You have shown me a strange image, and they are strange prisoners.

Like ourselves, I replied; and they see only their own shadows, or the shadows of one another, which the fire throws on the opposite wall of the cave?

True, he said; how could they see anything but the shadows if they were never allowed to move their heads?

And of the objects which are being carried in like manner they would only see the shadows?

Yes, he said.

And if they were able to converse with one another, would they not suppose that they were naming what was actually before them?

Very true.

And suppose further that the prison had an echo which came from the other side, would they not be sure to fancy when one of the passers-by spoke that the voice which they heard came from the passing shadow?

No question, he replied.

To them, I said, the truth would be literally nothing but the shadows of the images.

That is certain.

And now look again, and see what will naturally follow if the prisoners are released and disabused of their error. At first, when any of them is liberated and compelled suddenly to stand up and turn his neck round and walk and look towards the light, he will suffer sharp pains; the glare will distress him, and he will be unable to see the realities of which in his former state he had seen the shadows; and then conceive someone saying to him, that what he saw before was an illusion, but that now, when he is approaching nearer to being and his eye is turned towards more real existence, he has a clearer vision,—what will be his reply? And you may further imagine that his instructor is pointing to the objects as they pass and requiring him to name them,—will he not be perplexed? Will he not fancy that the shadows which he formerly saw are truer than the objects which are now shown to him?

Far truer.

And if he is compelled to look straight at the light, will he not have a pain in his eyes which will make him turn away to take refuge in the objects of vision which he can see, and which he will conceive to be in reality clearer than the things which are now being shown to him?

True, he said.

And suppose once more, that he is reluctantly dragged up a steep and rugged ascent, and held fast until he is forced into the presence of the sun himself, is he not likely to be pained and irritated? When he approaches the light his eyes will be dazzled, and he will not be able to see anything at all of what are now called realities.

Not all in a moment, he said.

He will require to grow accustomed to the sight of the upper world. And first he will see the shadows best, next the reflections of men and other objects in the water, and then the objects themselves; then he will gaze upon the light of the moon and the stars and the spangled heaven; and he will see the sky and the stars by night better than the sun or the light of the sun by day?

Certainly.

Last of all he will be able to see the sun, and not mere reflections of him in the water, but he will see him in his own proper place, and not in another; and he will contemplate him as he is.[10]

The main characteristics of the conception of conversion as a spiritual turning is its dynamic interpretation of life as a pilgrimage of the spirit over the long pull of the years as over against the concept of conversion as being solely the first and "stamping" encounter with God at the conscious level. In this view, there are many turnings in the way although there will probably be one initial one hundred eighty degree turn. The central act of conversion is the change of direction in life. In Prescott Lecky's theory of personality, the thrust of the self is to maintain consistency of values. When a new set of values is posed to an individual—or group, for that matter—conflict ensues over the ethical dissonance between the new way of life and the old way. Resistance to change must be overcome if a person is to grow, or, if not, to consolidate on a level already attained.[11] Responding affirmatively to the new value claims results in a conversion.

The spiritual turning of which we are speaking here is also pictured in the New Testament as a changing of the mind, a change of heart. These words are translated as "repentance" or "rethinking." The hearts of fathers are hardened, but they are "turned" to their children by the power of the good news of the coming of the Kingdom of Christ. Here is a turning from unteachableness to openness and teachability, from suspicion to trustfulness. In the Old Testament the meaning of *repent* is to turn back, as if to retrace one's steps back to God and the covenants one has formed with God. One has strayed and lost his sense of direction. To repent is to get on the right road going in the right direction. To do this one has faith in God. In the New Testament that God is revealed in Jesus Christ. In the contemporary church, repentance is the integral part of being converted.

CONVERSION AS AN ACT OF SURRENDER

One of the students in my class did a careful word study of the spectrum of literature on conversion, paying attention to the terms used for conversion as well as the grammatical forms the word *conversion* takes when used as a verb. He concluded that the verb *convert* is regularly used in the passive sense: "To be converted," "was converted," "have been converted," and so on are examples. This observation reflects one whole set of assumptions about the nature of conversion, namely, conversion takes place as a result of an act of surrender, a certain giving up, a release of aggressive discharges of personal power to a more receptive, relaxed, and submissive relation to reality and Reality as a Whole. One quits fighting, responds with trust, and recognizes the Power that is greater than oneself and at the same time has one's best interests at heart.

Kurt H. Wolff says that surrender is "cognitive love" in seed form. By this he means that all the fruits of love grow from cognitive love which expresses itself through the act of surrender. He says that other meanings of cognitive love spring from the acts of surrender. Several of these meanings are: *total involvement, suspension of received notions, pertinence, identifications, and the risk of being hurt.*

The person who surrenders becomes totally involved with the object of his love, having difficulty deciding where the boundaries of the self end and the boundaries of the Loved One end.

Furthermore, in the act of surrender one starts over by suspending all previous notions, beliefs, values, and rethinks afresh the whole of life as it relates centrally to the Loved One. This is a kind of "bracketing."

In the third place, in the act of surrender, a person assumes that all that comes to his attention is pertinent and related to the approval of the Loved One.

The fourth dimension of the act of surrender is identification with rather than mastery of the Loved One. He is changed or transformed into the same likeness through the power of the Loved One in his life.

Finally, risk characterizes the act of surrender. One makes oneself vulnerable to change by the Loved One. Yet, as did Job, he says: "Though I am slain, yet will I trust." The spirit of the young Hebrew captives of a king demanding that they worship foreign gods *is* the attitude of the person who is genuinely converted, who really surrenders to God: "Our God whom we serve is able to deliver us from the burning fiery furnace; he will deliver us out of your hand, O king. . . . that we will not serve your gods or worship the golden image which you have set up" (Dan. 3:17–18, RSV). This is the act of surrender in face of the risk of being hurt.[12]

These five dimensions of the act of surrender are all necessary to distinguish genuine conversion from specious conversion, spiritual transformation from an appeal for magical results or a bargain that is being struck with God.

Harry M. Tiebout, a psychiatrist who spent much time in the treatment of alcoholics, makes a distinction between the act of surrender and mere compliance to external demands. Surrender implies admission of powerlessness. Admission of the truth of one's finiteness and limitedness is "the blood brother of acceptance." One is able to incorporate a truth as part of oneself, not merely capitulate to a theoretical idea. Surrender produces the wholehearted acceptance of the self as one is. Compliance, on the other hand, "means agreeing, going along but in no way implies enthusiastic, wholehearted assent and approval." [13] This deep-running surrender is embodied in the first two steps of the Alcoholics Anonymous *Twelve Steps to Recovery:*

1. We admitted we were powerless over alcohol—that our lives had become unmanageable.
2. We came to believe that a Power greater than ourselves could restore us to sanity.

In increasing numbers, these persons mark these two affirmations as the turning point in their road to recovery.

In a careful study of the results of conversion in the treatment of alcoholism, C. Roy Woodruff says that there are four categories of conversion among the alcoholics who remained sober as a result of conversion. The first category is *psychosocial conversion* in which the person is changed in self-concept and relation to others. This is a horizontal conversion based on the love of people and enlightened self-interest. The second category is *restrictive conversion* which is similar to Salzman's regressive conversion but is different in that the person changes from drunkenness to sobriety but stabilizes at a level of arrogance, ambition-riddenness, and intolerance of others. A third category is called *limited Christian conversion*—the person remains dependent, indecisive about what is right and wrong. In essence, this person is inadequate, but the conversion experience removed the devastation of alcoholism. His possibility of becoming depressed or schizophrenic after his conversion should be watched closely. The fourth category Woodruff poses is the *comprehensive Christian conviction,* implying that the experience is deeply felt, total, transforming, releasing, and transcendent. The central focus is in the revelation of God in Jesus Christ. It involves a total involvement of the self in Christ.[14]

The perspective of conversion that presumes an act of surrender presupposes varying degrees of ability to commit oneself. In the studies of Bowlby, Erikson, Kenniston, and others, it was shown that this capacity varies from individual to individual in terms of the person's emotional deprivation. Some people, from a theological point of view, obviously "enter into life," as Jesus said, but they also "enter into life maimed," as Jesus also said. It is better to do the latter than to languish in hopelessness waiting for perfection or to assume that handicaps are not real at all. The psychologist of religion can identify emotional maiming or crippling in the lives of individuals and groups. He would ask: "Is there not room for these crippled-ones-in-the-spirit as well as the lame, the halt, and the blind in body?" As a theologian, my answer would be: "Yes!"

PROGRAMMED CONVERSION

No discussion of conversion is complete when separated from the institutionalization of conversion in the programs of the churches. The realist today cannot take the position of William James in considering religious experience from a purely personal, noninstitutional point of view. This is especially true of the phenomenon of conversion, because whole religious movements have been escalated on the presupposition that conversion is *the* via par excellence into the kingdom of God. The Great Awakening was a very vital frontier movement that drew its strength from the agreed upon expectation that *all* people must be converted. They were called "converts." Furthermore, the churches of the Great Awakening—Baptists, Disciples of Christ, the Church of God, the Assembly of God, and to a great extent Methodists, and so on—were established as denominations upon a doctrine of repentance, expectation of conversion, and the ritual of the revival as *the* model for becoming a Christian and a church member. This is still true in considerable force in all these denominations, regardless of the gradual slide downward of the age level of converts toward childhood and even infancy and regardless of the subtle shifts in church programming of great numbers of these churches.

Furthermore, in the 1950s and 1960s the resurgence of piety in America and to some extent in other parts of the world has been heralded by the mass evangelism of Billy Graham, Oral Roberts, and other less well-known persons. These evangelists use the institutionalized interpretation of conversion as *the* operating hypothesis of their appeal to large numbers of people.

Now in the 1970s, the nonrational aspects of the counterrevolution have grasped at the revival model of programming conversion experiences. Explo '72 in Dallas, Texas, for example, was a mass festival of the less radical youth of middle-class America in response to the programming ability of Campus Crusade. The packaging of conversion persuasion was the pattern of the approach of this movement as well as the less well-organized Jesus Movement.

The programming of conversion introduces several new factors into the basic nature of conversion. First, the revival creates a social expectation that persons will behave in a pattern of conversion. The possibility, though not the necessity, is that the conversion will be artificially induced due to external pressure. Second, the amount of external pressure may stimulate the person's need to be obedient and compliant or rebellious and nonconformed. Both phenomena have been observed. Third, other extraneous factors may take precedence over the need of the individual to be converted to a faith in God—the need to demonstrate the charisma of the evangelist; the need to maintain the public image and financial solvency of the revival team, the local church, or the denomination; and the need to recruit membership in mass movements and organizations. As in any mass production, the redirection of time with any individual person or thing tends to increase the amounts of impersonal authority for individual attention.

An excellent study of these and other dimensions of programmed conversions has been made by Professor Liston O. Mills of Vanderbilt Divinity School. He did a "one-year later" follow-up study of a revival that had lasted three weeks in a church in Indiana. He chose this particular revival because it had a spontaneous character, bursting out of the bounds of the traditional one-week pattern, and extended for three weeks. In these three weeks one hundred twenty-five persons responded to the invitation to make decisions for Christ. Of these, one year later, one hundred eight names were supplied by the church to Mills. Of these, ninety-three were chosen as having sufficient information to make contacting them possible. Of the ninety-three, attempts were made by random sample to contact sixty-one (64 percent). Interviews were completed with forty-one persons (44 percent). Fifteen refused to be interviewed (25 percent of the number contacted). Five (0.8 percent of the number contacted) could not be located.

Mills applied several criteria in evaluating the results of the interviews. Durability of religious participation in the life of the church was one criterion. For example, 7 percent made a profession of faith but did not seek baptism. Forty-one percent attended less than once a month, 39 percent attended more than once a month, and 12 percent attended more than once a month and had assumed responsibilities in the life of the church. A second criterion was the age of persons making decisions. No adults made *critical* decisions of religious commitment. They were all upon a statement of previous baptism and/or transfer of church membership. Sixty-six percent of those under age sixteen did not follow through to baptism.

Mills's conclusion that speaks most to the purposes of this book concerned the meaning of conversion. To these persons, conversion meant the *public* acceptance of Jesus Christ as Savior through responding to *the ritual of the invitation* which is extended by the preacher just before the singing of the last hymn, during which a person walks the aisle and by doing so *publicly* confesses Jesus Christ as Savior. This is the institutionalization of conversion. By this definition, the conversions of Augustine, the Apostle Paul, and the Ethiopian eunuch are weighed in the balances and found wanting! Concerning institutionalization of conversion through the revival and the invitation, Mills says:

> . . . symbols, forms, and procedures have a tendency to develop an autonomy of their own. Dependence upon them often leads to a denial of the very truths they were designed to communicate. Such would be the case with a revival. The symbolic act of coming to the front of the church ceased to represent the deep truth of conviction of and repentance for sin. . . . The impression is made that this is the *only* way to enter the church and the *only* experience which is saving.[15]

Such programming of conversion is far afield from the depth and transforming power of the experiences spoken of by James, Tiebout, and others. Yet the preaching at revivals dramatizes the experiences of Paul, the Ethiopian eunuch, and the Philippian jailer. But when one follows closely the results of even dramatic revivals today, one wonders if this preaching is not more of a sightseeing tour than an actual reenactment of the battle of the spirit with forces of evil and destruction. Nathaniel Hawthorne took John Bunyan's *Pilgrim's Progress* and satirized the New England church life of his day in a story called "The Celestial Railroad." In brief he describes the way between the City of Destruction and the Celestial City as having been changed into a sort of religious tourists' attraction for which, for a fee, people could ride in a railway car and *see* the Slough of Despond, the Iron Cage of Despair, the battle with Apollyon, and so on without having any risk or hurt threaten them. They could truly say they had made the trip without any change in themselves at all.

SECULAR CONVERSION

One of the reactions to the stereotyping of conversion in religious programming has been for .increasing numbers of people, including theologians, to drop the term from their vocabulary except when they are describing extremely conservative or dogmatic expressions of religion. An example of this is in Charles Stewart's book, *Adolescent Religion*. Whereas at the turn of the century, two psychologists, E. D. Starbuck and G. Stanley Hall, spoke of religious conversion as a typically adolescent phenomenon, Stewart in 1967 wrote a whole book on the subject of adolescent religion and used the concept of conversion only three times. In the first reference he likened conversion to one's first communion and confirmation, a sort of rite of passage to adulthood. In the second reference, he identified conversion with "more conservative Protestant children." The third reference was in a case study of "Diane, a conservative Protestant."

However, Stewart, having turned aside from any positive interpretation of conversion, nevertheless, used other meaningful categories to describe religious experiences that in a previous generation would have been discussed as conversion experiences. He talks, for instance, about vulnerability and invulnerability, the quest for identity and the lack of identity, coping with stress or succumbing to stress, faith and fantasy in adaptation, and so on. The coin of the realm in communication about religious faith and nurture is a distinctly psychological idiom that is exchangeable in both the sacred sanctuary and the secular marketplace.[16] As one student said, this is not so much a process of secularization as it is a rejection of a loaded term, a signal reaction word, namely, *conversion*, that would label one as a rigid reactionary if he used it.

This student's point of view is corroborated by Ralph Hood in a study of religious experience in which he observed that "indiscriminately anti-religious persons may actually have religious experiences but do not identify them as such." [17] On the other hand, proreligious persons may report as religious, experiences which are such only in name.

We seem not to be dealing with religious experience itself. A collapse of commonly agreed-upon ways of describing religious experience is the problem. The heavy pro and antireligious propaganda surrounding the programming of religious experience of all kinds creates the problem.

However, as one reads the works of Abraham Maslow as he describes "peak-experiences" in the lives of productive, healthy, and creative persons, one sees the psychological equivalents of the classical meanings of conversion discussed in this chapter. Maslow speaks of the resistance to being "rubricized," by which he means a "cheap form of cognizing . . . to place a person in a system takes less energy than to know him in his own right." [18] The following description by Maslow of the aspects of a peak-experience as an acute identity experience is an empirical description of what an earlier generation called conversion and a compact summary of the contents of this chapter. Note that at no point does he call peak-experiences conversion, but also note how similar the descriptions are:

The person in the peak-experiences feels more integrated (unified, whole, all-of-a-piece), than at other times. He also looks (to the observer) more integrated in various ways (described below), e.g., less split or dissociated, less fighting against himself, more at peace with himself, less split between an experiencing-self and an observing-self, more one-pointed, more harmoniously organized, more efficiently organized with all his parts functioning very nicely with each other, more synergic, with less internal friction, etc.

As he gets to be more purely and singly himself he is more able to fuse with the world.

The person in the peak-experiences usually feels himself to be at the peak of his powers, using all his capacities at the best and fullest.

A slightly different aspect of fully-functioning is effortlessness and ease of functioning when one is at one's best.

He is now most free of blocks, inhibitions, cautions, fears, doubts, controls, reservations, self-criticisms, brakes. These may be the negative aspects of the feeling of worth, of self-acceptance, of self-love-respect.

He is therefore more spontaneous, more expressive, more innocently behaving (guileless, naïve, honest, candid, ingenuous, child-like, artless, unguarded, defenseless), more natural (simple, relaxed, unhesitant, plain, sincere, unaffected, primitive in a particular sense, immediate), more uncontrolled and freely flowing outward (automatic, impulsive, reflexlike, 'instinctive,' unrestrained, unself-conscious, thoughtless, unaware).

In the peak-experiences, the individual is most here-now, most free of the past and of the future in various senses, most "all there" in the experience.

The person now becomes more a pure psyche and less a thing-of-the-world living under the laws of the world.

Expression and communication in the peak-experiences tend often to become poetic, mythical and rhapsodic, as if this were the natural kind of language to express such states of being.

All peak-experiences may be fruitfully understood.

People during and after peak-experiences characteristically feel lucky, fortunate, graced. A not uncommon reaction is "I don't deserve this." Peaks are not planned or brought about by design; they happen. We are "surprised by joy." The reaction of surprise, of unexpectedness, of the sweet "shock of recognition" are very frequent.

A common consequence is a feeling of gratitude, in religious persons to their God, in others to Fate, to Nature, to people, to the past, to parents, to the world, to everything and anything that helped to make this wonder possible. This can go over into worship, giving thanks, adoring, giving praise, oblation and other reactions which fit very easily into a religious framework. Clearly any psychology of religion, either supernatural or natural, must take account of these happenings, as also must any naturalistic theory of the origins of religion.[19]

Maslow says that a person "needs a religion or religion surrogate to live by, in about the same sense he needs sunlight, calcium, or love." He calls this the "cognitive need to understand." Life has to have some meaningful framework for a person to survive. The seemingly meaningless aberrations of the most acutely psychotic person serve to provide him with a shred of understanding with which to hold on tenuously to life. As Maslow says, "What man needs but doesn't have, he seeks for unceasingly, and he becomes dangerously ready to jump at *any* hope, good or bad. . . . We need a validated, usable system of human values that we can believe in and devote ourselves to (be willing to die for), because they are true rather than because we are exhorted to 'believe and have faith.'" [20]

However, the choice between a religion that exhorts and a surrogate religion that provides a freshly stated set of propositions is a hard choice for a person in the formative years of late adolescence and early maturity to make. He may be caught in a struggle—a storm and stress—between the religious tradition of his parents and the surrogate religion of a psychological system. In responding warmly to the latter, he may be simply establishing independence of mother, father, home church, and the past. He may be on a pilgrimage to a fresh restatement of his faith which he can understand and use. This is the best possible hope. The worst possible solution may be that he does not see that the psychological systems of today are in essence surrogate religions. Thus, his teeth will be set on edge against the religion of parents that has indeed lost its power and become a "grapes of wrath" kind of bitterness rather than love, joy, peace, long suffering, and kindness which are the fruits of the spirit.

NOTES

1. John Marsh, "Conversion," *The Interpreter's Dictionary of the Bible* (Nashville: Abingdon, 1962), 1: 678.

2. William James, *Varieties of Religious Experience* (New York: New American Library, 1958), p. 41.

3. Ibid., p. 157.

4. Clark Moustakas, *The Self: Explorations in Personal Growth* (New York: Harper & Bros., 1956).

8. Augustine *Confessions* 7. 6, 7, 11.

6. James, *Varieties of Religious Experience,* p. 144.

7. Edward D. Starbuck, *The Psychology of Religion,* pp. 224, 262.

8. Leon Salzman, "Psychology of Religious Ideological Conversion," *Psychiatry,* vol. 16, no. 2 (May 1953).

9. Andras Angyal, *Neurosis and Treatment* (New York: John Wiley, 1965), pp. 8, 29.

10. Plato *Republic* 7.

11. Prescott Lecky, *Self-Consistency,* pp. 245–56.

12. Kurt H. Wolff, "Surrender and Religion," *Journal for the Scientific Study of Religion,* vol. 2, no. 1 (Fall 1962).

13. Harry M. Tiebout, "Surrender vs. Compliance in Therapy," *Pastoral Psychology,* vol. 9, no. 83 (April 1958), p. 30.

14. C. Roy Woodruff, *Alcoholism and Christian Experience* (Philadelphia: Westminster Press, 1968), pp. 23–48.

15. Liston O. Mills, "Conversion Experiences in a Revival of the First Southern Baptist Church of Clarksville, Indiana" (Th.D. diss., Southern Baptist Theological Seminary, 1963), pp. 205–6.

16. Charles Stewart, *Adolescent Religion* (New York: Abingdon, 1967), pp. 180–83, 200–4, 266.

17. Ralph Hood, "Religious Orientation and the Report of Religious Experience," *Journal for the Scientific Study of Religion,* vol. 9, no. 4 (Winter 1970), p. 289.

18. Abraham Maslow, *Toward a Psychology of Being,* p. 126.

19. Ibid., pp. 104–14.

20. Ibid., p. 206.

QUESTIONS FOR FURTHER STUDY

1. Write a brief autobiography of your own conversion, conversions, or peak-experiences. If you have not experienced such events in your life, write your reaction to the ways other people talk about them.

2. What parallels to conversion in the Judaeo-Christian tradition can you find in a secular movement such as communism?

3. Do you think conversion is by definition a religious experience, or is it a form of human behaving in crises whether a person thinks of himself as religious or not?

4. Read Erik Erikson's *Young Man Luther* or John Henry Newman's *Apologia Pro Vita Sua,* and describe the conversion of these men from one religious persuasion to another.

6

MYSTICISM AND THE LIFE OF THE SPIRIT

Mankind's mystical involvement at the nonrational level of human experience in his encounter with the Infinite has more recently become a burning issue, not only in the life of religious people but also in the lives of people who have turned their backs on institutional religion. Persons who have been brought up in a distinctly secular setting, those of whichever generation who see themselves as opponents of the institutions of life—whether it be the church, the school, the state, or the home —are turning to mystical experiences. In short, by reason of the impact of the concerns for religion on American thought, the pervasive influence of the counterrevolution, and the use of psychedelic drugs there has been a renewed interest in mysticism and the life of the spirit.

Mysticism is a way of knowing. Mysticism moves upon the assumption that God, spiritual truth, and ultimately our faith may be known through immediate intuition, insight, or illumination in a way different from ordinary perception. Mysticism builds upon the heightening of sense perception through the discipline and development of all of the senses rather than overdependence upon one of the senses. For example, more recent mystical disciplinarians are calling attention to the conscious development and increased use of the senses of touch, taste, and smell as well as the senses of hearing and seeing. Evelyn Underhill speaks of mysticism as an art, "the art of union with Reality." The mystic "aims at and believes in such attainment." [1] A more recent definition is that of Hal Bridges who says that "mysticism is selfless, direct, transcendent, unitive experience of God or ultimate reality, and the experient's interpretation of that experience." [2] St. Augustine epitomizes such an experience in his *Confessions:*

> I entered even into my inward self, Thou being my Guide: and able I was, for Thou wert become my Helper. And I entered and beheld with the eye of

my soul . . . my mind, the Light Unchangeable. . . . He that knows the Truth, knows what that Light is; and he knows It, he that knows It, knows eternity. Love knoweth It. Oh Truth Who Art Eternity! And Love Who Art Truth! And Eternity Who Art Love! [3]

A SPECTRUM OF THE MYSTICAL EXPERIENCE

Not all mystical experiences are alike. There are different qualities of light and shade of meaning in the kinds of experiences that mystics describe. These fall into a spectrum which can be perceived in a variety of meanings if we take an analytical look at the different kinds of experiences which mystics describe. These various kinds of mysticism cannot be clearly demarcated from each other but blend into each other almost imperceptibly. This is why I use the figure of speech of a spectrum. Nevertheless, they can be differentiated from each other in a qualitative way. The different kinds of mysticism, as I perceive them, are somewhat as follows:

NATURE MYSTICISM

In nature mysticism the boundaries between the Self and Nature are obliterated; the Self blends with all natural objects within its vision. This kind of experience is described most vividly by Wordsworth in his poem "Lines Written a Few Miles above Tintern Abbey":

And I have felt
A presence that disturbs me with the joy
Of elevated thoughts; a sense sublime, a sense
Of something more deeply interfused,
Whose dwelling is the light of setting sun,
And the round ocean and the moving air,
And the blue sky, and in the mind of man;
A motion and a spirit, that impels
All thinking things, all objects of all thought, and rolls through all things.

In nature mysticism there is a confluence of subject and object almost like the union of an unborn child with its mother. It is like one lying on the seashore with shiny waters glittering in her eyes, stimulated by breezes and distance and nearness which become blurred into one. "Without and within glide into each other." The nature mystics speak of being "borne up" by the earth speaking to them, of the air giving them "something of itself," of the mystery and glory of the sea, of the light and brilliance of the sun and the "exquisite color and sweetness of the sky." They lay considerable emphasis upon the puniness of prayer and the inarticulate mass of the soul, as well as the complete inadequacy of language. From a philosophical point of view one might say that the nature mystics are more pantheistically oriented. R. C. Zaehner describes this type of mysticism as panen-henic. In this kind of mysticism "all creaturely existence is experienced as one and one as all." [4]

SELF-BLENDING MYSTICISM

A second kind of mysticism emphasizes the blending of the self into the All, the Infinite, or the Ultimate. Buddhism interprets all phenomenal things as being impermanent and in a constant state of change. No happiness abides in them. Pain is identical with the hungers and cravings of self. The only way to liberation or enlightenment is the extinguishing of all craving and desire, the escape from and transcendence of the self.

In self-blending mysticism the self blends gradually into the cosmos; this is the state of Nirvana, in which there is oblivion to pain, to care, or to external reality induced by joy, intoxication, and ecstasy, as in Buddhism. In Hinduism it is the extension of the fire of life through final emancipation from the self and reunion with Brahma. For example, Aldous Huxley says that if a person "persists in worshipping the beauty in art and nature without going on to make himself capable, through the selflessness of apprehending beauty as it is in the Divine Ground, then he is only an idolater." [5]

Huxley, with his preoccupation with mescaline as a drug that induces mystical experience, turned to a Vedantic form of Eastern mysticism that insisted that nature mysticism was a form of idolatry and that one must go further by losing the ego, the self, in a sort of disembodied consciousness that struggles even then against repentance and union with the clear light of the Void. Salvation comes in a total obliteration of the sense of personal identity. This is not a negative view of the self as in the orthodox moralisms of Christianity. Rather it is the attempt of the self to "lose its identity" in behalf of a greater identity with God, as in Brahma, and so on through the dying out in the heart of the fires of passion, hatred, delusion. This emancipation results in a beatific spiritual condition that frees the self from the necessity for future transmigration, as in Buddhism.

PLATONIC AND/OR NEOPLATONIC MYSTICISM

In this third kind of mysticism the individual spirit is separated from the psychosomatic complex of the temporal or mortal part of man. This particular kind of mysticism roots far back in the history of Western culture. It probably had its beginning in an attempt to turn the philosophy of Plato into a religious system. The parent of this form of mysticism was Plotinus (204–69). Its main emphasis is upon the hiddenness of God, namely, he is so transcendent that whatever we say of him merely limits him; hence we cannot attribute to God beauty or goodness or thought or will, for all such attributes are limitations and really imperfections. We cannot say what he is, but only what he is not. God is like the sun from which the light radiates; the farther we are from the sun, the nearer we are to darkness. Matter, creation, human personality, the body, the sense processes, and so on are all a fall from the perfect to the imperfect. God emanates in three stages—pure thought, the soul, and matter. Matter is farthest removed from God. There is no trace in it of God. It is darkness. The mystical way is a reversal of this process in which the soul goes through a catharsis in which all contamination of the body is removed. This purification is preparation for contemplation, or the immediate intuition of our death. Contemplation is superior to action because it brings the mystic nearer to the vision of God. However, contemplation has an objective: to bring the mystic into union with God through a state of ecstasy in which the soul transcends its own thought, loses itself in the soul of God, becomes one with God in a mystical return to God. This kind of mysticism has distinct Neoplatonic roots and is clearly influenced by such Eastern religions as Zoroastrianism in its transmission to contemporary life. It is often mistaken for the distinctly Christian or Jewish kind of relationship to God. Much of Catholic and Protestant fundamentalism is a popular expression of this particular kind of interpretation of the mystical way of life.

CHRISTIAN MYSTICISM

The Judaeo-Christian tradition has bequeathed to us a belief in the vitality of the individual as being profoundly related to God but uniquely distinguishable from God as a total psychosomatic unity with an individuality of its own. Matter is not evil but shares in communion with God through the shape of the human body which is a "temple of the Holy Spirit." Ultimately the whole man will be transformed in God, and God will be all in all. Thus the mystical way of life becomes a "walk with God," a fellowship with other human beings, and a pilgrimage in the individual's quest for identity and search for his purpose in life in relation to God. The essential relationship is that of the creation to the creator and not that of the natural to the supernatural in opposition to one another. God is always manifesting himself through the faces and forms of mankind, and even of plants and animals. Such a mystical experience is recorded by Rufus Jones, the Quaker mystic, in the following autobiographical account:

> I was walking alone in the forest, trying to map out my plan of life, confronted with issues which seemed too complex and difficult for my mind to solve. Suddenly I felt the walls between the visible and invisible grow thin and the Eternal seemed to break through into the world where I was. I saw no flood of light, I heard no voice, but I felt as though I was face to face with a higher order of reality than that of the trees or mountains. I went down on my knees there in the woods with that same feeling of awe which compelled

men in earlier times to take off their shoes from their feet. A sense of mission broke in on me and I felt that I was being called to a well-defined task of life to which I then and there dedicated myself.[6]

In this quotation one sees the presence of nature, the awareness of individuality, the sense of awe in the presence of God, a distinct sense of communion with God, and a clear-cut sense of vocation and identification with a purpose in life.

PRACTICAL MYSTICISM

The contemporary man is debtor to all four of the above types of mystical experience, and influences run as tributaries into his perception of reality. Therefore, I suggest a fifth type of mysticism, namely, practical mysticism, because so much of what has been written on the subject of mysticism seems to be so foreign to the mundane experience of the average student, professor, workman in the shop, businessman in the office, and parent and/or child in the home. Evelyn Underhill addresses the following comment to such persons about their lives:

Yet it is to you, practical man, reading these pages as you rush through the subway to the practical work of rearranging unimportant fragments of your universe, that this message so needed by your time—or rather, by your want of time—is addressed. To you, unconscious analyst, so busy reading the advertisements on the subway wall, that you hardly observe the stages of your unceasing flight: so anxiously acquisitive of the crumbs that you never lift your eyes to the loaf. The essence of mystical contemplation is summed up in these two experiences—union with the flux of life, and union with the whole in which all lesser realities are resumed—and these experiences are well within your reach. Though it is likely that the accusation will annoy you, you are already in fact a potential contemplative: for this act . . . is, indeed, the characteristic human activity.

Underhill speaks of the breakthrough of the Eternal into the ordinary experiences of life. There is the experience of which William James speaks when he says:

I am done with great things
And big things, great
Institutions and big successes.

I am for those tiny invisible
Molecular forces that work
From individual to individual
Creeping through the crannies of the world
Like soft rootlets
Or like the capillary oozing of water
Yet which, if you give them time,
Will rend the heartiest monuments of man's pride.

Or there is that kind of practical mysticism that one experiences when one observes a plant which breaks through the preoccupations of the daily routine and commends itself to one's attention. Tennyson had such an experience when he wrote:

> Flower in the crannied wall,
> I pluck you out of the crannies
> I hold you there, root and all, in my hand
> Little flower—but if I could understand
> What you are, root and all, and all in all,
> I should know what God and man is.

The busy student driven hither and yon by the demands of parents, teachers, and the programming of his life by other people, quite often reads material concerning mysticism in a textbook fashion and has a sort of not-me feeling. Such an experience applies to other people but not to us, we are likely to say. However, practical mysticism is built on many assumptions of a different kind, namely, that in between the lines of mundane experience are wide blank spaces of unexplored reality waiting to be understood by the student much as in the reading of a book he seeks to visualize what kind of human being an author is whose material he is reading. Thus, one goes beyond the written page to the one doing the writing. One goes beyond the mundane experiences of life to the realities that are not so mundane. God breaks through both the lines and the writer to the reader. God breaks through the schedules of "scheduled men looking for a schedule God" and reveals himself as a God who cannot be programmed, managed, or manipulated. Such revelations do await if we breathe deeply, think with abandon, and contemplate the meaning of life as well as the words of life.

CHARACTERISTICS OF MYSTICAL EXPERIENCE

Mystical experience, regardless of the particular color or hue that it takes, has been described by various persons as having certain common characteristics. An analytic approach to mystical experience identifies these characteristics and helps the reader to understand a bit more of what mysticism is all about.

William James identified four aspects of mystical experience as follows: First, *mystical experience is ineffable.* James says that "it defies expression, no adequate report of its contents can be given in words." He says that it is like music that calls for a musical ear to appreciate it; like love, one must have been in love to understand a lover's state of mind. Second, *mystical experience is a form of knowledge.* This knowledge is a form of insight, illumination, or revelation which carries with it "a curious sense of authority for later times." Third, *mystical experiences are transient in nature.* They cannot be sustained for long periods of time but tend to fade into the ordinariness of everyday experience. However, they can be remembered upon recognition if not recall. Fourth, *mystical experiences are passive in nature and are "received" more than they are "achieved."* One wonders if this does not relate more directly to the autonomic or involuntary nervous system than to the central or voluntary nervous system.[7]

Underhill says that mysticism is practical and not theoretical, is an entirely spiritual activity, and its business and method is love. Mysticism entails a definite psychological experience, and true mysticism is never self-seeking.[8]

Whereas William James denied having anything other than a second-hand knowledge of mysticism, Evelyn Underhill was a lifelong mystic and speaks confessionally rather than descriptively, although her confessional statements are down to earth and operationally clear.

Walter Pahnke, a medical doctor, in studying the effects of consciousness-expanding drugs such as psilocybin and LSD in producing mystical states of consciousness sought to summarize the measured criteria of genuine mystical consciousness which he drew from a study of classical mystical writings. His summary was ninefold in character as follows:

(1) Mystical experience produces an internal and external unity with one's self and with one's environment.

(2) Mystical experience blends objectivity and reality in a direct experience at a non-rational level of the essential nature of existence both through the world and of one's self.

(3) The mystic transcends space and time and receives a perspective of the timelessness of life.

(4) Mystical experience produces a sense of sacredness, or a non-rational, intuitive, hushed, competent response in the presence of inspiring realities. This is similar to Rudolf Otto's idea of the *mysterium-tremendum*.

(5) Mystical experience produces a deeply felt positive mood focused upon joy, love, blessedness, and peace.

(6) Mystical experience produces a paradoxical transcendence of the laws of logic in which the person "feels out of the body" while still being "in the body." This is similar to the experience that the apostle Paul described in II Corinthians 12:2–3.

(7) Mystical experience, as James said, is ineffable, and the person feels incapable of conveying his experiences into words without distorting them by rendering them finite and impure.

(8) Mystical experience produces a feeling of transiency, or the temporary duration of the mystical consciousness as compared with usual experiences. There is less continuity and durability to mystical awareness.

(9) Mystical experience results in positive changes in attitude or behavior that increase the trust and warmth one feels toward others, a sense of relatedness with others and a relaxation of habitual mechanisms of ego-defense.[9]

These identifying characteristics of mysticism outline the speculative side of mysticism and help the analytic-oriented person to get something of a working rationale of what the philosophical stance of the mystic is in relation to reality in general. One should not assume that mysticism is a late comer to the world of philosophy, theology, and science. For example, during the fourteenth century there were two branches of mysticism, a Latin mysticism which was quite submissive to the Catholic church and a Germanic mysticism which assumed a more independent attitude toward the church. The Latin mystics were represented by such persons as Pierre d'Ailly (1350–1425), his pupil John Geurson (1363–1429), and Raymond of Sabunde (c. 1434). The Germanic school included such persons as Meister Eckhart (1260–1327), Johannes Pauler (1300–61), Gerhard de Groot (plus 1384), the Brethren of the Common Life, and Thomas à Kempis (1380–1471), the celebrated author of *The Imitation of Christ*. There has been a continuous heritage of mysticism in Quakerism dating back to George Fox (1624–91). Fox was followed by the American Society of Friends or Quaker preacher and author, John Woolman (1720–72). In our times the Quakers have been warm exponents of a practical mysticism that is demonstrated by a keen social consciousness in the work of Rufus Jones, Thomas Kelly, and Douglas Steere. One does not get a clear grasp or a keen feeling for mysticism by discursive thought but by reading descriptions of autobiographical experiences that people have had in relating themselves mystically to their universe.

MYSTICISM: A WALK WITH GOD IN EVERYDAY LIFE

We have seen that one of the most important characteristics of mysticism is that it is indescribable, ineffable, and beyond words. On this all who speak from firsthand experience about mystical happenings in their lives are agreed. Therefore, it is somewhat self-contradictory to write a discursive analytical treatise on mysticism. The reality of the experience eludes the page of print. To the contrary, one must move into the realm of poetry, poetic prose, and the slicing fire of prophetic utterance in order to describe even partially what the mystical experience is. Such epiphanous experiences as that of Moses at the burning bush, Isaiah in the temple, and Jesus on the Mount of Transfiguration are luminous expressions of mystical encounter with God. Moses experienced the presence of God in the everyday work of his care of flocks of sheep. Isaiah experienced the revelation of God and his commissioning as a prophet from God in a time of great political crisis and in a place of reverent worship—the temple. The disciples experienced the revelation of Christ as the son of God in a time of fatigue and heaviness with sleep. None of these persons programmed or caused to happen any of these experiences. Consequently, the place to look for being laid hold of by the spirit of mystical experience is in the serendipitous breakthroughs of the Eternal into the commonplace, the routine, and even the drudgery of daily existence. The Eternal incarnates Reality in these mundane, everyday experiences. The difference between a mystic and a person who is not a mystic, in this sense, is not that one is, as William James said, a "sick soul" and the other a "healthy minded soul." The difference lies in the capacity to perceive. As Browning put it, "some persons see every common bush as a revelation of God, but others see only blackberries!" Walt Whitman, in his *Leaves of Grass,* says it this way:

> I see something of God each day each hour of the twenty-four,
> and each moment then,
> In the faces of men and women I see God and in my own
> face in the glass,
> I find letters from God dropped in the street, and
> everyone is signed by God's name,
> And I leave them where they are, for I know that
> wheresoever I go,
> Others will punctually come forever and ever.

Yet, the student who is pushed from class to class by a heavy schedule and probably carrying a part-time job along with his program of learning has a right to ask how this mystical, luminous event actually happens in living life daily. As a practical mystic myself and as one who has taken the lives of persons like Walt Whitman, Rufus Jones, Thomas Kelly, Howard Thurman, Douglas Steere, and many others seriously, let me venture the following suggestions as an answer to this important concern.

First, each person has a life story, a history, a memory. That memory is a kaleidoscopic succession of one's own self-in-relation to the universe above him. As one contemplates this history he is likely to experience the kind of thing that Howard Thurman describes in an autobiographical passage:

As a child I was accustomed to spend many hours alone in my rowboat, fishing along the river, when there was no sound save the rapping of the waves against the boat. There were times when it seemed as if the earth and the river and the sky and I were one beat of the same thoughts. It was a time of watching and waiting for what I did not know—yet I always knew there would come a moment when beyond the single pulse beat there was a sense of Presence which seemed always to speak to me. My response to the sense of Presence always had the quality of personal communion. There was no voice. There was no image. There was no vision. There was God.[10]

As one contemplates the twisting turns of his pilgrimage from the dawning of consciousness until the present moment, one is likely to say, as an elderly teacher of mine on his seventy-fifth birthday said, "As I think on the events of my life and unfold the memories of my years, I am overwhelmed with awe and feel that God has kept his angels up late at night redeeming my life from destruction and charting out my destiny for me." Pastoral psychologists and psychiatrists today are laying hold of the power of memory to create new life as one takes the spiritual pilgrimage or religious history of persons seriously. We have been over-educated to look back at our histories with shame and fear and find only the traumatic, the pathological, and new reasons for self-pity. However, to take the same look backward at the times of destruction from which one was delivered, at the times one has received refreshed and renewed senses of direction from God, and at the times of answered prayer tends to mobilize our human potential and stimulate fresh experiences of depth in face-to-face relationship with God.

In the second place, I have discovered that the mystical consciousness is a saving backdrop for the conversations we have with people who are in crucial human situations and seek our counseling, affirmation, and empathic understanding. Naïveté, a suspension of our own frame of reference, and participation in the being of another person who is suffering also brings us into direct, face-to-face encounter with God in the crucial human situations of life. Browning describes the intentionality that I have felt as a counselor in my search to understand those who open themselves vulnerably to trust in me:

> I would I could adopt your will,
> See with your eyes and set my heart
> Beating by yours, and drink my fill
> At your soul's springs,—your part, my part
> In life, for good and ill.[11]

Empathic listening can itself be a mystical experience in which the boundaries between selves as objects are relaxed and selves as subjects begin to flow back and forth into each other with such depth that a Third Presence soon becomes vivid and very real even if names for this Presence are never called.

The process of listening I have described is very kin to Harry Stack Sullivan's description of reverie. He says:

> Reverie continues to be relatively untroubled by grammatical rules, the necessity for making complete sentences, and so on. . . . A great deal of covert living . . . can go on without the use of words. The fact is, as I see it, that most of living goes on that way.[12]

Such wordless thinking and living as a living being often issues in indistinctly mystical experience. As William Wordsworth said, in times of reverie:

> There are in our existence spots of time
> That would distinct pre-eminence retain
> A renovating virtue . . .
> Our minds are nourished and invisibly repaired.[13]

The Christian experiences this in his participation in the love of God through the Holy Spirit. We live in a galaxied universe in which "there is no speech, nor are there words; their voice is not heard; yet their voice goes out through all the earth, and their words to the end of the world" (Ps. 19:3–4, RSV) . Such an event came my way as follows:

I sat with a preadolescent child who was in the depths of grief. Neither she nor I could talk much, yet we seemed to understand each other. She asked if I were in a hurry. I said no; as we both watched it rain outside, she asked why I was not in a hurry. I said that rarely did I find opportunity to be in the presence of a little girl who was not herself in a hurry. We sat in reverie and watched the sun come through the clouds. Then in a sparkling array a rainbow appeared on the horizon. It made no noise as it appeared, and no words cluttered our knowledge of grief, merely friendship and freedom from hurry and fear. Little did I know or have any information by such knowledge than that I was speechless. I was worshiping God through the Holy Spirit.

However, one does not have to be a highly verbal enthusiast for Christian faith in order to be aware of the mystical depths of human life and to be freed of his fear of that which lies beyond the reach of words and deep categories to describe. It was Gardner Murphy, a research psychologist at Menninger Clinic, who said about the future of the psychology of personality:

> In a future psychology of personality there will surely be a place for directly grappling with the question of man's response to the cosmos, his sense of unity with it, the nature of his aesthetic demands upon it, and his feelings of loneliness or of consummation in his contemplation of it. There may be a touch of neurotic phobea and the persistence with which modern study of man has evaded the question of his need to come to terms with the cosmos as a whole . . . our study of man must include the study of his response to the cosmos of which he is a reflection.[14]

The autobiographical data which men and women report concerning mystical experience are data in and of themselves. They are pertinent to the study of man's response to the cosmos of which he is a reflection. One cannot simply write these experiences off as an aberration in the constitutions of a few people, as attempts of sick souls to heal themselves by autosuggestion. If one tries, he may at the same time be revealing the touch of neurotic phobia in evading a considerable body of data from the lives of creative and productive people. For, as Walter Houston Clark has said, "No experience will bring to the individual a vividness of religious certainty equal to that enjoyed by the mystic." [15] And as it has also been said, religion cannot be reduced to mystical experience, nor can it survive long without it.

NOTES

1. Evelyn Underhill, *Practical Mysticism: A Little Book for Normal People* (New York: E. P. Dutton, 1914), p. 1.
2. Hal Bridges, *American Mysticism from William James to Zen* (New York: Harper & Row, 1970), p. 4.
3. Augustine *Confessions.*
4. R. C. Zaehner, *Mysticism: Sacred and Profane* (New York: Oxford University Press, 1961), p. 168.
5. Bridges, *American Mysticism,* p. 94.
6. Rufus M. Jones, "Why I Enroll with the Mystics," *Contemporary American Theology: Theological Autobiography,* ed. Vergilius Ferm (New York: Round Table Press, 1932), pp. 196–97.
7. James, *Varieties of Religious Experience,* pp. 3, 71–72.
8. Thomas S. Kepler, ed., *Evelyn Underhill Reader* (New York: Abingdon, 1962), pp. 34-37.
9. Walter N. Pahnke, M.D., "Drugs and Mysticism: An Analysis of the Relationship between Psychedelic Drugs and the Mystical Consciousness" (Ph.D. diss., Harvard University, 1963), p. 242.
10. Howard Thurman, *Disciplines of the Spirit* (New York: Harper & Row, 1963), p. 96.
11. Browning *Two in the Campagna* 9.
12. Sullivan, *Interpersonal Theory of Psychiatry,* pp. 84–85.
13. Wordsworth *The Prelude* 12. 208.
14. Murphy, *Personality,* p. 921.
15. Walter Houston Clark, *Psychology of Religion* (New York: Macmillan, 1958), p. 262.

QUESTIONS FOR FURTHER STUDY

1. Do you know anyone who is a mystic? Describe this person, the kinds of experiences he had, and how you learned of them.

2. Quite apart from whether it was a distinctly religious kind of event that happened to you, have you ever experienced a mystical state of consciousness? If so, describe it in detail. If not, describe how you feel about not having had such an experience.

3. Choose a representative of at least two of the types of mysticism described in this chapter. Study some things they have written and write a comparison.

4. Do you think the classification of types of mysticism is adequate? How would you change this classification?

7

THE EXPANSION OF CONSCIOUSNESS

Build thee more stately mansions, O my soul
  As the swift seasons roll!
  Leave thy low vaulted past!
Let each new temple, nobler than the last,
Shut thee from heaven with a dome more vast,
  Till thou at length art free,
Leaving Thine outgrown shell by life's unresting sea! [1]

Men have merely translated, not erased, the holy language of religious experience being written daily as a human document of man's true being. Recently, although we do not call it the "religious consciousness" as did J. B. Pratt, the searchlight of public attention has been focused upon the ways in which the human consciousness has been narrowed and restricted and needs expansion and elevating. We have tended to exclude the animal, plant, and inanimate world of human consciousness as a matter of unwritten policy. Not only have we tended to exclude these realms of being, we have also tended to exclude great portions of human being by calling them the unconscious, animal nature, not-me, or unacceptable self. Furthermore, studies of the closed self indicate that when placed on a continuum between the closed self and the open self most people tend to be biased by our semantic constrictions. Our particular frames of reference are so confining that expanding our consciousness to include the richness and variety of the universe has become an acute concern.

This acute concern has manifested itself in several ways in contemporary life and thought. First, the most romantic and sensational emphasis on the expansion of consciousness has been the experiments with psychedelic drugs, such as LSD and psilocybin. Such outstanding personalities as Walter Houston Clark, in his book, *Chemical Ecstasy*, have asserted that these drugs are significant and valuable stimuli to profound religious experience. Walter Pahnke has done an elaborate study of the relationship between psychedelic drugs and religious experience. He says that these drugs "might illuminate the dynamics and significant worship of God. . . . Theologians must evaluate the light that such resource could shed upon the doctrine of incarnation, the Holy Spirit, the presence of Christ, and God's *gratia activa*." [2]

Second, the emphasis on the expansion of consciousness has been furthered also by the impact of the counterculture of the late 1960s. People reject mind-constricting role performance, social class lock-stepping, and alienation from and the pollution of the natural environment of the earth. Late adolescents insist upon psychological moratoria from premature closure in making life commitments. They challenge a success-oriented, competitive, and military society. Many take part in a resurgence of interest in Eastern mysticism.

Third, the interest in the expansion of consciousness has been intensified by the upsurge of liberation movements such as black power, women's liberation, and so on. These movements have been characterized by the attempt of their enthusiasts, leaders, and sympathizers to raise the consciousness of the whole population to the basic humanity of minority groups, such as blacks and women, quite apart from their assigned roles and restricted functions in society. We are especially indebted to the women's liberation movement and to black power. They make us aware of the expanded human potential of interpersonal relationships between the sexes and the races when the exploitation of women and blacks is summarily called off. Rather, they are encountered, understood, and accepted as human beings in their own right without the unnatural constrictions that the taboos, superstitions, and vested interest that a white, male-oriented society has placed upon them.

Finally, an upsurge of interest in the expansion of consciousness has been brought into being by the vitality and organization of what is now known as the human potential movement. It has its conceptual base in the field of theory formulations of Kurt Lewin and in the research of Abraham Maslow in his exploration of the productive personality. In its operational and more popular expression, persons like William Schutz have emphasized the untapped resources of joy available to persons through an expanded human consciousness. This can occur without the use of psychedelic drugs but through the use of specific group sensitivity disciplines under adequate leadership.

PSYCHEDELIC DRUGS AND THE EXPANSION OF CONSCIOUSNESS

In a double-blind study of experimental groups, Pahnke administered psilocybin to one group, and a control group received a placebo under the same set-and-setting conditions. He found statistically important elevations of the mystical consciousness in the lives of subjects who did receive the psilocybin as over against those who did not. The sense of deeply felt positive moods of joy, blessedness, and peace were expressed as love on a very human level, but not as love of God. The sense of reverence or sacredness was awe in the pure sense of the word without necessarily being directed toward God. The most positive changes were in a development of a distinct philosophy of life, the knowledge that there is a new and depth dimension in life and an increased sense of the preciousness of life. There was more sensitivity and authenticity with other people and a relaxation of the need to play-act, put on appearances, and generally to be phony in one's behavior. Pahnke says that the most striking single phenomenon was the emergence of an awareness of a death-birth experience, of having died to an old life and then being born to a new, and this new life is a lasting sense of new significance and meaning to the rest of life.

However, another significant discovery was found. The drug alone was not sufficient. Pahnke insists that a meaningful religious setting is also necessary to produce these kinds of results. This leads to a conclusion that the value structure of the person using the drug has much indeed to do with the kind of outcome that the psychedelic-drug experience produces. This kind of experimentation with drugs under controlled conditions raises the integral and crucial issue about drug use and religious experience. The values of the use of drugs for inducing religious experience—such as Walter Clark in his book, *Chemical Ecstasy,* and Aldous Huxley in his book, *Doors of Perception,* assume—presuppose a highly disciplined intellectual and spiritual life with a heritage of religious instruction and exploration. As Pahnke's results indicate, the form of experience following the use of psychedelic drugs is shaped by the set and setting of religious values which are provided out of the heritage and contemporary religious framework that a person brings to the use of drugs prior to the time at which they are used. A hypothesis may be formed which needs confirmatory research: a drug-induced expansion of consciousness is not necessarily religious, but may intensify the chaos of the ethical values of a person who brings such chaos to the use of drugs. A devout religious person may have one kind of experience, a person with a confirmed idolatry of sexual orgasm may have another kind of experience, and a person with a rapacious desire to make money without work may have even another kind of experience.

Regardless of the kind of background and value structure a person brings to the time of using consciousness-expanding drugs, what William James said in 1902 concerning the nature of consciousness as such, after he himself used a kind of consciousness-expanding drug, is still basically true. He says:

Some years ago I myself made some observations on [the metaphysical] aspect of nitrous oxide intoxication. . . . One conclusion was forced upon my mind at that time, and my impression of its truth has ever since remained unshaken. It is that our normal waking consciousness, rational consciousness as we call it, is that one special type of consciousness, whilst all about it, copied from it by the filmiest of screens, there lie potential forms of consciousness entirely different. We may go through life without suspecting their existence; but apply the requisite stimulus, and at a touch they are there in all of their completeness, definite types of mentality which probably somewhere have their field of application and adaptation. No account of the universe in its totality can be final which leaves these other forms of consciousness quite disregarded. How to regard them is the question—for they are so discontinuous with ordinary consciousness. Yet they may determine attitudes though they cannot furnish formulas, and open a region though they fail to give a map. At any rate, they form a premature closing of our accounts with reality. Looking back on my own experiences, they all converge toward a kind of insight to which I cannot help ascribing some metaphysical significance. . . . those who have ears to hear, let them hear; to leave a living sense of its reality only comes in the artificial mystic state of mind.[3]

The real issue at the heart of the use of consciousness-expanding drugs, it seems to me, is twofold: first, the relationship between the religious heritage and education of a person and chemical ecstasy; and, second, the ways in which the American law society has collided with the American criminal society over drugs. This collision has produced a power struggle between organized law and organized crime that grinds up naïve and unsuspecting young people. Mutually excruciating demands for law and order on the one hand and the rapacious desire for money on the other hand move with an equal relentlessness. This becomes a social problem of international proportions which prostitutes and distorts imputed religious and therapeutic values associated with the use of drugs. It is a poignant reality to see young people of the counterculture becoming drug enthusiasts opposing with might and main the tyranny of the Establishment. At the same time they become victims of the worst form of the Establishment in the money moguls of the underworld who provide different types of drugs to the street-pusher. The moguls and the pushers are in it, not for religious experience or any other such elevated thing, but for the cold cash on the line from hooked victims.

THE COUNTERCULTURE AND THE EXPANSION OF CONSCIOUSNESS

After the initial exploration of William James into the hinterlands of consciousness, the thinking of Sigmund Freud concerning the expansion of consciousness became a prevailing mode of understanding of the need for an expanded ego structure of the individual. Freud saw the dark continent of the unconscious as the source of repressed mentation which goes on quite without regard for our rational thought processes. At first he used hypnosis as a way of dilating the consciousness of a person. The results proved capricious and short-lived. Therefore, he moved, on the basis of his own autobiographical exploration of his personal dreams, to what he called the "royal road to the unconsciousness," namely, dreams. He took the dreams of his subjects and used a modified form of associationism which he termed free association. This technique enabled him to decipher the code of the symbolism of the dreams and thereby to make sense of the nonsense of one's deeper-level, sleep experiences of dreaming. On the foundation of the findings of dream analysis, Freud built the imposing edifice of psychoanalysis. This science is a late nineteenth-century and early twentieth-century attempt at the laborious and highly ritualized expansion of the human consciousness.

PSYCHOANALYSIS

Later psychoanalysts modified the findings of Freud. Harry Stack Sullivan focused them on neglected, peripheral, and nonverbal aspects of the human experience of other human beings. Karen Horney, also, for example, emphasized the way in which the cultural heritage and surroundings of a person must shape his experience quite unbeknowing to the individual. The effort of the individual to become just that—an individual—is restricted by the taboos, the prohibitions, the commands, and the compelling forces of the set and setting of one's cultural framework. Of course, religion and morality are crystallized expressions of this culture. The forms of religion without the power thereof, to quote the Apostle Paul, become constricting forces on the consciousness of mankind. Liberation from these bondages to the laws of culture into the freedom of a more spontaneous and creative life widens the horizons of a person and enables him to be genuinely free. It is significant indeed that Karen Horney in her latter years turned to an Eastern religion, Hinduism, as the apt psychological expression of her basic convictions concerning the nature of human experience in its religious framework. It is as if she expanded her own religious awareness by disengaging herself from the Western Christian tradition and reaching out toward Hinduism.

Furthermore, Harry Stack Sullivan spoke of the ways in which we in our normal course of events "selectively inattend" those parameters of our daily experience which disturb the stereotypes of our thinking. These constricted modes of our behavior create anxiety. He spoke of the great realm of "the uncanny" which we experience as being beyond ourselves, as our "not-me." He saw therapy as the effort to produce a wider human awareness of those selectively inattended experiences, to establish kinship with others in a relationship freed of constricting stereotypes, and to acknowledge the unacknowledged not-me feelings we have toward ourselves as selves. He identified the sense of mysteriousness and horror that we experience when we come alongside the great realm of the uncanny.

To work out of our molds of conventionality and become conversant with this realm of the uncanny results in a widening of our consciousness and a production of human courage.

However, psychoanalytic approaches to the expansion of consciousness themselves, by the nature of the expense involved in psychotherapy of a psychoanalytic type, are culturally conditioned and bound. They tend to produce a distinctly upper-class and at best middle-class kind of mentality which is divorced from the great wide expanses of humanity in the lower-middle class, the upper-lower class and especially the lower-lower class. Furthermore, the psychoanalytic understanding of the expanded consciousness tends to leave the impression—quite unintentionally—that the unconscious represents the animal nature of man's sexual and aggressive impulses which are supposed to be brought into conformity and adjustment to a conventional society. Even this psychoanalytic effort at the expansion of consciousness, so characteristic of pre- and post-World War II psychological frames of reference, is itself in need of expansion.

Therefore in the middle 1960s, exponents of the counterrevolution such as Marcus G. Raskin, Charles A. Reich, and Theodore Roszak began to develop distinctly sociological modes of understanding consciousness and its expansion. No discussion of the expansion of consciousness, therefore, in a book on the psychology of religion published in the 1970s is complete without a focused appreciation of the impact of these representatives of what has now come to be called the counterculture.

THE COUNTERCULTURE

Marcus G. Raskin insists that we need a new vocabulary and new analytical tools to break out of the incapsulated insights which have become the common coin of what he calls the new industrial state. In the new industrial state, being a citizen, being a human being, is caught up into a new form of colonization in which consciousness and the state come to be one and the same. He says that consciousness of the average American, for example, has been clamped into the forms of four distinct colonies of the mind: the *Violence Colony,* which could be equated with government and governmental authority; the *Plantation Colony,* which could be equated with the gross national product and the economy; the *Channeling Colony,* which can be equated with the meritocracy and exclusivism of the educational institutions of the land; and the *Dream Colony,* which can be equated with the mass communications of television, radio, and newspaper. All of these colonies have heavy expressions in the bureaucratization of society. The aim is to create a human being who acts in such a way as to perpetuate the colonies. The individual who has been properly programmed, bureaucratized, and colonized has a set of constricting controls working within him and not merely upon him from the outside. Therefore, as a human being he can best be understood as a bundle of roles and is controlled by being pushed into role socialization. By the term *role,* Raskin means a practice defined by the service it performs for the larger organization behind which there is an explanation of the individual in behalf of the organization. The individual is taught to dance to the tune of the prototypes of the organization. The "exit to consciousness" is no mere repetition of private rights, Horatio Alger individualism, or compulsive bucking of the system.

Rather, an "exit to consciousness" is to become aware of the pyramidal structures of the colonies of society. Even if an individual has great latitude in his life style and his personal choices, he is then also wistfully aware that he is living according to forces external to his choices and to the relationships which he might otherwise freely choose. In fact, the art of growing old means gradually to use one's accumulated seniority and prestige to become free of the colonization of his life and the life of those younger than he. The wise old person refuses simply to perpetuate and represent those forces which externally constrict the consciousness and awareness of the living human being. A person is no colonial subject. He belongs to an intimate community which disallows the constrictions of the self to the external symbols of the colonies such as governmental position, economic success, educational position, and artificial dreams inevitably produced. One supposes that the development of wisdom and the capacity to have a humor free of cynicism that can poke fun objectively at the colonization process is the secret of what Raskin calls "being and doing" as a human being.[4]

One wonders whether Raskin would include the religious education of the population in his "channeling colony." Does he simply omit the church and the forces of religion generally from the scheme of things? He may agree with Theodore Roszak who says that when he speaks of religion he is not referring to that of the churches or to the religion of belief and doctrine, "which is . . . the last fitful flicker of the divine fire before it sinks into darkness." [5]

Another approach to the counterculture definition of the expansion of consciousness is that of Charles Reich, a professor of law at Yale University, who adopts what he considers to be a distinctly sociological model of consciousness. He separates himself from the Freudian psychobiological view of consciousness, from the Marxian economic theory of consciousness as being social class, and from the psychedelic view of consciousness expansion. Consciousness, according to Reich, gains meaning from all of these but should be seen as distinctly different. Consciousness is not a set of opinions, information, or values, but a total configuration of attitudes given any one individual which makes up his perception of reality, his world view. Consciousness is within a substantial degree, but not necessarily entirely, socially determined. Reich moves on the assumption that once a man's beliefs on certain subjects are determined a whole range of his other beliefs can be predicted. This is obvious in the way in which our culture stamps out the stereotyped awarenesses in masses of people. However, it is misleading to say that this is always true. One set of a person's beliefs does not necessarily determine what his other beliefs will be. Reich here overlooks the tower of compartmentalization in personality and seems to underestimate the power of denial in the belief structure of persons.

Reich identifies three kinds of consciousness: Consciousness I is that type of mentality formed in the nineteenth century, the traditional outlook of the American farmer, small businessman, and worker who was or is trying to get ahead in the rat-race for success. Consciousness I is characterized by individualism. Hard work always succeeds, and if you want something done, you do it yourself. Consciousness I attaches more faith to winning and succeeding than to loving and caring. Reich feels that Consciousness I led to corruption and competition in which great numbers of people lost a sense of reality as their belief in self-interest led to self-destruction.

Reich suggests a second kind of consciousness which he entitles Consciousness II, which emerged with scientific technology and the massive programming of commodities that came along with and after World War II and produced a consumerism psychology. Consciousness II grew up as a reaction to the failure of Consciousness I with its competition, inequality, and chaos of individualism. Consciousness II was a militant reaction against gangster psychology of tycoons in the business world and dictators in the political world. These inordinate expressions of individualism in capitalism gone-wild, fascism, and communism brought a breach in the existing Consciousness I. The social good of the larger group, organization and coordination of well-arranged establishments, and training go beyond the self to sacrifice for the corporation or organization as the highest good. This particular type of Consciousness II reached its limits in John F. Kennedy's "call to the colors": "Ask not what your country can do for you, but what you can do for your country."

The characteristics of Consciousness II may be listed as follows:

a. What man conquers by reason constitutes reality (law, technology, and institutions).

b. The institutional organization has priority over the individual, and the individual subordinates his will to that of others.

c. The individual must fit into a role-oriented hierarchy of the organization. Prefabricated roles for individuals and groups of individuals require a role-oriented consciousness that is constricting, narrowing, and confining.

d. Meritocracy is the order of the day in which emphasis is placed upon credentials, degrees, certification, and other "self-rights of access without which one is an outsider to the action."

e. Change is determined by social engineering, organizing, planning, and consultation with experts. Consciousness II is the attitude of expertise.

f. Power is a necessary element for effect but it must go through proper channels, proper procedures; a hierarchical priesthood controls the channels.

g. Equal opportunity is a romantic, religious ideal to which Consciousness II mentalities all give credence, but there actually is no equality because equality is always at war with excellence.

h. Consciousness II submerges the sense of the personal, private, intimate values in official roles and public images.

i. The end result of Consciousness II has been the emergence of a certain kind of constricted personality—the organization man or woman on the one hand, the corporate state on the other—composed of technology and big business. Thus Consciousness II stamps out a certain kind of mass-produced personality. That personality is worth just the cost of the product it produces in a production-oriented society and no more.

Reich points out that the counterrevolution is an opposing valence to Consciousness II which rises out of imminent self-destruction of Consciousness II because of two forces: the promise of an abundant life in an affluent culture and the threat to life caused by consumer orientation of products which we are programmed to believe that we must have.

Consciousness III is a revolution against this kind of destructiveness and has the following characteristics:

a. Rejection of and liberation from bondage to prefabricated roles on the job, in the home, in the school, in the church, and in the government. Role constriction is the source of narrowed consciousness. If consciousness is to be expanded, one must take a more existential view of the self than the constricting confining of the narrowed and prefabricated roles of Consciousness II.

b. The individual self is the primary reality, and life is founded in individuals and not in organizations.

c. The generalized standards and the effort to classify individuals according to certain stereotypes is rejected and refused.

d. Work roles, sex roles, and public roles of persons are blurred into each other as is apparent in the way persons of different sexes wear similar clothing, similar hair styles, and contend with each other as to who is to do the dirty work in the commune, in the home, and in the school.

e. A new attitude toward decision is adopted. Persons refuse to make fixed decisions for all of life but emphasize the possibility of constant change and growth of the individual. Thus, consciousness is kept open and closure is avoided in terms of the future. This is exemplified in the decisions of many Consciousness III persons who "simply do not get the idea of one man and one woman living together for the rest of their lives."

f. The group becomes the thing as a source for energy and spontaneity but the group ambition is not a norm for success. Rather, the group becomes a source of intimacy, mutual support, and processing of decisions.

g. The goals of status, security, power, respect for a public image, money, a place in the meritocracy, and so on are not only wrong, but they are unreal. Therefore, a studied nonchalance toward these goals is the order of the day with Consciousness III.

h. Consciousness III folk resist paternalism and being patronized. They are contemptuous of people who try to "do everything for them" and reserve the right (1) to make decisions for them without consultation and (2) to refuse to permit them to be a part of the decision-making process.

i. Work must be meaningful in order to be done. The idea of duty to a distasteful task is taboo. This different attitude toward work is not necessarily laziness although that has not been proved not to exist. Rather, Consciousness III persons insist on doing work that is creative and interesting and refuse to let their work come between them and other people. This seems to be a reaction against the work addiction syndromes of Consciousness II parents who have let their work come between them and their sons and daughters.[6]

One asks the question as to what are the religious implications of the Reich theory on Consciousness I, II, and III? First, Reich's emphasis on Consciousness III represents a revival and widening of the Hebrew idea of the consciousness of a corporate personality. Whereas Consciousness II had an idea of corporate personality whereby the individual is given over to a superorganization, Consciousness III expands this awareness and insists upon a larger kinship of all nations and all people. Therefore, it is not difficult for Consciousness III people to see that the North and the South Vietnamese are in the same plight. In the second place, Reich's recommendation of Consciousness III refines the kinship of man with the rest of creation. God redeems all men and all the earth and does not destroy one part of his creation in the effort to improve another part of his creation. Reich is more Dionysian in emphasizing a natural creativity coming out of the chaos of life and the self as the part of a greater over-soul in nature mysticism. In doing so he writes off orthodox Western Christianity and turns to some forms of Eastern religion.

In the third place, the heavy insistence of Reich upon a sharp distinction between Consciousness II and Consciousness III, in deed and in fact, seems to be a rehashing of the old theological problem of law and grace. For example, before his conversion Paul was a Consciousness II person, highly organized in Judaism as a highly ordered person who put down the insurrection of threatened chaos proposed by those of the Christian way. He was converted to a kind of Consciousness III in Christian experience which was at that time an unorganized, but creative, mystical group living very close to nature, hiding in caves. They insisted upon living by the Spirit rather than the law.

In the fourth place, from the point of view of organized religion, the conception of the religious offices such as that of a minister and/or pastor changes when one shifts from a Consciousness II perspective to Consciousness III. In Consciousness II a person is called to be a body to fill up a role. If he does not fill the socially expected role, he will be seen as not being "called." Consciousness III personality seems to march to the beat of a different drummer, to negate the importance of a heavily stylized role for ministers, and to insist upon a much more spontaneous and less programmed expression of care and concern for people and of ways of communicating that concern to others in such a way that they will listen.

As a form of expanded consciousness the counterculture or Consciousness III type of personality is not alone. He belongs to "the tribe," to pick up on the name of counterculture given by the authors of the Broadway musical *Hair*. As Theodore Roszak says, "The counter-culture is scarcely [a] disciplined movement. It is something in the nature of a medieval crusade; a variegated procession, constantly in flux, acquiring and losing members all along the route of the march." [7] Actually the counterculture is a "politics of consciousness." These crusaders are boisterously, persistently, and aggressively trying both to become aware themselves and to make others aware. The rape of nature by industry, the kinship of people of all nations to be bound together against the enemy of war, and a settled resolve against being pushed into the mold of the roles assigned to people which make things of persons instead of human beings—these are causes.

However, the most trenchant criticism of this effort at the political expansion of consciousness is the ephemeral nature of the commitments. As Roszak again says about the fadlike enthusiasms of counterculture exponents,

> . . . run them together as one may, they have not the continuity and comprehensiveness demanded by a way of life. And it is a way of life the young need to grow into, a maturity which may include political activity, but also embraces more fundamental needs, love, family, subsistence, companionship. Political action and organizing cannot even provide a fulltime career for more than a handful of apparatchiks, let alone a pattern of life for an entire generation. What, then, do the disaffiliated young have to grow toward? What ideal of adulthood has the world to offer them that will take the place of the middle class debauch they instinctively reject? [8]

My own reaction to Reich and Roszak's analyses of the expansion of consciousness through political awareness is that one very important element, although referred to by Roszak, is not pronounced clearly. That element is time. One of the tests of an extended consciousness is the awareness of the bounds of one's habitation in time and space. There is a certain timeless quality to the political consciousness of Consciousness III, for example. This is exemplified in the much-touted phrase of the counterculture which rejects the thought of "anyone over thirty." However, if one is quite well past the age of thirty, let us say in his fifties, he has heard that phrase for over ten years, and some of the people who are saying it are themselves either "very thirty" or well past thirty. The incongruity of this lack of awareness of the threescore or fourscore and ten years of man's life is itself a kind of constricted awareness. The counterculture enthusiasts quite often remind one of what Kierkegaard had to say about the preachments of his day. He said religious shibboleths were mouthed by many loud and long while the hall clock ticked away in the setting of eternity. For example, furthermore, if a person delays premature closure in making decisions about his life commitments, time will tend to make many of these decisions for him without participation of either his rational or mystical consciousness. This disclaimer needs to be entered at this juncture in these discussions of the counterculture as a type of expanded consciousness.

A different application of the test of time is to ask whether Consciousness III itself is not an interpretation of a temporary phenomenon. For example, Reich's book was written in 1970. As I write these words on the threshold of 1973, already we see a considerable number of young people joining the status seekers, becoming very authoritarian in their closedness of mind as Jesus Freaks, members of the God-movements, and so on and using the symbols of long hair and the hippie uniform to maintain rapport with drug users whom they exhort to "turn on for Jesus." One asks whether, by the time this book is published a few months hence, Reich's categories will really describe accurately what is happening then. Such skepticism—hopefully wholesome—should attend the apparent bandwagon impulses created by Reich's *Greening of America* and his fellow Yale professor, Eric Segal's book, *Love Story*.

The long-term evaluation of Reich would place his book in a long train of books on utopia or a primitivistic yearning to return to a Garden of Eden where food is free, clothing is not really needed, avarice is absent, and men and women live so close to nature that the sense of guilt is nonexistent. This nostalgia seems always to be with us as it was with Whitman when he said he wished he could live as cattle do, for they are composed and serene and do not lie awake at night in remorse over their sins.

A final comment about the counterrevolution has been raised by students: Where does the expansion of consciousness end without the annihilation of any clear sense of focus of selfhood? Are we to ask for a sort of Nirvana in which purpose, goal, will, and intention are absent? Is this the *summum bonum* of life? This seems to be the crucial question. If Consciousness III persons want a part of the action and want to be a part of the decision-making process, what will the decision be and will they take also a part of the implementation of the action? Or, do they expect Consciousness II people to do the relatively uninteresting and boring drudgery that it takes to stay by a decision once it has been made? My own commitment is to be a "bridge over the troubled waters" between Consciousness II and Consciousness III. The former have a challenge and a discipline to be open to, listen to, and willing to include Consciousness III persons in things that affect their lives. Consciousness III people have a challenge and a discipline to make a few clear decisions, communicate them clearly, and stay by them until they are implemented.

LIBERATION MOVEMENTS AS FORMS OF ELEVATED CONSCIOUSNESS

The expansion of consciousness has another and unique meaning in contemporary life. Minority and oppressed groups have gone and are still going through at least three phases of the expansion of their personal awareness and sense of identity. For example, first black people and women of all races became aware of the possibility of breaking out of the heavy legal and social confines that segregated them. Second, they have waged and are waging a war for equal opportunity in work, play, worship, and love. This equality of opportunity has elevated their awareness of their humanity. Third, they have begun to realize afresh the uniqueness and power of their own position in the world. One might say that these three phases consist of the removal of caste, the exercise of equality, and the discovery of personal power. As such they are varied facets of an expanded self-awareness not only for blacks and women but on the part of whites in the case of blacks and men in the case of women. Inherent in these expanding awarenesses is the collapse of fixed roles for blacks and women as persons. A fluid and continuing negotiability of the place and function of these very important groups has emerged. As a result of this increased awareness, both blacks and women are becoming articulate forces in the formation of a new human ethic and a new political force in this country.

In the religious community these minority and oppressed movements have been challenges to old religious sanctions and the stimulus for the development of a more dynamic and less static kind of religious experience. The challenges have been felt especially keenly in the areas of family living and in religious and public education. In the face of such movements one can no longer think of the religious consciousness as a private tête-à-tête of an individual with God. Religious concerns must also include an agonizing appraisal of the meaning of creation in terms of God's created order of persons of different colors and different sexes. As such, one moves out of the tradition of Pratt in his interpretations of the religious consciousness and into the arena of George Albert Coe and the thought of Anton Boisen in their empirical evaluations of religion in crisis and custom.

THE EXPANSION OF CONSCIOUSNESS AND THE HUMAN POTENTIAL MOVEMENT

Another vital force which contributes to the contemporary jet stream of concern for the expansion of consciousness is what has come to be called the human potential movement. One of the most important theoreticians of this movement is Abraham Maslow. In his posthumous book, Maslow describes the core of this movement in what he calls the "Jonah Complex." He says that all of us have a fear of our own greatness. We tend to evade our destiny by running away from our own best talents. In contradistinction to Freud he says that "we fear our best as well as our worst, even though in different ways." He calls attention to our unused potentialities and those which are not fully developed ones. He assumes that we have constitutionally suggested vocations which in religious language could be identified as a call, a destiny, a task in life, or a mission.

> So we run away from the responsibilities dictated (or rather suggested) by nature, by fate, even sometimes by accident, just as Jonah tried—in vain—to run away from *his* fate.
>   We fear our highest possibilities (as well as our lowest ones). We are generally afraid to become that which we can glimpse in our most perfect moments, under the most perfect conditions, under the conditions of the great courage. We enjoy and even thrill to the god-like possibilities we see in ourselves in such peak moments. Yet we simultaneously shiver with weakness, awe, and fear before these very same possibilities.[9]

On the basis of this assumption, Maslow developed a view of Being-Values and Being-Cognition persons whose awareness of their potential brought them to a peak-experience from time to time throughout their life. He called them self-actualizing people. These persons are

> involved in a cause outside their own skin, in something outside themselves. They are devoted, working at something, something which is very precious to them—some calling or vocation in the old sense, the priestly sense. They are working at something which fate has called them to somehow and which

they work at and which they love, so that the work-joy dichotomy in them disappears. One devotes his life to the law, another to justice, another to beauty or truth. All, in one way or another, devote their lives to the search of what I have called the Being-Values, the ultimate values which are intrinsic, which cannot be reduced to anything more ultimate.[10]

The person who has taken the intricate and highly elaborated conclusions of Maslow and formulated them into a form of positive therapy for normals is William C. Schutz in his book entitled *Joy: Expanding Human Awareness*. He and the other colleagues of his at the Esalen Center in California insist that joy arises from full development of one's personal functioning. We meet our own and other people's need for being included, for feeling a sense of control over one's destiny. We learn to express affection toward others and to receive affection from others. Shutz develops specific techniques of the expansion of human consciousness by enabling a person to experience physical release in his body to intensify that personal functioning. He uses such freeing experiences as the deliberate exploration of fantasy, empathy with others, and practice of solitude. He suggests wordless meetings of people as a form of developing nonverbal expression and deeper communication. He uses dramatic and sensitivity methods of getting in touch with persons whom we have lost, such as what he calls the "guided day-dream."

Genuine joy, according to Schutz, is the potential of being more of a person than one thinks one could be. The potential for being more significant, competent, and lovable enables one to be a more meaningful individual who is capable of coping more effectively with the world and therefore better able to give and receive love. The human-potential enthusiasts insist that human consciousness can be expanded with joy and without the use of artificial substitutes such as drugs. Their conviction is that there is no substitute for meaningful persons in one's life. The expansion of consciousness is not merely a subjective experience of a private soliloquy with God. It is equally as objective in one's encounter with other persons as he sees himself mirrored in his relationship to them.

The significance of the human-potential movement for the psychology of religious experience can best be appreciated by a historical look. The great revivals of religious concern have tended to have their beginning in small groups where definite rituals were devised for enabling the individuals to become more totally aware of each other's needs for care, comfort, confrontation, and the sheer joy of fellowship with others. A love that knows no barriers is experienced in these groups. In the midst of this expanding awareness of other people, the knowledge of God tends to break forth, shattering the dead forms of the past and becoming intimately real in the present. People participate in each other's dreams of what they might become under God. They take each other's dreams, hopes, callings, and commitments seriously. They drop the face work of the shams of respectability and are willing to be known even as they know themselves to be known by God. Although specific religious categories are not used, the human-potential movement has become a vital force generating what Howard Clinebell has called "the people dynamic" in all sorts of institutional settings and not just the church.

Naturally, as in all religious awakenings, the human-potential movement in its sensitivity training exercises has its excesses and offbeat confusions. Nevertheless, the whole movement cannot be negated on the basis of these vacillated experiences. To the contrary the central emphasis of the movement, namely the experience of joy and self-actualization in the expanded awareness of one's total environment, is very akin to the highest and best that religion has offered through the ages. One could with real profit restudy the relationship that Jesus had to the disciples and the intimate company of those who knew him best from the point of view of the positive psychology of Maslow and the practical, group interaction of the human-potential movement.

The concluding question for this chapter is also raised by Maslow in several places in his work. We need to ask about all of the contemporary movements that have emphasized the expansion of consciousness: At just what point in time does one cease to expand consciousness and decide to focus consciousness upon specific movements in time and in place? Another way of asking the question is: What is the relationship between expanded awareness and the feeling of personal responsibility before God? As we move into other chapters of this book, we will continue to examine such problems as nonverbal communication, magic, sleep and revelation, ritual and habit. However, these two questions will not become genuinely focused until we begin dealing with the problems of decision making and responsibility, temptation and fantasy, sin and forgiveness, commitment and uncommitment, loyalty and disloyalty, cowardice and hate.

NOTES

1. Oliver Wendell Holmes, "The Chambered Nautilus," *The Autocrat of the Breakfast Table.*

2. Pahnke, "Drugs and Mysticism," p. 242. A summary of this research is found in the article by Walter N. Pahnke, M.D., Ph.D., and William A. Richards, S.T.M., "Implications of L.S.D. and Experimental Mysticism," *The General Religion and Health,* vol. 5, no. 3 (July 1966), p. 22.

3. James, *Varieties of Religious Experience,* pp. 378–79.

4. Marcus G. Raskin, *Being and Doing* (New York: Random House, 1972).

5. Theodore Roszak, *Where the Wasteland Ends* (New York: Doubleday, 1972), p. xx.

6. Charles Reich, *The Greening of America* (New York: Random House, 1970).

7. Theodore Roszak, *The Making of a Counter Culture* (New York: Doubleday, 1969), p. 48.

8. Ibid., p. 202.

9. Abraham Maslow, *The Farther Reaches of Human Nature* (New York: Viking, 1971), pp. 35–36.

10. Ibid., pp. 43–44.

QUESTIONS FOR FURTHER STUDY

1. From your encounters with the drug culture, do you think that consciousness can be expanded by natural means and without drugs?

2. Contrast the point of view of William Glasser in his books, *Reality Therapy* and *The Identity Society*, with that of Freud on the unconscious.

3. To what extent does organized religion colonize the consciousness of its communicants?

4. What kind of Consciousness I, II, or III are you and your parents? Does Reich help you understand your parents better?

5. When does consciousness expansion stop and decision making begin?

8

NONVERBAL COMMUNICATION
AND PRAYER

. , ; ! ? (——) An author is very contradictory to use words to talk about nonverbal communication. As one student said when this subject was discussed, "It seems strange that the first thing we do in thinking about nonverbal communication is to write a brief comment at the beginning of class as the basis for a discussion to follow." Such is my dilemma also. Therefore, I began the chapter with the nonverbal elements in the printed page. The period has a tone of finality about it. The comma is a pause, a chance to catch one's breath between words. The semicolon is a stop sign, but not a stoplight, as the period is. The exclamation point conveys emotion, excitement, and an elevated mood. The question mark is an invitation to dialogue, and one's tone of voice rises to a crescendo at the end of a sentence that is a question. And, have you ever noticed how you will pay a little closer attention to what is in brackets or parentheses, as if the writer is on stage but turns aside and speaks in a stage whisper?

Therefore, the printed page is not without its own specific form of nonverbal communication. More subtle and less specific is the way a writer puts meaning between the lines rather than in them, the way he deals in innuendo, and the way we give thanks for blank spaces on the page with which to rest us from words.

Nonverbal communication seems to be a vital part of religious experience, both personal and public. The study of mystical experience emphasized again and again that such encounters with the reality of the Eternal are ineffable, inexpressible, beyond words. The Jewish people hold the name of God, YHWH, never to be spoken. Instead, they substitute the name *Adonai* and hold the name that signifies God's unutterable holiness as too sacred to put into words. In their psalms, one reads:

> Day to day pours forth speech,
>   and night to night declares knowledge.
> There is no speech, nor are there words;
>   their voice is not heard;
> yet their voice goes out through all the earth,
>   and their words to the end of the world (Ps. 19:2–4, rsv).

The prophets were not the wordy persons we perceive them to be as we talk about them in the religious marketplace. Ezekiel did prophetic acts such as "sitting where his people sat" and being "hurt for his people's hurt." Jeremiah conducted a listening campaign among his people, a far cry from the noisy rhetoric of the political and religious campaigns of our day. Likewise, in the life of Jesus, his silences were dramatic. When he stood before Caiaphas and was asked by him to respond to the charges of the witnesses against him, "Jesus was silent" (Matt. 26: 63, rsv). Pilate said to him, "Do you not hear how many things they testify against you?" Jesus "gave him no answer, not even to a single charge; so that the governor wondered greatly" (Matt. 27:13–14, rsv). In the face of the magnitude of the gift of redemption in Christ, the Apostle Paul exclaims, "Thanks be to God for his inexpressible gift" (2 Cor. 9:15, rsv). Paul frankly admits the basic limitations of words in the authentic prayer life. He says, "Likewise the Spirit helps us in our weakness; for we do not know how to pray as we ought, but the Spirit himself intercedes for us with sighs too deep for words" (Rom. 8:26, rsv). Jesus, in speaking of prayer, said, "And in praying do not heap up empty phrases as the Gentiles do; for they think that they will be heard for their many words. Do not be like them, . . ." (Matt. 6:7–8, rsv).

It is hardly likely that the Judaeo-Christian heritage would be quite this specific about nonverbal communication if the nature of authentic experience with God were not deeply involved. Before the discovery of the New World, Mediterranean countries were prone to stamp a picture of the Pillars of Hercules on their coins with the words underneath, *Ne Plus Ultra,* "there is nothing beyond." After their discovery of the New World, they removed the word *Ne,* and their coins read instead, "There is more beyond." The discovery of the world of nonverbal communication is to the religious life of a person like the discovery of a whole new world. There is indeed more beyond the spoken word because behind the word lies the tone of voice, the facial gesture, the movement of the body in an organ language, and the tacit meaning of the words to the individual in his internal frame of reference as he speaks them. Listening to what one means is a more exciting but a more difficult discipline than listening legalistically to what one says. Therefore, the thrust of this chapter is to answer the question: How does one get in touch with the world of the nonverbal?

THE DISCIPLINES OF THE NONVERBAL

THE DISCIPLINES OF BODY LANGUAGE

The nonverbal level of life and the life of prayer are at one in the demand for a discipline of the language of the body. Alfred Korzybski speaks of "pointing one's finger" as one example of the language of the body, the language with a difference:

> This difference, being inexpressible by words, cannot be expressed by words. We must have other means to indicate this difference. We must show with our hand, by pointing with our finger to the object, and by being silent outwardly as well as inwardly, which silence we may indicate by closing our lips with the other hand. . . . On this last level, we can look, handle, but must be silent.[1]

The pointed finger may mean such hushed reverence in identifying the ineffable depths of one's wordless communication. On the other hand, as the transactional psychotherapists suggest, the pointed finger may mean the attempt of a person to "parent" another as a "child" with his authority. The meaning of body language such as this may change with cultural shifts. For example, the *V* finger sign in World War II, especially when accompanied by some notes from Beethoven's Fifth Symphony, was a prayer of determination for victory. During the Vietnam War it became a peace sign. Ray Birdwhistle, in his book, *Kinesics and Context,* observes that body language, like verbal language, varies from culture to culture almost as a dialect.

Yet, the life of prayer has tended to universalize certain kinds of body language: kneeling on one's knees in prayer, bowing one's head, closing one's eyes, looking upward, lifting one's arms upward, clasping one's hands together, prostrating oneself face down, lying in the form of a cross, facing to the east (as in Mohammedanism), and joining hands with the person next to one.

Similarly, the milieu in which body contact between persons takes place provides a context of prayer for persons' communication which, in other contexts, would be interpreted quite differently. For example, a beautiful young woman has just been told that her husband was taken as a prisoner of war or killed in combat. The male members of her personal community may touch, embrace, or even kiss her in ways that on the happy occasion of a picnic or a superficial social encounter in a church foyer would communicate something quite different! [2]

From a clinical point of view, one can observe the ways in which "the voice of illness" is itself a way of expressing the deeper prayers of some persons who cannot put them into words. I have observed two cases of hysterical tremors of the hand, for example. Careful medical diagnosis had ruled out the possibility of organic origins of the symptoms. Under hypnosis one of the patients confessed that God was punishing him for forbidden acts he had performed with his hands and arms. The tremor was a sort of "public confession." The other patient had more specific awareness of the meaning of his symptoms. Without hypnosis, he said that God was making him "tell the whole world what he had been doing." Such cases tend to verify to some extent Sigmund Freud's assumption that neurotic behavior is a private religious ceremony, unsupported and unvalidated by the community. On the other hand, public religious ceremonies meet some of the same neurotic needs in a way supported and sustained by the religious community.

Other more distinctly psychophysiologic disorders also provide a kind of prayer language of the body. The anorexia nervosa patient, that is, one who refuses to eat at all, is often crying out at the injustice he or she —usually she—is experiencing at the hands of family members. Furthermore, a fundamental rejection of one's sexuality may often be at stake in this disorder. It is as if a young girl's prayers are saying, "Why did you make me a girl, God? I am going to do away with every sign of my femininity by not eating."

Obesity, alcoholism, and drug addiction are forms of nonverbal communication of rebellion against one's situation in life, or of protecting oneself from the unwanted responsibilities of life by incapacitating one's self through the compulsive use of food, alcohol, and/or drugs.

Body language, unhealthy person or well, is, as Paul Pruyser says, elevated into distinctly religious body language:

> Instead of having one's own body to love, the person is given the body of his church, the body of the faithful, the body of Christ, and the body and blood of the sacraments to cathect. They are all nurturing "bodies," they feed and give warmth with a tenderness that cannot fail to remind the individual of his first love relation. Church, Christ, and sacraments can be eroticized, as the mystical literature with its words "bride" and "groom" amply shows.[3]

THE DISCIPLINE OF HEIGHTENED SENSES

Thorleif Boman, in contrasting Hebrew psychology with Greek psychology, says that Hebrew psychology has a heightened emphasis on hearing. Therefore, obedience is the key to the Hebrew understanding of behavior in relation to God. Obedience is ranged in order of submission to authority. Husbands, fathers, and slave owners are to be submissive to God; wives, children, and slaves are to be submissive, as unto the Lord, to husband, father, and slave owner. Considerateness of wives, refraining from harassment, and justice toward slaves is required of the man of the house in the male-oriented Hebrew home. The thing they have in common, regardless of station in life, is obedience to the word of the Lord. Consequently, the Hebrew-Christian tradition has become a word-oriented, sermon-producing heritage, demanding obedience of its adherents.

On the other hand, says Boman, Greek psychology emphasized the role of seeing in knowing, and insight became its central concern. To be able to see beyond the visible world to the invisible world was to renew the inner person. To be able to see the Eternal in all the faces and forms of things was to pray.[4] This motif appears in the thought of the Apostle Paul, who confessed himself to be debtor both to the Jew and to the Greek. He said, "So we do not lose heart. Though our outer nature is wasting away, our inner nature is being renewed every day. For this slight momentary affliction is preparing us for an eternal weight of glory beyond all comparison, because we look not to the things that are seen but to the things that are unseen; for the things that are seen are transient, but the things that are unseen are eternal" (2 Cor. 4:16–18, RSV) .

Therefore, the Greek way of searching for the Eternal through sight and insight as well as hearing and obedience increases the discipline of the senses in encounter with God. This way of communication with God is channeled through at least five media: symbolism, music, art, architecture, and clothing.

Symbolism. A symbol is a sign that represents something else that has an existence independent of the symbol. This varies from religion to religion. In Egyptian religion a symbol of a god appeared more often than the likeness of the god himself. Greek religion seems to have preferred the image of the god himself rather than the symbol that simply referred the imagination to the god. In Judaism and Christianity symbolism is variantly used. The symbol of the burning bush is the Jews' way of saying that the revelation of the Law began with Moses' calling to liberate the Hebrew people from bondage in Egypt. The Sabbath was a symbolic ritual to commemorate weekly, not only the seventh day in which the creator God rested, but also the way in which God delivered his people up out of the slave pits of Egypt.

Likewise, in Christianity, the symbol of IXΘUS, the fish drawn in the sand, was a nonverbal sign of obedience to "Jesus Christ, God, Our Savior."

The cross has taken an elaborate array of cultural forms throughout history to represent nonverbally the crucifixion of Jesus as the central act of man's redemption. The crucifix—the cross with Jesus upon it—is to this day a universal in Roman Catholicism. Protestants have abandoned the crucifix in favor of an empty cross "pointing" to the resurrection of Christ. Protestants add another nonverbal medium—music—to words to epitomize the cross in such hymns as "When I Survey the Wondrous Cross," written by Isaac Watts to the tune of a Gregorian chant arrangement by Lowell Mason. The cross was a symbol of the Crusades, of many orders of knighthood, and more recently a symbol of the anti-Vietnam War movement. The cross has many shapes, representing the cultural milieu which gave it context in history. There is the

Latin cross, with a longer upright than crossbeam; there is the arch-
episcopal or patriarchal cross, a Latin cross with two crossbeams; there is
the papal cross with three crossbeams; there is the cross with a slanting
upright and two crossbeams; there is the Greek cross, with equal length
beams, apparent in the symbol of the Red Cross of our day; there is the
St. Andrew's cross which is shaped like an X and often appears with a
superimposed rho, or *P*, to symbolize "Christ, King"; the tau cross is like
a *T*; the Celtic or Iona cross bears a circle, the center of which is the
intersection of the crosspieces; the Maltese cross and swastika have recent
historical meanings in World War I and II uses of them by the German
military.

The ways in which the cross has been used to symbolize meaning in
relation to war and peace is a significant, nonverbal kind of message
in which "there is no speech, nor are there words; their voice is not heard;
yet their voice goes throughout all the earth, and their words to the end
of the earth." This changes the context of Psalm 19, but it is evidence
that context changes the meaning of a powerful symbol like the cross,
also.

Another pair of Christian symbols is less well known than those of the
cross. That is the symbol of the descending dove and the tongues of fire
which point to the reality and/or presence of the Holy Spirit. With the
recurrent upsurge of interest in ecstatic experiences which involve the
seminonverbal experience of speaking in unknown tongues, or glossolalia,
these symbols of the dove and the flames of fire become nonverbal bases
of identity in fellowships where the Holy Spirit seems to be the primary
concern.

Music. Another powerful purveyor of meaning without the necessary
use of words is music. Music is essentially perceived through auditory
and kinesthetic senses. As such, music heightens the senses over and
above the use of words. Music is a time art and a motion art as well as
an experience of tones. One catches the significance of timing, cadence,
and bodily movement in music. The point at which the nonverbal
communication of music has unnecessarily become disruptive in worship
is when the tone and the timing are split away from the cadence and
rhythm that music produces in the body. The black church has successfully avoided this split and has kept the auditory experiences of music
wedded to the tactual and kinesthetic senses of the total body as well
as the ears. The folk-festival approach to the mass in Catholicism, the
revival in the Free Church tradition, and the small group experiences in
Protestantism seem to represent movement toward reuniting the wholeness of the experience of music. Recently a young Catholic girl said to
me: "I go to sleep in church because the ritual meets the priest's needs
but not mine. I go to white Protestant churches with my friends, but
staying still stifles me. I was really opened up when I went to a black

church with a friend of mine." She, being eighteen, spoke for many young persons for whom any bodily movement to music has been banished as evil. The senses can be heightened by a reappraisal of the life of prayer and worship in the union and heightening of the use of all the senses possible in the expression of prayer and music. Not only Salome, the daughter of Herod, danced, but so did David dance "before the Lord with all his might" (2 Sam. 6:14), and Jesus paid enough attention to children playing in the marketplace that he memorialized their game of dance in one of his comments (Luke 7:32).

Sam Keen speaks of the joylessness and staid lack of movement in a "religion of nostalgia" which sits inert and speaks of remembrance of preserpentine Eden or in anticipation of a hope deferred into the future. He sets this over against the worship of God in both discipline and spontaneity, in decision and in ecstasy, in promise and the immediacy of realized gratification. He reassesses the more native sources of the religious life which, like primitive religion, are not believed as a creed as much as they are danced as a rhythm and timing too easily forgotten when life is ruled too much by intellectualizations.[5]

Art. Today art is a widely variegated form of nonverbal communication. The nonverbal, inarticulate realm of the divine-human encounter is often interpreted negatively as a weakness. The creative dimensions are missed. We lay such store by the verbal that inarticulateness is culturally stamped as inferior by a word-laden society. As Margaret Mead has said,

> The artist and the photographer are still not only paid less than the writer but those who are gifted in a thousand other ways are penalized, for if they do not have a "degree," they are debarred from one activity after another. . . . all the "degrees" are based on an ability to use words. People cannot graduate from anything today because they can paint a beautiful picture, restore a disturbed child to health, comfort the dying or design a new kind of computer.[6]

The painting, the photograph, the sculpture, and the invention are ways of expressing one's inner concerns and prayers both to God and to man. In my own family we are blessed with one son who is exceptionally proficient as a photographer and another who is equally proficient as a cabinetmaker—a user of tools and a mechanical engineer. I find that they express their sense of the infinite, of human compassion, and of human fellowship through these media more profoundly than in the use of God-talk. The kind of photograph one takes during a summer in New York and the kind of art object the other brings back from one of his tours of duty in Vietnam say a volume to one about each of their senses of the Eternal in each place. I, being hyperverbal as the reader of this book can tell, have had my own sense heightened by their active use of art and invention skills in nonverbal communication.

Architecture. Man is not just a speaker in his prayers; he is also a builder. His prayers tend to take shape in what he builds. As Winston Churchill said, "We shape our buildings; thereafter our buildings shape us." The senses are heightened in the use of light, color, line, space, temperature, and type of material—stone, wood, mortar, cement, cloth, and so on in building. A message of a whole community of prayer or learning is communicated in the architecture of the people at worship and study. For example, the Quaker meeting house is bare of images, crosses, communion tables, altars, but the seats are arranged in a square or circle, and the one who speaks stands on an even level with those to whom he speaks. The churches of the Great Awakening, to whom the revival is the central ritual, are built with an aisle which bespeaks nonverbally the forthcoming invitation to "walk the aisle" and make a profession of faith in or rededication to Christ.

A school's history and philosophy of education tend inevitably to take literal, nonverbal shape in its buildings. An era when the lecture was the thing is epitomized in large rooms with high platforms for the lecturer. Another era, when the seminar was the mode of communication, will be expressed in buildings with small rooms and tables. Another time, when group interaction and sensitivity learning predominate, multiple purpose rooms with versatile uses will be the architecture of learning. A school with educational equipment from the nineteenth century and administrative equipment of plush executive business offices as one would find in a business establishment conveys its preoccupation with promotional work, processing, packaging, and marketing rather than teaching and learning. This is the message that gets through to students without voice, language, lecture, or sermon. Yet, whatever the form architecture takes, a meaning consonant with the things people consider most important is conveyed by it.

Clothing. The ancient story of temptation in Genesis 3 tells that when Adam and Eve came to know good and evil "the eyes of both were opened, and they knew that they were naked; and they sewed fig leaves together and made themselves aprons" (Gen. 3:7, RSV). In their new estate in life before they were driven from the Garden of Eden, "the Lord God made for Adam and for his wife garments of skin and clothed them."

The dialogue of mankind and womankind with God and with each other is expressed nonverbally in attitudes toward the body and practices of clothing. Noah, furthermore, was the "first tiller of the soil," and he planted a vineyard, made wine, drank it, and became drunk, so drunk that he failed to clothe his nakedness. His son Ham saw him, told his brother, and earned the curse of his father for doing so. Nakedness and clothing must have something to do with our divine-human and human-human dialogues and trialogues which we conventionally call prayer! About this several things can be observed.

The need for confession and the need to be an open self are both literally and symbolically related to being clothed or naked. Job, though suffering dreadfully, insisted that he had nothing to hide, that he had not sinned, nor did he charge God with wrong. Rather, he said in his prayer as he fell upon the ground and worshiped: "Naked I came from my mother's womb, and naked shall I return; the Lord gave, and the Lord took away; blessed be the name of the Lord" (Job 1:21, RSV). He insisted on laying his life bare before God.

This is in contradistinction to the association of guilt and shame with nakedness found in the stories of the sin of Adam and Eve and the shame of Noah.

The development of priestly and nun garbs to cover the whole body except the hands and face submits itself to a variety of interpretations of which modesty about and shame of the body are only a part. In the Protestant tradition, similar ascetic ideas of the sin of the exposed body accompany those of the rhythmical or dancing body. Strictures against swim suits, coeducational swimming, women's shorts, and so on fall in this category.

Clothing is a nonverbal vehicle of protest. Isaiah, when Ashdod was besieged by Assyria in 711 B.C., walked the streets of Jerusalem naked. He went and loosed the sackcloth from his loins and took off his shoes from his feet. He did this for three years to symbolize the garb of a slave in order to bear his witness and to protest against the Egyptianizing party in Jerusalem. His intent was dramatically to impress on the people of Jerusalem the foolishness of relying upon Egypt (Isa. 20:1–6). Both Egypt and Isaiah's countrymen would be stripped naked and made slaves of Assyria.

Protest movements more recently are using clothing and hair as a kind of protest against affluence, against meritocracy, against the military-industrial complex, against involvement in wars like the Vietnam War, and, more often than any of these, against parental control. Symbols of clothing also are used to protest the exploitation of women as sex symbols and of men as willing buyers because of the use of sex as a sales pitch in advertisement. If prayer is "the soul's sincere desire, un-uttered or expressed," then these are nonverbal ways of expressing prayer for freedom from bondage and exploitation.

Clothing is used as a way of removing the option from one's com-mitment, whether it be a religious commitment to God, as in the case of the clerical garb and the Amish and Mennonite distinctive garb, or a commitment to a cause from which one cannot back out, such as the military uniform, the nurse's uniform, or, to a lesser extent, the hippie garb. When one wears these garbs, habits, or uniforms, he takes a position. Every move he makes is publicly identified. As long as a person wears this clothing, his position is one of optionless commitment. Furthermore, the problem of identity of the individual is covered with a larger identity with one's commitment to his God and/or cause. Therefore, clothing is not just a medium of nonverbal protest but also a form of identification in which one rules out the option of being anonymous about it or retracting one's vows by inner speculation.

The changing of clothes is a way of symbolizing one's changed relationship to God and man. As such, it is a form of nonverbal prayer. This, too, may be literally or symbolically true. Literally, the changing of a military uniform to civilian garb may represent a change of affiliation or heart, especially if accompanied by a resignation from the service. To wear the Nazi brown shirt and swastika after having worn civilians in the Germany of the 1930s and 1940s was to show a change of heart.

The New Testament uses the figure of speech of changing clothes to symbolize the experience of redemption in Christ, and especially entering into the resurrection after death. Paul says, "For we know that if the earthly tent we live in is destroyed, we have a building from God, a house not made with hands, eternal in the heavens. Here indeed we groan, and long to put on our heavenly dwelling, so that by putting it on we may not be found naked" (2 Cor. 5:1–3, RSV). In Ephesians, the Christian is enjoined to "put off" the old nature which belongs to a former manner of life and to "put on" a new nature "created after the likeness of God in true righteousness and holiness" (Eph. 4:22–24, RSV). Furthermore, the Christian is urged to "put on the whole armor of God" and each piece of armor is identified as symbolizing the equipment of the Christian for life.

The final among many ways in which clothing is a form of religious nonverbal communication is the way clothing becomes a form of sham, avoidance of communion with God, and an expression of a desire to take God's place. Jesus spoke contemptuously of persons who dressed "in soft raiment and dwelled in kings' houses" (Matt. 11:8). The Book of James contrasts the person with gold rings and fine clothing getting all the attention in the assembly of Christians with the man dressed in shabby clothing getting nothing but niggardly care (James 2:1–7). Jesus also revered the great tradition of loving God with one's whole being and one's neighbor as oneself. This was written on the phylacteries worn on the forehead. He spoke grimly of the pride of those who "do all their deeds to be seen by men; for they make their phylacteries broad and their fringes long, and they love the place of honor at feasts and the best seats in the synagogues, and salutations in the market places, and being called rabbi by men" (Matt. 23:5–7, RSV).

Clothing in this sense becomes a substitute for personhood. Against this a considerable number of young persons in the early 1970s have reacted. However, one is also impressed with the way the most expensive clothes are now copies of the earlier austerity of young hippies. Styles of clothing thus can become so faddish that money is wasted on clothes for the fashion's sake, and one fears to refer to it in a book lest the styles change several times for pride's sake before the book is published!

THE APPRECIATION OF INTIMACY AND DISTANCE

The discussion of the disciplines of the senses as a form of nonverbal communication and communion in prayer leads to the literal and symbolic meanings of closeness and distance. Symbolically, persons speak of being close to God, being far from God, and drawing near unto God. Admittedly, these are anthropomorphic expressions, but they symbolize intimacy and distantiation in Erikson's categories. The psalmist asks of God why he is so far from helping him (Ps. 22:1) and says elsewhere that God's salvation is far from the wicked (Ps. 114:155). Jesus tells the man who asked which commandment was greatest that he was not far from the Kingdom (Mark 12:34). God is spoken of by the psalmist as near, and Israel is spoken of as a people who are near to God (Ps. 148:14).

One who does much pastoral counseling repeatedly encounters persons whose complaint is that they feel far from God, that they cannot reach God, that the Spirit has left them and they feel abandoned. One does not listen long until the same sense of psychic space appears characteristic of their relationship to persons other than God. They quite often are people who have been repeatedly abandoned. Their relationship with God is that of an absentee God. Their prayers are hindered by this almost spatial feeling of isolation.

The Greek idea of the soul probably is a formulation based on an attempt to solve the problem of space. Is God in here or out there? Does the soul enter the body at birth and leave it at death? Greek gnosticism said that Jesus, for example, only seemed to have been crucified, for the real Christ descended on Jesus at his baptism and departed before he died on the cross. This separation of the soul was challenged by the Christian belief in the resurrection, a belief that Athenian Greeks took very lightly. Yet, the nonverbal sense of the separateness of one's selfhood hangs tenaciously to the contemporary mind.

The nonverbal sense of space and distance is a developmental task of young adults in relation to each other. The paradox between a husband and wife being intimate with each other so completely as to enter and encompass each other bodily and at the same time to respect each other's private space, individuality, and prayers before God is a paradox of distance and relation. The Apostle Paul struggled to put this mystery into words in 1 Corinthians 7. To him, too, it was a mystery. Martin Buber, a contemporary Jew, grapples with this paradox of distance in all human relations, not just marriage: "Man's art of setting at a distance is no more to be understood as primary than his act of relation which is bound up with it." [7] He says that the need of man for distance is his need for the universal and his need for relation is his need for the personal. Both are a twofold, inseparable principle of life. God is perceived as hidden, other, unknowable, *and* revealed, personal, and knowable. Dialogue brings these together in communion because even for men and women to be in relation within and between sexes "means the acceptance of otherness." We become genuinely human in genuine meetings. It is from one person to another that "the heavenly bread of self-being is passed."

Yet, speaking less philosophically and more concretely, Edward Hall has said that such meetings pose nonverbal threats of invasion of privacy to people. He says that space has a language of its own, a silent language. The distances in human relations can be measured. "Intimate space" has two phases, near and far. Intimate distance-near is the distance of love making and wrestling, comforting, and protesting. Communication is by muscle, skin, olfaction, and the sense of warmth or cold. Intimate distance-far is about six to eighteen inches, within easy half-arm distance. The voice may be used but a whisper will do.

The second phase of distance Hall calls "personal distance," which has also a close phase of one and a half to two and a half feet. This is the kind of distance a husband and wife ordinarily can stand in relation in public. The far phase is two and a half to four feet—"arm's distance"—which may communicate personal respect for another's dignity or general respect for another's territory.

The third phase of distance is "social distance," with a close phase of four to seven feet. This is the "impersonal business" phase, a common distance for casual social gatherings. The far phase of social distance is seven to twelve feet, a kind of distance for formal social dealings. The voice level is high enough to sound formal. This kind of distance insulates people from each other.

"Public distance" is the phase of distance in which persons are well outside the circle of involvement with each other personally. At the near phase of twelve to twenty-five feet verbal communication calls for careful enunciation; nonverbal communication calls for large muscle use. The far phase of public distance is twenty-five feet or more. This is the kind of distance public figures such as presidents of the country maintain. Not only the voice but all bodily movements must be magnified to communicate. It calls for a rather frozen, rigid style of speech and gesture.[8]

Expressions of religious faith call for ethical as well as devotional adaptation of the meaning of space to man and man, and man and God. Forms of group worship are intimate, personal, social, or purely public in terms of Hall's categories. Religious adaptations of sensitivity and personal growth groups make much of this in reeducating religious people to a more intimate involvement with each other. Prayer is measured in its informality or formality on the axis of these perceptions of space and interpersonal relationships. This awareness in the planning of prayer and worship experiences is indispensable.

From an ethical vantage point, the whole problem of a crowding population explosion is involved in the way housing, even in rural slums, huddles people together. The gradual erosion of space-availability chips away at the sense of being an individual. Seward Hiltner relates the rise of monasticism as a search for privacy in the overcrowded conditions in people's "one room shed(s) with a dirt floor." Children were exploited sexually as a rule rather than the exception. "In such households, rich or poor, how could one ever get a spot of privacy? Or freedom from watching sex relations in the same room? For a long time, the one answer was monasticism in some form." [9] In the contemporary scene, Hiltner observes that "today we value privacy highly. But we also dread privacy. . . . Even suburbanites know that the line between desired privacy and enforced isolation may be very thin." [10]

This search for a balance between intimacy and privacy has nonverbal roots in mankind's ambivalence about reaching out to people and "standing on his own two feet." Suburbanite people will firmly deny in a church meeting that there are any people with disturbing family problems in the church. On a private telephone wire later they may ask desperately for private counseling about a marriage conflict and/or a severe rebellion of an adolescent son or daughter. A late adolescent may want desperately to be independent of parents, have a room or apartment of his own. Yet, he does not want to work or develop a responsible marriage relationship. His search for distance, privacy, and independence outweighs the deep hunger for intimacy, closeness, and genuine communion.

The struggle of the soul for a balance between individuality and community, solitude and fellowship, integrity and comradeship, isolation and intimacy, is essentially a religious quest and is made tangible in what Kant called one of the inherent categories of the mind—space. Space can best be described nonverbally.

NOTES

1. Alfred Korzybski, *Science and Sanity*, 3d ed. (Lakeville, Conn.: Institute of General Semantics, 1948), p. 417.

2. Julius Fast, *Body Language* (London: Pan Books, 1971).

3. Paul Pruyser, *A Dynamic Psychology of Religion* (New York: Harper & Row, 1968), p. 304.

4. Thorleif Boman, *Hebrew Thought Compared with Greek Thought* (Philadelphia: Westminster, 1960), pp. 201 ff.

5. Sam Keen, *To a Dancing God* (New York: Harper & Row, 1970), pp. 5, 51.

6. "Dr. Mead Scores Degree Criteria," *New York Times,* 18 July 1965.

7. Martin Buber, *The Knowledge of Man,* ed. Maurice Friedman (New York: Harper Torchbook, 1965), p. 63.

8. Edward T. Hall, *The Hidden Dimension* (New York: Doubleday, 1966), pp. 107–22.

9. Seward Hiltner, *Theological Dynamics* (New York: Abingdon, 1972), pp. 134–35.

10. Ibid., p. 90.

QUESTIONS FOR FURTHER STUDY

1. This chapter has been written primarily from the Judaeo-Christian point of view. What emphases do Buddhism and Hinduism place upon nonverbal prayer?

2. Devise specific small group procedures based on Howard Clinebell's book *The People Dynamic* for developing nonverbal experiences of worship.

3. In what ways have you and your family members developed ways of communicating awareness of the presence of God in nonverbal ways?

4. Have you revolted against verbal prayer without saying so in words or even admitting it to yourself? If so, do some of the nonverbal approaches to prayer and a heightened use of the senses offer a positive alternative to that which you have outgrown?

9

MAGIC AND PERSUASION

Magic is the art or group of arts which claims to be able or to have the power to compel unknown forces, the deity, or supernatural powers to do something to change the order of natural events. The magician claims to produce effects by the assistance of a power greater than himself. Witchcraft, sorcery, or diabolism is evil or *black* magic. The supernatural collaboration is with the satanic powers of darkness. *White* magic is the cooperation with natural and supernatural powers of a more benevolent, healing character. No reference by the author is intended toward racial factors in this definition of black and white magic, but superstition *has* associated black magic with the voodoo of the Haitians, for instance, and white magic with healing miracles of white Christian evangelists. Underlying some of these assumptions about magic, also, seems to be an older influence of Zoroastrianism which associates the good god with light and the evil god with darkness. The two gods are evenly matched and constantly at war with each other. Of course, the darkness-light motif pervades much of Judaeo-Christian thinking as well.

My contention in this chapter is that magic cannot be classified as the opposite of religion, as evil in itself, whereas religion is free of all magic and, therefore, good in itself. Rather, magic is like any other ability of human beings—it is either brought into consecrated relationship to God, or it is used in alienation from God as a means of self-aggrandizement and cleverness and as an attempt to supplant or take God's place. Vetter rightly says that the attempt to rarify religion apart from *any* tangible consequence, practical result, or end aimed to benefit us as persons is (a) the way to make religion insipid and uninteresting to people, and (b) the way to encourage people to go off after cults and sects that are predominantly focused on providing health, wealth, and freedom from undue anxiety for persons.

Therefore, my hypothesis will be that the power to persuade is rooted in the same kind of soil among sophisticated and technologically oriented peoples as what is commonly labeled magic among primitive persons. Persuasion does effect changes in the behavior of people and as such is the technological equivalent of magic in both religion and medicine today. Frank admission of this hypothesis opens up, therefore, a wider and more honest appreciation of both religion and science.[1]

THE COMPONENTS OF MAGIC

In whatever kind of magic one examines, at least three components tend to appear—the spell, the rite, and the condition of the magician. These need some explanation.

THE SPELL

When the parent, the magician, the showman, the witch doctor, the prophet, the therapist, the minister, or the teacher utters a set of words in a set order according to a formula, this can and often does amount to a spell. The parent says, "You will never amount to anything!" or "You will either wind up in jail, the crazy house, or the poor house!" These can amount to a spell in a growing child's life. They ring in his ears. He never forgets them. As such they have incantation power as curses or even a hex. Similarly, a blessing can have equal power. Parents can say, "You may have all sorts of obstacles, but you have a destiny to fulfill and you will overcome them!" The magician may cast a spell on a garment, a pet, a cow, and so on. A knife of a warrior may be made a special knife by a spell. To use it as an ordinary knife is to desecrate it. The prophet says, "Thus says the Lord . . ." The therapist says, "You are sick, but you can get well."

THE RITE

A spell is conveyed to a person, ordinarily, through a set of acts in order to get the desired effect. Elisha told Naaman to go wash in the river. A healed leper, according to the rites of the law, was required to go show himself to the priest. The patient of the psychoanalyst goes through the rites of the appointments for therapy sessions. The teacher has an array of obligatory rites—note taking, class attendance, prerequisite courses, majors and minors, grading and graduation. All of these can become exercises in magic in and of themselves to produce the desired effect of blessing or curse, the formulae of certificate. The degree itself has a certain magical quality in the rites of the school system.

Rites draw much of their power from habit, tradition, and institutionalization. Where religious rituals are heavily sanctioned by the community—such as the Catholic confessional, the Protestant revival, and pastoral visitation—these rites have inherent power when performed by a person of prestige, credibility, and unquestionable commitment to what he is doing.

THE CONDITION OF THE MAGICIAN

This leads to the assessment of the quality and character of the person who performs the powerful act of magic.

The magical personage himself is the central component of magic. He accepts faithfully and believes himself in the sanctions and taboos of his system. He disciplines himself according to the code held up for him. He cannot insist on being an ordinary person. He sees himself as extraordinary and does the things required in the nonrational codes of people that make him unusual, different, and endowed with special power. If he is a Nazarite, as was John the Baptist, he remains unshaven and does not touch alcohol. He, as Jesus said, "came neither eating nor drinking." He honestly does these things. As Jan Ehrenwald says, the scientific person today, especially the psychotherapist, lives in an analytical world of fact *and* a mythological world of belief, assumption, and intuition. These beliefs, assumptions, and intuitions themselves are facts. As Wolfgang Kohler says, values exist in a world of fact. The reverse is also true: Facts exist in a world of value. One must be honestly aware of, committed to, and able to function in relation both to facts and values. Ehrenwald speaks of the element of the magical residing in contemporary, scientific personages such as psychotherapists. For example, a psychiatrist uses hypnotism, that curious phenomenon that combines faith, science, and magic. The psychiatrist is "donning the mantle of the magician" when he hypnotizes a person. Ehrenwald says that it is not enough that he simply "role play" as a magician. He must not just "pretend to be playing the role of hypnotist. He must project himself, heart and soul, into it." [2]

In an old book, Gustave Le Bon speaks of the power vested in a leader of crowds. He says that the leader must have the mysterious force known as prestige. Prestige dominates the mind of the followers of a leader. This domination paralyzes critical abilities and "fills our soul with astonishment and respect." Le Bon distinguishes between acquired and personal prestige. Acquired prestige comes from inheritance, family name, position and office, title and rank. These may be enhanced by literary or artistic prestige. For example, reading Homer can be very boring, but who would dare to say so? Such prestige is standardized, stereotyped, crowd prestige. As Le Bon says, "Crowds always, and individuals as a rule, stand in need of ready-made opinions on all subjects." These opinions are solely regulated by their prestige, not the measure of truth or error they contain.

But the most important kind of prestige, that factor so elemental to the condition of the magician, is personal prestige. "It is independent of all titles, of all authority, and is possessed by a small number of persons whom it enables to exercise a veritably magnetic fascination on those around them, although they are socially their equals and lack all means of domination." [3] Le Bon places Jesus in this latter category.

A more recent author, Hollander, calls this personal prestige "idiosyncratic credit" which comes from having productively served the community of which one is a part. An individual within a group has a number of group-awarded credits. These credits give permission to the person to vary from commonly accepted norms of the group. The individual who performs with excellence the primary functions of the group then is permitted a latitude of behavior not allowed the person who fails to produce. If this occurs over an extended period of time, the symbolic power of the person increases in geometric proportion. For example, in a school setting the person with seniority who nevertheless fails to do his job with zest and creativity is often written off and not taken seriously. The person with the seniority and an increasing productivity develops a massive, personal prestige. In essence, this point of view is that of E. P. Hollander in his book, *Leaders, Groups, and Influence*.[4]

KINDS OF MAGIC

There are several kinds of magic and identifying them is a form of clarification.

SYMPATHETIC MAGIC

The principle on which sympathetic magic works is that "like affects like." Two tuning forks that are alike will pick up each other's vibrations. Persons are prone to imitate people they like. Therefore, change can be created in another person by stimulating the desire to be like you. In group relationships a spirit of kinship, free of disharmony, can be created that causes the members to resonate with each other. The alchemy of the phenomenological approach to psychology seems to be in the discipline of one person in becoming like or feeling with another person to such an extent that the person changes his sense of self-worth, attitudes, and behavior. The more mundane example of sympathetic magic is the prankster who stands in the front of a moving bus and yawns long and conspicuously. Five or six persons seated in the bus will yawn sympathetically! The magic of television advertising is a sympathetic one. Behavior patterns of the buying public are affected by beautiful people drinking Coca Cola, stunning persons smoking Winchesters, fun people squeezing bread or paper tissues, and so on. The power of peer-group pressure to program drinking habits, drug use, and ecstatic behavior is a form of sympathetic magic.

DIVINATION

Divination is an esoteric means of gaining hidden knowledge. As Levy-Bruhl says, in ordinary life a person depends upon ready explanations for the meaning of events. He may even depend upon dreams, omens, hunches, intuitions to make difficult decisions and choices. Yet, there come times when common sense and dreams, omens, and so on, are found wanting. In order to overcome such impediments, the person consults someone with prestige, esoteric knowledge, in short, the power of divination. This consultation is aimed to use the mystic powers to bear upon that which interests him strongly. Whether one is primitive, technologically oriented, religious, or secular, this process of divination goes on, I would say.[5] The contemporary upsurge of interest in astrology is based upon the assumption of both hidden knowledge and power in the solar system, the relation of the moon and the stars to human behavior. The almanacs we read are filled with predictions and instructions based upon the esoteric relationship of the stars. One plants one kind of seed at one time of the moon and another at another. Much folklore and folk behavior is geared by this kind of magic. For example, among the Navajo Indians it is believed that if a pregnant woman sees an eclipse of the sun or moon her baby will either be crazy or have convulsions.[6] Today the conception that persons are likely to become psychotic at a full moon time is seriously discussed in literature and on psychiatric wards. Astrology is at this time quite vogue in respectable circles and is a highly lucrative business as well.

Clairvoyance is another form of divination. The shape of things to come is of intense interest to most persons, and we have uncanny and magical feelings about the future. We are only half amused by fortune cookies at an Oriental restaurant. We are drawn to the palmist. We teeter in indecision and consult counselors with a hidden expectation that this person will say or do just the right thing to assure us that a certain path of action is the inerrantly correct one. The frankly magical personage—the palmist, the fortuneteller, and the reader of cards or tea leaves—is not the most pervasive person who is turned to for divination. The medical doctor, the psychotherapist, the pastoral counselor, the marriage counselor—regardless of how they perceive themselves—are perceived by patients and counselees as having powers of divination.

NECROMANCY

The consultation of and communication with the dead is a form of divination, also. The bereaved person has magical experiences in which he perceives messages from the loved one who is dead. A bereaved person often lurches awake at the half-sleeping sensation that his dead loved one is alive and present. The loss of a person by death is sometimes felt as a phantom part of one's self, as if he had lost an arm or a leg. The person who loses someone suddenly and does not get to tell him good-by, does not get the chance to reconcile a grievance, or simply does not get to tell him how much he loves and cares for him often has a yearning need to get in touch with him after he has died. Shakespeare immortalized this need in Hamlet's need to communicate with his father's ghost about the manner of his death. Dickens's *Christmas Carol* depicts Scrooge getting alarmed at Marley's ghost. It does not take a primitive or unsophisticated person to experience the restlessness of the spirits of the dead.

Among the Shona of Southern Africa "it is imperative for a person who is sick—and equally important to the survivors if he dies—to consult the divine to learn the reason for the illness or death. Otherwise the anger or wrath of the departed relative or of the witch will continue unabated, and more unhappiness will come to the family. A very large part of the witch doctor's duties are concerned with divination."[7] This is among unsophisticated and primitive persons. I have been in a conference where a prominent and erudite theologian told of having consulted a medium in a seance in order to get in touch with his deceased wife. He was facing the decision as to whether to remarry, and he needed his first wife's opinion of what he was contemplating doing. She gave him her blessing and approval in the seance, he said.

The Gestalt-therapy technique of having a lost person imaginatively to sit in an empty chair during a counseling session gives the counselee the opportunity—with assistance from the counselor—to abreact emotions, articulate messages, and even to receive messages from the spirit of the departed dead. In this sense, contemporary psychotherapy relies empirically upon divination procedure whether the actual mythology of magic is accepted by either them or their clients. It is astonishing to see the results of this psychodramatic procedure.[8]

THAUMATURGY

Thaumaturgy is what is popularly thought of as magic. It is legerdemain or sleight of hand. One could say it is the art of making the hand work more rapidly than the eye. It is the Houdini type of tricky wonderworking. Here magic mixes with entertainment. Artistic handling of these rituals has often been used by religious leaders in order to get the attention of audiences before preaching or teaching. It is a sort of side show to the main event. However, the necessary degree of magical power of the leader spills over from the side show to the main event. The aura of the mysterious is blended into the religious exposition, and the audience tends to continue under the spell of the magician. On the surface, however, thaumaturgy seems to be the least serious form of magic.

INCANTATION

Incantation as a form of magic represents the blend of suggestion and hypnosis, on the one hand, and specific rituals of words and acts, on the other hand. The repetition of a formula of words, the repetition of a series of acts, repetition of a particular pattern of music—these are examples of incantations. A certain evangelist always says precisely the same words when he gives an invitation at the end of his sermon. These words are followed by the singing of exactly the same gospel song in exactly the same way each time. The members of the evangelistic team assisting the evangelist make exactly the same movements each time the invitation is given. The whole event has a precision choreography to go with the repetition of the words. As a unit, it has powerful incantation value, hypnotically enhancing the likelihood that people will do as requested.

Incantation is a vital part of exorcism. Babylonian exorcists invoked the names of the cosmic deities, and their magician invoked the names of pagan gods. Jewish exorcists invoked the name of Jehovah in their efforts to drive out evil spirits. Josephus reports that God granted Solomon "knowledge of the art used against demons for the benefit and healing of men. He also composed incantations by which illnesses are relieved and left behind forms of exorcism with which those possessed by demons drive them out never to return." [9]

PERSUASION: THE COMMON DENOMINATOR OF MAGIC, RELIGION, AND SCIENCE

Le Bon's and Hollander's discussion of prestige focuses the power of persuasion as the common denominator of magic, religion, and science. For the magician, priest-minister-rabbi, or scientist to have any power or effect he must be credible, believed in, trusted. This means that he is persuasive and convincing, that his audience, patient, or communicant heeds or listens to what he does and says. At this point of persuasion, magic, religion, and science intersect—both to meet and to part company with each other. This can be demonstrated from studies of persuasion in its relation to magic, religion, and science.

Persuasion, in the New Testament sense, means "to prevail upon" or "win over." Paul, at Ephesus, "persuaded and turned away a company of people, saying that gods made with hands are not gods" (Acts 19:26, RSV). Paul, in his powerful witness before Agrippa, had such an effect on Agrippa that Agrippa said, "In a short time you think [or almost persuade] to make me a Christian" (Acts 26:28, RSV). In its more intransitive sense, the word *persuade* means "to trust, have confidence, or be confident." In Romans 2:19 it is translated "to be sure." In the passive or middle voice, it means "to believe" or "to be persuaded." This is found in Romans 8:38 (RSV): "I am sure that neither death, nor life, nor angels, nor principalities, nor things present, nor things to come, nor powers, nor height, nor depth, nor anything else in all creation, will be able to separate us from the love of God in Christ Jesus our Lord."

The source of this persuasion, according to the New Testament, is in the "free gift" or charisma of redemption from sin by God through Christ and in the "call of God," both of which are irrevocable (Rom. 11:29). Therefore, the persuader is a charismatic person in the classical sense of that word. The charismatic person has power, is convincing, is credible, for several reasons.

First, he is consecrated to God and accepts his humanity. The free gift of God is a treasure, but it is in the earthen vessel of the humanity of the person. The purpose of the charismatic person is that whatever power or excellency he demonstrates in action be clearly from God and not himself.

Second, he goes through a discipline of self-perfection of his motives. He renounces legerdemain, underhanded ways, and the practice of cunning. Whatever cleverness he has is dedicated intelligence. He enters the sacred relationship with clean hands and a pure heart. He does not lift up his soul to vanity nor swear deceitfully.

In the third place, the charismatic person does not guarantee a specific outcome but sees whatever outcome of his work to be inseparable from the longer purpose of God. He may be cast down, but he is not forsaken; he may be perplexed, but not unto despair. He is a harbinger of hope, given to continued experimentation, and confident of an ultimate triumph that not even death can thwart.

Such confidence is the beating heart of the power of persuasion described in the New Testament. Healing, miracle working, reconciliation of alienated brethren, and the resistance to persecution are all outgrowths of this charisma, productive of deep credibility and ecstatic responses of faith. Whereas these dimensions of the persuasive religious personage have been predominantly from New Testament accounts of the life of Paul, all the great living faiths tend to produce in their own ways these characteristics of the persuasive leader.

Scientific studies of persuasion provide another angle of vision of the relation of persuasion to human behavior. Jerome Frank provides research of his own and reviews other research. He concludes that every person imposes some kind of order on the experiences that impinge upon him. Therefore, he creates for himself a set of assumptions which serve as guides and bases for action. Frank calls this set of assumptions the person's "assumptive world." Much of this assumptive world is unconscious. These assumptions cannot be dealt with by purely rational measures. Yet, at both the conscious and unconscious levels, persons experience threats to their existence in the form of disease or disaster.

They experience ambiguity and uncertainty. They feel that no one cares about them. The goal of the psychotherapist is to appeal to both the conscious and the unconscious, to stabilize the anxiety with a measure of certainty, and to communicate the hope of recovery. The "psycho-therapist, as a socially sanctioned expert and healer and a representative of the larger society, may be able to mobilize forces sufficiently powerful to produce beneficial changes . . ." [10] The element of persuasion, often bordering on magic, lies in the fact that he is "a socially sanctioned expert and healer." Frank further says that revivalism provides "emotionally charged methods of influence that offer detailed guides to behavior based on an inclusive, infallible assumptive world which also arouses hope." [11]

In experimental studies Frank discovered things about the nature of persuasion which are reminiscent of what has been said here of magic. For example, the persuader-healer requires an act, some initiative, some exerted demonstration of confidence on the part of the person being influenced. Furthermore, a person can be influenced by nonverbal cues of approval or disapproval by the listener. Finally, the listener's memory and recall of the person's previous conversation or behavior enhances his credibility and power to influence.

Another experimental study of persuasion reflects that behavior is changed in whatever desired direction in keeping with several factors: (1) high credibility of the communicator; (2) the clear, nonambiguous statement of one's own conclusions and recommendations rather than leaving the person or group to make up their own mind; (3) the provision of reasons for possible failure as a basis for preparing for, accounting for, or discounting failure; (4) the provision of group support of decisions and behavior change; (5) the creation of opportunities for the person to enact the behavior in role performance in relatively safe surroundings.[12]

An Unscientific Postscript on Charisma

When one adds together the data presented here, a close relationship between religion, magic, and science is seen in the way in which all three rely upon the heavy credibility of the communicator—whether that person is magician, priest-minister-rabbi, or scientist. All three of these rely upon spell, rite, and incantation. All three produce effects that can only be explained in terms of the power of persuasion.

One asks then, what is the difference? A tentative answer could be that charisma is consecrated magic or power of persuasion. Charisma is an ethically purged power of persuasion or magic. A power of persuasion lived in ethical responsibility both to God and to the well-being of one's subject calls for a self-emptying, a taking on of the condition of the other person. Empathy precedes such persuasion. Understanding is the stuff of which it is made. We are back to the essential charisma of an incarnational approach to life.

Yet, these same gifts can be practiced apart from and in defiance of God. Thus, creativity and the power to influence others can become a means of self-aggrandizement, exploitation, and deception. Scientific ethics can replace the sense of responsibility to God with the antiseptic technique and code of the physician. Thus, the charisma can be maintained at a humanistic level with dignity and love among men. In all three instances, the stuff of credibility, achievement of certainty, provision for failure, group support, and opportunity to behave instead of just talk remain constant in magic, religion, and science.

NOTES

1. George B. Vetter, *Magic and Religion* (New York: Philosophical Library, 1958), pp. 156 ff.
2. Jan Ehrenwald, *Psychotherapy: Myth and Method, The Integrative Approach* (New York: Grune and Stratton, 1966), pp. 145–46.
3. Gustave Le Bon, *The Crowd: A Study of the Popular Mind* (London: T. Fisher Unwin, 1896), pp. 147–59.
4. E. P. Hollander, *Leaders, Groups, and Influence* (New York: Oxford Press, 1964), pp. 26–29, 161–78.
5. Lucien Levy-Bruhl, *Primitive Mentality* (Boston: Beacon Press, 1923 and 1966), p. 160.
6. Bert Caplan and Dale Jones, "The Social Meaning of Navajo Psychopathology and Psychotherapy," *Magic, Faith, and Healing*, ed. Ari Kiev (New York: Free Press, 1964), p. 208.
7. Michael Gelfand, "Psychiatric Disorders As Recognized by the Shona," *Magic, Faith, and Healing*, p. 157.
8. William Schutz, *Joy: The Expanding Human Awareness* (New York: Grove Press, 1967).
9. *Interpreter's Dictionary of the Bible*, 2: 199.
10. Jerome Frank, *Persuasion and Healing* (Baltimore: Johns Hopkins University Press, 1961), p. 35.
11. Ibid., p. 80.
12. Carl Hovland, Irving L. Janis, Harold H. Kelley, *Communication and Persuasion* (New Haven, Conn.: Yale University Press, 1953), pp. 260–300.

QUESTIONS FOR FURTHER STUDY

1. Do you agree or disagree with the idea that the prestigious scientist today has magical power?
2. What is your understanding of the meaning of charismatic power?
3. Search out the relationship between incantation and extrasensory perception. Look for such authors as Gardner Murphy and J. B. Rhine.
4. If you were choosing a counselor with whom to talk about a bothersome habit of yours, to what extent would you expect him to have magical power?

10

SLEEP, DREAMS, AND REVELATION

Magic and persuasion, religion and science, have a common focus in the need of the human being to rest, to relax, to sleep. Primitive man associated death and sleep. He believed that a man who died continued to live under new conditions and to influence his neighborhood. In the same way, when a man slept and dreamed, his spirit was thought to leave his body.[1] This is, many think, where the idea arose of the soul being separate from the body. It was Shelley, following the lead of Homer, who said

> How wonderful is Death,
> Death and his brother Sleep!
> One pale as yonder man and horrid moon,
> With lips of lurid blue,
> The other glowing like the vital morn,
> When throned on the ocean's wave
> It breathes over the world:
> Yet both passing strange and wonderful! [2]

This sense of mysteriousness and fascination with death and sleep still fills the mind of more persons than just primitive persons living in an animistic world. In the world of technologically developed peoples, the data of neurology, physiology, psychology, psychiatry, and psychoanalysis are heavily interspersed with the relation between sleep, dreams, and insight. The living religions have extensive involvement with the relation of sleep states to the waking directions of life and vice versa.

BIBLICAL EMPHASES ON SLEEP, DREAMS, AND REVELATION

One of the Jewish understandings of sleep is that it is a distinctly creaturely function. A qualitative difference between God and man is

164

that God "will neither slumber nor sleep" (Ps. 121:4). God does not "faint or grow weary" (Isa. 40:28). Yet when man is troubled, his "sleep leaves him" (Dan. 2:1). He is caused to sleep by God (Gen. 2:21). God deals profoundly with man as a creature during his sleep. Jacob received a covenant from God in his sleep (Gen. 28:10–17). Jacob wrestled in a wakeful night at the river Jabbok (Gen. 32:22–32). Joseph dreamed dreams of grandeur about his leadership of his family (Gen. 37:1–11). These dreams earned his father's fear and his brothers' hatred. When sold into slavery and later imprisoned, he interpreted the dreams of his fellow prisoners and won the right to interpret the dreams of Pharaoh (Gen. 40, 41).

In the New Testament, sleep and dreams are also significant in the interaction between man and God. Joseph had it revealed to him in a dream that he should stand by and care for Mary, the mother of Jesus (Matt. 1:20). Joseph was warned in a dream to take Mary and Jesus to Egypt, out of reach of Herod (Matt. 2:13). Pilate's wife had a dream and warned him not to have anything to do "with that righteous man" because, she said, "I have suffered much over him in a dream today" (Matt. 27:19). The disciples of Jesus had much interaction with Jesus through sleep. As Jesus, Peter, John, and James had gone up on a mountain to pray, Jesus remained awake, and the three disciples "were heavy with sleep but kept awake" and saw Jesus transfigured (Luke 9:28–36). Yet it was Jesus who was asleep in the boat when the severe storm frightened his disciples. They felt that he did not care (Mark 4:35–41). To the contrary, however, when Jesus was praying in the Garden of Gethsemane, his disciples were asleep. "When he rose from prayer, he came to his disciples, and found them sleeping for sorrow" (see Luke 22:39–46).

In the ministry of Jesus, the seesaw reaction as to whether a person was dead or asleep appears. The crowd laughed at him when he told them Jairus' daughter was not dead but asleep (Matt. 9:18–26; Mark 5:35–43). To the contrary, Jesus said that Lazarus had fallen asleep, and his disciples said, "Lord, if he has fallen asleep, he will recover." Then Jesus told them plainly, "Lazarus is dead" (John 11:14).

This same duality of sleep and death appears in Acts and in the Epistles. The angel of the Lord appeared to Peter as he slept between two soldiers. He was miraculously delivered from bondage (Acts 12:6). He did not know whether what had happened was real or not. He came to himself only a little later. Here sleep was actually sleep and unconfused with death. Paul speaks in Acts 13:36 of David as having "fallen asleep," meaning that he died, was "laid with his fathers and saw corruption." In 1 Corinthians 15:20–51 and 1 Thessalonians 4:14, the idea of sleep is used to refer to death also.

Several conclusions can be drawn concerning these biblical references to the nature of sleep, dreams, and revelation. First, sleep is used as a symbol or a paradigm for death. Second, sleep and dreams are consistent avenues of revelation. Man's dealings as spirit with God do not cease when he goes to sleep. Third, God appears most vividly in dreams and sleep when persons are troubled, when real danger is at hand, and when deliverance is greatly needed. Many of the biblical dreams, such as Joseph's dreams, were literally deliverance dreams. Fourth, sleep is a therapy for sorrow, as was true of the sleep of the disciples at the Garden of Gethsemane. Depression, grief, disappointment, heartbreak, and disillusionment are signaled by the loss of sleep and healed by the power of sleep. As Shakespeare says,

> Sleep . . . knits up the ravell'd sleave of care
> The death of each day's life, sore labour's bath,
> Balm of hurt minds, great nature's second course,
> Chief nourisher in life's feast.[3]

Finally, disturbed sleep and its dreams in the biblical scene are indicators of anxiety. Pilate's wife suffered over Jesus in her dreams. Nebuchadnezzar's sleep was disturbed by his fears. The modern conflict-theory of dreams is evident in and supported by the biblical accounts.

In these respects, the religious interpretations of sleep, dreams, and revelation are prescientific preludes to scientific formulations of today. The "assumptive world" of the Bible is distinctly related to God. The mythological assumptions of science today do not necessarily include or exclude the God reference. Yet, their empirical findings are not thereby negated. To the contrary, these findings can be raw material for the religious interpreter.

One need not restrict himself to the Judaeo-Christian tradition for the religious understanding of sleep, dreams, and revelation. Both a religious and a scientific concern for this may be found in Greek culture. The Greeks had ritualized sleep treatment in the incubation sanctuaries. The Greeks went through the rite of sleeping on a skin or on the ground in order to commune with the gods of the underworld through dreams. They held to the belief that the gods prescribed medicine or granted healing through sleep. The Asclepian temples used baths, massages, and sleep as forms of religio-therapeutic technique. Plato speaks of dreams as being the sleep-behavior of good men who go to sleep and dream of doing what bad men actually do in their waking hours. When the ruling power of one's reason and humanity is asleep, "then the wild beast within us . . . goes forth to satisfy his desires; and there is no conceivable folly or crime —not excepting incest or any other unnatural union, or parricide, or the eating of forbidden food—which at such time, when he has parted company with all shame and sense, a man may not be ready to commit." [4]

Yet the dark picture is not the only possibility in sleep, according to Plato. When a person lives a rational and temperate life and feeds his rational powers on noble thoughts, in sleep he can indeed aspire to knowledge of the unknown, attain truth most nearly, and be least likely "to be the sport of fantastic and lawless visions." [5]

EMPIRICAL STUDIES OF SLEEP

The more recent scientific community has developed a considerable body of technical data on sleep. They have experimentally identified—through the use of electroencephalograms and electrooculograms—two different kinds of sleep. Under ordinary circumstances, these two kinds of sleep alternate in cycles during a night's sleep. The first stage is the beginning Stage 1 EEG (a low-voltage, fast, random pattern). During this stage of the EEG and type of sleep there are alternating spurts of rapid eye movement. This kind of sleep is called REM sleep, or rapid eye movement sleep. The second kind of sleep has no such eye movement and is called NREM sleep or nonrapid eye movement sleep. It goes through three EEG stages. Stage 2 has no "D" waves on the EEG. Stages 3 and 4 do have "D" waves. In a typical night's sleep, a person will begin with about one and one-half hours of NREM sleep, followed by about ten to fifteen minutes of REM sleep. REM sleep is filled with mental activity and 80–90 percent of the subjects awakened during REM sleep report dreaming. NREM sleep has mental activity, but it is more reality based, more plausible, less fantastic and bizarre, and more concerned with contemporary waking life. During a typical night of sleep, there will be a total of three cycles of alternation between REM and NREM sleep.[6] The intuitive insights of Plato described poetically these two types of sleep. The psychoanalytic dream analyses of Freud separated the more bizarre kind of dream from the ones related realistically to everyday happenings and immediate physical stimuli such as cold, dampness, and so on. Individual differences, age differences, differences in amounts of sleep, and so on appear in these sleep patterns. The basic rhythm of the REM-NREM is somewhat constant. Serious scholars probe the causes of the BRAC (basic-rest-activity cycle) and note that the 85.5 minute cycle is also the "value of Schuler's constant for the gyrocompass and is equal to $\frac{1}{2} \pi \sqrt{\frac{R}{g}}$ where R is the radius of the earth and g is the acceleration—due to gravity at the earth's surface. Ninety minutes is also the approximate period of revolution of artificial satellites fairly close to the surface of the earth." [7] The sleep disturbances and perceptual distortions of persons who fly long distances in short spans of time seem to indicate that Luce and Segal are right when they say that "somewhere within our chemistry there must be a clock, the metronome of our circadian rhythm that puts us to sleep once in every 24 hours."[8] Other persons represent the sleep cycle as being like the ebb and flow of the tide. The rhythm of the tide can be measured, and so can that of sleep.[9]

REM sleep is very important for the health and spiritual perspective of a person. This is the time of dreaming. In ancient as well as modern times, dreams have been looked upon as bearers of tidings of the spiritual realm of life. Today, psychoanalytic theory has interpreted dreams as revelations of the inner self. Residual in the meaning of anxiety dreams is the theme of interpersonal conflict and the need for reconciliation. Apart from simple wish-fulfillment dreams and physiological-response dreams, the most significant kind of dream is the dream that points to disturbed human relationships. The biblical dreams mentioned previously tend to be this kind of dream.[10] Consequently, the religious interpreter can with safety look for the conflict theme and take dreams seriously in the ministry of reconciliation.

There is some less firm evidence that deprivation of sleep, particularly REM sleep, raises the level of possibility that the perceptual and thinking order of the person will become paranoid. REM sleep seems, at least, to "discharge potentially harmful tensions that are unable to find release in waking experience. When this mechanism is blocked, these harmful tensions may accumulate and eventually force their way into waking expression in the form of mental disturbance."[11] Although this has not been definitively proved, it is a worthy hypothesis for further research. W. Dement, however, concludes that the problem is much deeper than just the deprivation of "the right to dream" in Stage 1 sleep. Specific biological functions are affected by deprivation of REM sleep. Some biochemical substances are accumulated during waking hours which are discharged and eliminated during REM sleep.[12]

One is prone to relate these data to more recent studies of stress in which the 17-hydroxycorticosteroid is identified as the particular substance that accumulates in stress situations and produces fatigue, anxiety, and the effort syndrome.[13] Conflict produces stress, and the stress remains until a solution of the conflict emerges. Breger and others hypothesize that "dreams may serve a unique function in the integration or assimilation of affectively aroused information into the 'solutions' embodied in the memory systems." When a person goes to sleep with conflicts aroused, memory systems related to the conflicts are activated during REM periods. Almost in a computer fashion *the present conflict is blended with its historical roots . . . , and solutions, frequently of a symbolic nature, are displayed.*[14] Stress management could use sleep therapy as a technique and prevent many of the depressions and psychophysiological disorders which are now being treated with shock therapy and anti-depressant and antianxiety drugs.

Additional data concerning sleep and stress reveal that marked variations appear between long and short sleepers. Short sleepers, in one study, were all either employed full time—often more than full time—or were in school full time, and often both. Several reported working seventy to eighty hours per week. Histories indicated that they had usually started sleeping their short hours about age sixteen to eighteen. Pressures increased from school and work. Unlike most persons, however, they had found that they could do it and manage easily and even enjoy getting shorter amounts of sleep than previously.

These short sleepers were in engineering, business, carpentry, and contracting. They appeared to be successful and relatively healthy. They kept busy and avoided problems, relying upon hyperactivity, denial, avoidance, and keeping busy. One might assume, I should think, that other people had to adjust to them rather than vice versa.

In contrast the long sleepers were less active, less conformist in their views. They were creative and more reflective. They showed a great variety of psychological problems. They were shy, tended to be mildly depressed, and registered considerable anxiety. They had minor medical and psychosomatic problems. They were not as good sleepers as the short sleepers. Their sleep was disturbed more often, and they did not get as much refreshment from their sleep.[15]

Foulkes mentions conflict as being the content-theme of many REM dreams. Dement points to the build-up of biochemical substances due to the absence of REM sleep. Stress studies seem to point to the way in which 17-OHCS is such a biochemical substance caused by stress. Could it be, therefore, that short sleepers use up their stress-produced biochemicals through large muscle activity and a minimum of introspection, whereas the long sleepers do little physical activity, ruminate much, and experience much conflict that must be drained off in somewhat troubled sleep? Putting the empirical data together makes this seem plausible.

A closer look at the conflict itself, furthermore, may even be between the different kinds of sleepers, the doers and the thinkers, the men of action and the men of contemplation. One counselee of mine gave me a clue to this when she said, "I used to stay awake and have my sleep disturbed by thoughts of all my opponents. Then one day I realized that while I was wrestling with my sheets over them *they* were sleeping like babies! I decided that if they could sleep well *I* could too!"[16]

This seems to me to be a clue at least to some of the conflicts that plague the religious community. If the spiritual director of such communities would take the A.M.-P.M. variations, the sleep patterns, and the dreams of people more seriously, he could be more perceptive of the deeper meanings being revealed in their conflictual relationships. At least, he would have a more profound and less obvious kind of index than to worry quite so much about their verbal statements of their disagreements.

RELIGIOUS SIGNIFICANCE OF SLEEP AND DREAMING

This leads to several hypotheses about the significance of sleep and dreaming for the religious life.

First, wherever we learned to think of dreams as the "idle sputtering of the brain or meaningless bits of mental fluff," we did not learn it from the documents of living religions, great philosophers, or empirical scientific research on sleep. A case can be made at every point for a serious religious psychology of sleep and dreaming. If the study of theology, as Calvin saw it, is to learn of both God and the self, then the sleep experience of mankind cannot be excluded from the quest.

Second, sleep and dreaming are fertile sources of creative religious imagination. Foulkes makes much of the ways in which voluntary and active imagining, and even semivoluntary daydreaming, are accompanied by rapid eye movements.[17] The presence of active REM recall of dreams is positively related to "waking story-telling ability." The process of problem solution is hastened through such a cycling of sleep. A mathematical problem that will not come right often falls easily into place after effective sleep. The proverbial ritual of sleeping on a decision seems to have real validity from an experimental point of view.

From a revelational point of view, a person who believes that God makes himself known through the creative processes of the mind and of human history can with real justification rely upon sleep and dreams as one of the important media of the knowledge of God. As such, they can be to the modern person as they were to young Samuel (1 Sam. 3:1–18). In days when "the word of the Lord is rare" and "there is no frequent vision," a reexamination of the religious significance of sleep and dream experience has much to offer.

In the third place, an adequate cycling of sleep has a way of clearing and defogging the perception. Deprivation, particularly of REM sleep, increases paranoid distortion. Shakespeare was right when he called sleep "the balm of hurt minds." The role of sleep in restoring the soul seems to be that it is one of the way stations of meditation and prayer. When one, by circumstance, suffering, and exhaustion, is "made to lie down," as the psalmist puts it, then restoring to the soul has a chance to happen. Activistic forms of religion overlook this and become stressors in and of themselves. For example, in a recent survey of a group of theological students, it was found that fully one-third of the students were working a full forty-hour week over and above their full class load. There was little or no time for study outside class, meditation, making love, or sleeping, to say nothing of three cycles of REM sleep in each twenty-four hours!

In the fourth place, the restorative power of sleep and dreams is directly related to the prevention, diagnosis, and therapy of depression. Depression is the antithesis of hope, both of which have a biochemistry related to the sleep cycle. The primary problem the religious counselor deals with is that of despair. The main psychological component of effective religion is hope. If the personal and organized expressions of religion are to remain in force, images, forces, and energizers of hope must continually be generated. A specific form of ministry with which to begin is the sleep needs of persons.

The manufacturers of drugs seem to know this. We begin with the caffeine in coffee and the pills students take during exam week, continuing with alcohol used both to stimulate and relax the organism; we conclude with downers—narcotics, barbiturates, and so on. These and many more are the pharmacopoeia of sleep. We can rightly ask, "Shall we teach or medicate?" A person under barbiturates cannot be fully himself. Persons can be taught to do without drugs, except in severe instances, for ordinary coping with anxiety and tension that disrupt sleep. In fact, complete freedom from sleeplessness is as dangerous as complete freedom from the sensation of pain.

The task of an effective religion, it seems to me, is to teach people how to experience the joy of life with hope. The accessible data concerning sleep are excellent points of contact with persons in individual counseling, group interaction, and spiritual retreats for the renewal of the hoping dynamics of life.

NOTES

1. Levy-Bruhl, *Primitive Mentality*, p. 99.
2. Shelley *Daemon of the World* 1. 1. 1.
3. Shakespeare *Macbeth,* act 2, sc. 1, 1. 36.
4. Plato *Republic* 9
5. Ibid.
6. Gerald Vogel, David Foulkes, and Harry Trosman, "Ego Functions and Dreaming During Sleep Onset," *Altered States of Consciousness*, ed. Charles T. Tart (New York: John Wiley, 1969), pp. 75–76.
7. Arthur Shapiro, "Comments on the 90 Minute Sleep Dream Cycle," *Sleep and Dreaming*, International Psychiatry Clinic (Boston: Little, Brown, Co., 1970), vol. 77, no. 2, p. 23.
8. Gay Goer Luce and Julius Segal, *Sleep* (New York: Lancer Books, 1967), p. 181.
9. Harmon S. Ephron and Patricia Carrington, "On the Functions of the Sleep Phases," *Sleep and Dreaming*, p. 270.
10. David Foulkes, *The Psychology of Sleep* (New York: Charles Scribner's Sons, 1966), pp. 96–98.

11. Ibid., pp. 204–5.

12. W. Dement, "Studies on the Function of Rapid Eye Movement (Paradoxical) Sleep in Human Subjects," *Anatomical and Functional Aspects of the Physiology of Sleep* (Paris: CNRS, 1965), pp. 571–608, quoted in Foulkes, *Psychology of Sleep*, p. 207.

13. Peter G. Bourne, *Men, Stress, and Vietnam* (Boston: Little, Brown, 1971), pp. 21, 92–94, 118–20.

14. Louis Breger, Ian Hunter, and Ron W. Lane, *The Effect of Stress on Dreams* (New York: International Press, 1971), p. 22.

15. Ernest Hartmann, M.D., Frederick Baekaland, M.D., George Zivilling, and Patrick Hoy, "Sleep Need: How Much Sleep and What Kind?", *The American Journal of Psychiatry*, vol. 127, no. 8, (February 1971), pp. 1001–8.

16. Foulkes, *Psychology of Sleep*, pp. 18–19.

17. Ibid., p. 186.

QUESTIONS FOR FURTHER STUDY

1. The data on sleep are related to the contemplative life. Find the work of Thomas Merton, *The Seeds of Contemplation,* and develop the relationship between rest, sleep, and contemplation.

2. The data concerning sleep are related also to muscular relaxation and spiritual discipline. The Oriental religious practice of Yoga is significant at this point. Relate Yoga to Edmund Jacobson's teachings in his book *Anxiety and Tension Control* (Philadelphia: J. B. Lippincott, 1964).

3. In what ways are the drug abuses of younger persons with illegal drugs and older persons with prescription drugs related to basic disorders of the Basic Rest Activity Cycle (BRAC) of their lives?

11

HABIT AND RELIGIOUS RITUAL

The word habit *is a venerable word with distinct religious connotations* in its more archaic sense. Formerly it referred to one's dress, garb, attire, and so on. The particular costume indicative of rank, calling, or immediate pursuit was called a habit. More recently than this, the word *habit* was used to refer to one's bearing, deportment, and demeanor. It was used almost as a synonym for a person's character. It referred to one's mental or moral constitution or bearing, his disposition, or the prevailing character of one's thoughts and feelings, in other words, one's mental make-up. Speaking psychologically, however, an even more recent definition of *habit* is an aptitude or inclination for a particular kind of action, acquired by frequent repetition, and showing itself in increased ease of performance or in decreased power of resistance. In other words, it is an acquired pattern of behavior.

The particular hypothesis of this chapter is that much religious behavior is built on the assumption of a psychology of habit. The habit is usually called either law or ritual among religious people and in religious literature. Therefore, in order to appreciate habit both psychologically and religiously, one must focus the discussion on the relationship between habit on the one hand and law and ritual on the other hand. However, a disclaimer needs to be entered lest we see habit too narrowly defined. Alfred North Whitehead, for example, said that "moral progress is impossible apart from the habitual vision of greatness." This seems to suggest that habit is a much larger concept than just this, that, or the other set of acquired behaviors. It may even refer to the larger psychoanalytic concept of identification of a person with other persons and ideals upon whom he has lastingly fixed his total affections. This is what William James referred to as "the habitual center of personal energies"; conversion consisted of a radical shift in this habitual center of personal energies. Therefore, the discussion here will have a macroscopic perspective of the larger style of life or way of life of a person's habitual center of personal energies and habitual vision of greatness. This will be followed by a microscopic view of the particular substructures of persons.

SOME LAWS OF HABIT: WILLIAM JAMES

William James in his *Talks to Teachers* encouraged teachers and students alike to see that the great thing in all education is to teach the nervous system to be our ally instead of our enemy. In order to do this "we must make automatic and habitual, as early as possible, as many useful actions as we can, and as carefully guard against the growing and the ways that are likely to be disadvantageous." In this sense, James saw habit as deliberately making desired patterns of behavior automatic, unconscious, and thereby releasing energy and time for learning new data and forming new habits. He said that "the more of the details of our daily life we can hand over to the effortless custody of automatism, the more our higher powers of mind will be set free for their proper work. There is no more miserable human being than one in whom nothing is habitual but indecision." Therefore, says James, the cornerstone of the formation of acceptable habits and the reconditioning of unacceptable habits is the capacity of an individual to make decisions. With this as background, James identifies five great laws of habit.

Law 1: "The acquisition of a new habit, or the leaving off of an old one, requires that we must take care to launch ourselves with as strong and decided an initiative as possible." One gets into conditions that encourage the new habit. He makes commitments that are contrary to the old commitments. He enlists the support, affection, and cooperation of all the people he knows and develops the resolution to form the new habit or break the old one with every aid that he knows. Underlying this law seems to be a morality of commitment, an ethic in which a person makes promises first to himself and then to his significant community of faith.

Law 2: "Never suffer an exception to occur 'til the new habit is securely rooted in your life." The unbroken record is an important incentive in the formation of new habits and in the reconditioning of old habits. One needs a series of uninterrupted success until repetition of the habit has fortified it to such a degree as to provide coping devices for dealing with any opposing temptations. Underneath this law of habit seems to lie an assumption of a psychology of temptation as the warring of unacceptable tendencies to act with the resolve to act acceptably to oneself and others.

Law 3: "Seize the very first possible opportunity to act on every resolution you make, and on every emotional prompting you may experience in the direction of the habits you aspire to gain." The objective of this law is to produce motor effects, brain changes, new neurological pathways. There is a definite neurophysiology to habit formation. Therefore, James cautions against letting "a resolve or a feeling" go by and "to evaporate without bearing practical fruit." This is not only a chance lost but hinders future resolutions and emotions from "taking the normal path of discharge."

Law 4: "Don't teach too much about habits or abound in good talk in the abstract." Instead one should grab practical opportunities to work good habits into the organic tissue of one's being. This is reminiscent of an observation of Freud who said that talk reduces the tendency to act. Therefore, Freud took the route of the "talk cure" for tendencies toward antisocial behavior and the acting out of habits that were dangerous to a person and other people. However, William James's emphasis in this fourth maxim concerning habit formation is that talking about one's own or another's good habits tends to reduce the intention to act in the actual formation of those habits.

Law 5: "Keep the faculty of effort alive in you by a little gratuitous exercise everyday." Alcoholics Anonymous have this law built into their treatment of alcoholic habits. They live on a twenty-four-hour basis. They do not promise to be sober tomorrow, but they do promise to be sober today. Therefore, they concentrate all their efforts in the gratuitous exercises toward sobriety in the day in which they are living. William Osler called this living life in day-tight compartments. The formation of positive habits, as well as the breaking of negative habits, calls for this "exercise every day." For example, Kenneth Scott LaTourette formed the habit of writing by allocating himself a certain number of words each day. If he did not keep up with his word quota, he would pass the work that he did not do today to tomorrow's quota and double his effort and exercise in writing on that day.

James's laws of habit seem to be somewhat tedious for those who lay their whole case for the transformation of character on the assumption of a sudden reform or conversion. They might even assume that the five laws of habit are the substitutions of work for faith in God. However, James answers this by saying that sudden conversions unquestionably do occur, regardless of how infrequent they may be. He insists that the most startling sudden alterations of character can be a sort of launching of the laws of habit formation into motion with "new stimuli and new excitements." The experience of conversion, in James's thought, consisted of a shift in the center of one's habitual personal energies. This conversion ordinarily consists of the expulsive power of a new affection, a new identification, and the creation of a new loyalty. Nevertheless, "the general laws of habit are no wise altered thereby, and the physiological study of mental conditions still remains on the whole the most powerful ally of ethics." We are in a constant state of becoming "walking bundles of habit," and our nerve cells and fibers are made up of molecules. They register and store up the results of our behavior to be used for or against us "when the next temptation comes." James concludes by saying that "as we become permanent drunkards by so many separate drinks, so we become saints in the moral, and authorities and experts in the practical and scientific spheres, by so many separate acts and hours of work." [1]

CLASSICAL CONDITIONING: IVAN PAVLOV

Ivan Pavlov (1849–1936) was a Russian physiologist, the son of a village priest of the Russian Orthodox church. He did research on the problems of digestion, cerebral activity, and the theory of reflexes. His work has been translated into English under the title *Conditioned Reflexes*. It was first published in Russian in 1907 and concerns such problems as salivation and digestion. Then it was published in French in 1914, and finally was published in English in 1927. Pavlov's famous experiment with the salivating dog consisted of the pairing of one stimulus, namely food, with another stimulus, namely the ringing of a bell, as a planned event within a given time span. The purpose was to produce a conditioned response, namely, salivation. A dog was placed in a fixed position; a bell was rung. Shortly afterward food was presented to the dog. Upon repetition of this process, the dog was so conditioned to expect the food when the bell rang that even when the food was not presented the dog salivated. The experiment produced salivation as a "conditioned reflex." Further note needs to be made that at the outset the experiment was made possible because the dog was hungry. Therefore, a conditioned response presupposes a deprivation as a precondition. Furthermore, if the dog becomes oversatiated with food, the results of the experiment diminish. If the dog is presented with a ringing bell and no food is forthcoming even though the dog is hungry, the conditioned response will tend to be extinguished. Commenting on this, B. F. Skinner, a later scientist of habit formation, says,

> The process of conditioning, as Pavlov reported in his book *Conditioned Reflexes*, is a process of *stimulus substitution*. A previously neutral stimulus acquires the power to elicit a response which was originally elicited by another stimulus. The change occurs when the neutral stimulus is followed or "reinforced" by the effected stimulus. Pavlov studied the effect of the interval of time elapsing between stimulus and reinforcement. He investigated the extent to which various properties of stimuli could acquire control. He also studied the converse process, in which the condition stimulus loses its power to evoke the response when it is no longer reinforced—a process which he calls "extinction." [2]

This relatively simple process of habit formation has been called classical conditioning. As one associates this kind of classical conditioning with the prophetic need for challenging and reconditioning human behavior, his mind races to the account of Jesus and his disciples found in Mark 2:23–28. They were going through the grain fields. His disciples began to pluck ears of grain. The Pharisees criticized them to Jesus saying, "Look, why are they doing what is not lawful on the Sabbath?" Then Jesus answered them by saying, "Have you never read what David did, when he was in need and was hungry, he and those who were with him: how he entered the house of God, when Abiathar was high priest, and ate the bread of the Presence, which is not lawful for any but the priests to eat, and also gave it to those who were with him?"

In this encounter with the Pharisees, Jesus was confronted with one of the Sabbath laws, a set of habit patterns into which faithful Jews had been classically conditioned. They were to refrain from gathering grain for food, even though they were hungry. However, Jesus pointed out to the Pharisees that acute deprivation of a need such as hunger causes old conditions to become extinct and new types of behavior to come into being. He insisted that the laws of the Sabbath were established on the basis of men's needs; they manifest, therefore, the need for rest and food and loving care of the Lord of life. The laws of the Sabbath were subordinate to these needs of man. "The Sabbath was made for man, not man for the Sabbath." Whitehead's comment about moral progress being built upon the "habitual vision of greatness" comes into focus in Jesus' comment that "the Son of Man is Lord even of the Sabbath." Pavlov's experiment is described in detail in many places in the literature of habit formation, but rarely is it mentioned that the dog was related to his master. Ultimately, the experiment would be made for the dog and not the dog for the experiment! When one translates this into human terms, one could say that the laws and rituals of religious behavior are always subordinate to the Lord of the rituals and the behavior. The important item dropped out of much discussion of classical conditioning is the relationship between "the conditioner and the conditionee." This relationship itself must be entered in any empirical description of habit formation that is complete.

In the contemporary religious scene, such classical conditioning is often used to motivate persons to make religious confessions and commitments. Food is known to have been used as a deprivation-stimulus to get homeless alcoholics to attend church services. In the nineteenth century, Rice Christians were made in the Far East. Persons were motivated to unite with the Protestant mission in order to get rice as food. More subtle is the person who relates to such a mission today in order to learn to speak the English language. Yes, the satiation of these desires may extinguish the newly formed habit of participating in religious worship.

A comment on the relationship of codes of ethics versus situational ethics is in order at this point. Jesus set aside the sublegislation to the commandment concerning the Sabbath. Acute human needs, and even the suffering such as that of an ox in a ditch, have a way of suspending the ordinary validity of many laws, habits, or rituals. The overwhelming deprivation or satiation of a need of man or animal produces a purposive suspension of these rituals, a reeducation of old habits. This reeducation becomes the religious concern with the weightier matters of the law as over against the minutiae. Yet, another relationship problem emerges: The interpretation of these changes in ritual and habit must take place on the basis of trust and openness of understanding such as existed between Jesus and his disciples. The catching-convicting-punishing relationship of distrust such as existed in the Pharisees' relationship to Jesus and his disciples would tend to mobilize the chaotic destruction of whatever is good in a given law, ritual, or habit. The prevailing context of relationship, in my opinion, in the formation or reformation of habits and laws is just as important as the parent stimuli aimed toward a conditioned response.

OPERANT CONDITIONING: B. F. SKINNER

In the 1930s B. F. Skinner, now a professor of psychology at Harvard, pointed out that most learning behavior does not fit the classical conditioning model of Pavlov. Whereas some learning does take place this way, most learning behavior does not fit this model. Behaving human beings do not merely respond mechanically to stimuli but learn to make active efforts that will enable them to achieve a goal or reward and to avoid pain or punishment. This conditioning is instrumental and enables an organism to gain a reward and to avoid punishment. Concerning the difference between his approach and that of Pavlov, Skinner says:

> In the Pavlovian experiment . . . a reinforcer is paired with a *stimulus;* whereas an operant behavior is contingent upon a *response*. Often reinforcement is, therefore, a separate process and requires a separate analysis. In both cases the strengthening of behavior which results from reinforcement is appropriately called "conditioning." In operant conditioning we "strengthen" an operant in the sense of making a response more probable, or in actual fact, more frequent.[3]

Operant conditioning depends upon the kind, amount, and immediacy of reinforcement. For example, operant behavior begins with certain controls, such as a given deprivation of something like food. As Skinner says, "Our control over the response of a pigeon stretching its neck is simply to make it hungry." Operant behavior can be extinguished when a given behavior no longer pays off. There are two types of reinforcements of behavior: Positive reinforcement, such as rewards, consists of presenting a stimulus such as food, water, sexual contact, and so on to a situation of hunger, thirst, or sexual need. Negative reinforcement consists of removing something, such as a loud noise, a very bright light, extreme cold or heat, or electric shock, from the situation. Both cases of reinforcement produce the possibility of a response being increased. In a word, they are the conditioning reinforcers of reward and punishment, positive and negative reinforcement. There is such a thing also as intermittent reinforcement in which the chances that a person is rewarded or punished or not rewarded or punished are varied. For example, instead of presenting a stimulus and its reward every time a presentation is made, the reward is presented every fifth or fiftieth time. This paces the reward, which is contingent upon responses. Also, interval reinforcements are related to time.

Satiation and deprivation are related to operant reinforcement, and Skinner says, "There is inevitable connection between the two processes: the effect of operant reinforcement will not be observed if the organism has not been appropriately deprived. The net result of reinforcement is not simply to strengthen behavior but to strengthen it in a given state of *deprivation*." Oversatiation, as has been said, may extinguish a response.

One of the great contributions that the behavioral psychologists have made to religious life and practice has been in the area of teaching us the laws of habituating people to what the community has agreed upon as redemptive and nourishing types of behavior patterns. On the other hand, a considerable amount of preoccupation in the life of the religious community is focused upon relieving, redeeming, and counterconditioning noisome habits which bring considerable disaster in people's lives. Behavioral therapy is a kind of therapy that can be learned in the simplest forms by lay persons. It does not take the amount of time that other types of therapy consume and, therefore, offers productive results in dealing with large numbers of people as is true in a religious community. All of which raises the question about what are some of the techniques most commonly used in habit breaking.

TECHNIQUES OF HABIT CHANGE

The first technique is that of the *incompatible-response* in which a given habit is replaced by another behavioral pattern that is opposed to it. Harry Emerson Fosdick tells of a man who owned a dog which consistently chased his car each morning when he drove out of the driveway to go to work. One morning a variation took place. The dog went in another direction and did not chase the car. The owner noticed that the dog had spied a cat sitting on a neighbor's porch and had taken

off after the cat. It is impossible to chase a car and a cat at the same time!
The Alcoholics Anonymous meetings for example are famous for their
consumption of coffee, Coca Colas, and so on. Their thirst is counter-
conditioned in this way. The drug culture is built, for example, not only
on the need of a young person for drugs but also for the companionship
of people who accept him, appreciate him, and do not hassle him.
The religious community that provides such a companionship for the
person has taken the first step in the direction of enabling the person
to break a habit by developing an incompatible-response community.

A second technique of habit breaking is *exhaustion*. One of the best
examples of this I can remember is having smoked several cigars in a
row when I was fourteen years of age. I became so very, very sick that
I have never had the ability to form the habit of smoking since then.
In the treatment of alcoholism, Antabuse is a deterrent therapy of no
mean proportions. A person who takes Antabuse very soon exhausts his
taste for alcohol.

A third method of habit breaking is *toleration*. The stimulus on which
the undesirable habit is based is presented in small doses so that a
person can tolerate the presence of the stimulus without being destroyed
by it. This is particularly a form of therapy used by Wolpe in his retro-
active inhibition therapy. An example of this would be a person who
fears rats will be presented the verbal name of a rat in conversation first,
then a picture of a rat is presented, then a toy rat is presented, and then
a small, defenseless baby rat is presented. If positive reactions are gained
through this increased tolerance technique of habit breaking, then the
fear can be overcome.

Another example of this is the problem of the inability of a very shy
person to participate in religious groups and activities. This could be
overcome through pleasant social experiences with one or two people
at a time who would then become ministers of introduction of the person
to one or two more people at a time until the shyness was gradually
overcome.

A fourth technique of habit breaking is *the change of environment*.
Thus, for example, a grudge war between an eighteen-year-old working
girl is causing her to engage in rebellious types of behavior that punish
and spite her mother. A change of jobs, or beginning a program of
school, or simply either starting to church or changing churches may
introduce a change of environment that will dislocate the bad habits.

A fifth method of habit breaking is *punishment*. In this sense the religious community ordinarily does not engage in punitive behavior in
order to change people's habits. Of course, several examples of punishment such as exclusion, snobbery, and verbal tongue-lashings do occur.
More concrete forms of punishment are meted out by the courts in legal
process when young people get into trouble. Religious leaders and

sponsors can take advantage of this type of punishment by avoiding the temptation to fix tickets or use influence to spring people from the results of their behavior. Jesus never told us to spring people from prison but only to visit them! If, however, a young person is allowed to go through the whole process of confronting the judge, paying a fine, and so on and at the same time have the presence and affection of people who care what happens to him, he is likely to think longer and harder before he engages in a bad habit again.

A sixth form of breaking habits is that of *affirmation and reward* of habits contrary to undesirable ones. This feeds the good habit and starves the bad habit. This could be called reward, but the word *reward* implies that tangible tokens or gifts are presented to the person. Probably the more intangible token or gift would be undivided attention, given on periodic but regular schedule, without the use of much money or material reward.

A final technique of habit breaking is the *use of money* in relation to productive work. The token system is used in some mental hospitals as a technique of motivating withdrawn and drifting patients to take initiative to do ward work and so on around the hospital. These tokens then can be exchanged for things that the patient wants to buy. The side effect is that the habit of sitting, ruminating, and daydreaming is broken somewhat in behalf of a more active initiative and involvement in the environment. Religious communities can help middle and late adolescents a very great deal in this respect by getting into the act of teaching them the relationship between money and work. Lay leadership in a church, for example, could take an active interest in the search of these young people for jobs in the community. Young people who have recently finished either high school or college or who are dropouts quite often get involved in the drug community because of the need for and interest in money. Drug pushing becomes a substitute for other types of more acceptable work. Similarly, sexual activity on the part of young women quite often expresses itself in substitutes for work as a means of getting money. This may or may not go the whole way in the direction of prostitution. However, for some women prostitution becomes what seems to them to be the only alternative for income.

RITUAL AND HABIT IN THE RELIGIOUS COMMUNITY

All that has been said thus far may seem to the reader to be somewhat tangential to a focused concern for the role of religious habit or ritual in the religious community. However, far from being tangential, the psychology of habit formation and reformation is integral to the ordered life of the religious community. Religious habits tend to take the form of religious laws, ceremonies, and rituals. Underneath these laws, ceremonies, and rituals are the basic principles of habit formation and habit breaking which we have just been discussing. Paul Pruyser makes several observations concerning ritual in his discussion of religion and the motor system of the human organism. First, Pruyser calls attention to the way in which rituals vary in the pace and scope of motor movements. The different forms of baptism, for example, take more or less motor movements, and the pace varies accordingly. An arm raised fully in a benediction is quite different from a snap salute of a soldier. In the second place, rituals, says Pruyser, are "measured, precise, specified in great detail, highly stereotyped, and often very repetitive." For example, when Billy Graham offers the invitation at the end of his crusade meetings, it is always done in precisely the same way in careful detail and is a repetition of the many, many times he has done this.

In the third place, Pruyser calls attention to the fact that "rhythm and number are important in ritual." We say "Holy, Holy, Holy" *three* times. Joshua and his people circled Jericho seven times before the walls would fall down. One denomination will have an observance of the Lord's Supper every Sunday of the year. Another denomination will have the same observance on a specific Sunday each month. Another group of churches within the same denomination will have the Lord's Supper once each quarter, four times a year. The cyclical numbering and rhythm of ritual has always the effect of intermittent conditioning. One does not notice the power of habit until he tries to change the number, the timing, and so on of these rituals.

Finally, Pruyser says that spontaneity and efficiency are variable relatives in the religious life but they are "suspended in rituals." They capitalize on inhibition, delay, and many different control devices.[4]

I would add another factor to the general description of ritual which Paul Pruyser presents. If one is interested in spontaneous expression of religious living, then he needs to be very aware that the meaning of spontaneity itself is intensified by the break in the routine of the regular rituals of the fellowship which it represents. Without this backdrop of ritual, then the spontaneity tends to extinguish rather quickly and become ritualized itself. Spontaneous occurrences are the dessert in the regular rituals of the religious community. They represent a break in the monotony without which regularity there would be no break.

Arnold Van Gennep, to whom reference has been previously made, points out that the rites of passage which constitute the rituals of the ongoing community, sacred or secular, represent efforts on the part of the community to enable individuals to separate from one station in life as they make the transition to another station in life and become securely incorporated in that station in life. These rites may be territorial rites in which a person moves from one place to another, or they may be social rites in which one moves from one status, role, age group, or position to another in life. Gennep points out that there are recurrent themes in these rites of separation, transition, and incorporation. There is the death-rebirth theme. This pageant of death-rebirth is reenacted in the act of baptism by immersion, for example. The theme symbolizes the regeneration and renewal of life. Again, there is the ablution or cleansing theme whereby a person is cleansed of an old way of life and brought into a new way of life washed and purified. One might add that there is the clothing or investiture theme whereby a person either literally or symbolically changes vestments as a symbol of his transition from one place of being in life to another. This clothing theme is reenacted each year at the Kentucky Derby when the horse that won the race is draped with an elaborate blanket of roses. Another name for the race is the Run of the Roses.

The Largest Significance of Habit and Ritual in a Psychology of Religion

Several basic principles can be formulated as to the largest significance of habit and ritual in the psychology of religious experience.

First, habit and ritual, on the one hand, and spontaneity and freedom, on the other hand, represent a rhythm between law and grace. Habit and ritual tend to provide structure for life, and grace enables life to function spontaneously. The laws of the Hebrew religion, the Apostle Paul tells us, were formulated as tutors to lead us to the life of grace in Christ. Participation in a purely structureless religious life is a fond imagination but not a reality. Whatever spontaneity of grace we may experience in the spirit, with the passage of time, begins to take form in the specific habits and rituals. The Quaker community, for example, leans hard against the coercive power of ritual. However, their simplified, nonverbal, and disciplined forms of worship themselves have a patterning of what may be called a high form of ritual.

Second, effective habits and rituals are based upon a commonly agreed upon interpretation of their meaning in a religious community. For example, if a Roman Catholic were totally deaf but understood the common interpretation of the rituals of the mass, he could participate without having anyone tell him in words what this great event in the life of a Catholic is. In this sense a ritual is a commonly agreed upon form of behavior which is no longer questioned but participated in as a means of being a part of the community.

Third, ritual that is effective is built upon some great needs of people. When it ceases to be built upon these great needs, the ritual itself begins to be questioned and sooner or later is extinguished. Needs, for example, of communicants for initiation into the community are met by participating in the ritual of baptism. The religious community that keeps its rituals, habits, and practices in relation in close proximity to the basic needs of people is likely to be a vital religious community. The one that does not do so is likely to be more sterile. Listening to sermons, for example, or going to confession is each in its own way related to the assuagement of guilt and the need for support and reassurance. Rituals, also, are built upon the great need for companionship in the presence of the threat of separation imposed by the normal process of life which ends with death. Little wonder is it that Paul Radin has identified the closeness or proximity of the great rituals of primitive religions with the crises in the developmental cycle of life.

Third, the formation of a religious tradition calls for habituation. Religious rituals and habits are ways of communicating the message of that tradition to the most people in the shortest possible length of time. For example, the ritual of the sermon is a much more rapid way of conveying Christian counsel than sitting individually with people in the pattern of personal counseling or individual inquiry roles. Nevertheless, pastoral counseling itself is a very private personal kind of ritual and is a way of communicating the message of the Christian faith when sermons are too general and public.

Fourth, ritual and habit in the life of the religious community provide ways of reenacting events of the religious community's history for the sake of memory. The instruction of the young prevents a generation from arising that, as the Old Testament says, "does not know Joseph." The laws, the rituals of the Passover, and so on among the Jewish community are ways which the father, the head of the house, teaches his sons and daughters the great heritage of the Jewish community. These are the people who were delivered up out of Egypt, whom God sustained in the wilderness, who were kept in communication with each other through their faith in spite of their dispersion and the Nazi death camps. The Jewish faith has used ritual as the Jews' way of staying together as a people and of transmitting their faith from generation to generation. The camp meeting at Anderson, Indiana, at Anderson College and School of Theology is a time when the people of their faith gather together in order to renew memories of the frontier society that gave their religious community its being. The Lord's Supper, when observed by a little boy or a little girl, quite often becomes an instrument of teaching and learning when the child asks the question: What is that? Then whoever is near him has an opportunity to explain the crucifixion of Jesus Christ in behalf of us.

Finally, habit and ritual are reliable ways of stabilizing anxiety and facing the grief of separation. The great anxieties of death, of separation, of abandonment, are spoken to in the rituals of the wedding, the funeral, and the homecoming habits of various religious communities. When rightly perceived and carefully observed, religious ritual can and does become a form of renewal among people of a religious faith. They cushion the blow of death, they desensitize the power of loneliness, and they provide ways of celebration at times such as weddings and commencements. If we did not have these rituals, we would make some. People have always done this. They probably always will and for these reasons.

NOTES

1. William James, *Talks to Teachers on Psychology and to Students on Some of Life's Ideals* (New York: Dover Publications, 1962 ed. of 1899 publication), pp. 31–45.
2. B. F. Skinner, *Science and Human Behavior* (New York: Free Press, 1953), p. 53.
3. Ibid., p. 65.
4. Paul Pruyser, *Dynamic Psychology of Religion*, pp. 185–86.

QUESTIONS FOR FURTHER STUDY

1. As you look back into your religious history, what rituals did you form as habits? Which were positive experiences for you? Which were negative experiences for you? Do you practice them now?
2. Read B. F. Skinner's *Beyond Freedom and Dignity*. See whether his system there differs from his earlier statement of it as found in *Science and Behavior*.
3. What part does music have in the formation of habit and ritual in or out of the church?
4. Explore behavior therapy with such authors as Schaeffer, Martin, and Yates.

12

FANTASY AND TEMPTATION

The psychology of temptation is built upon the psychology of fantasy or "imagining," as the Old Testament puts it. The relation between this psychological concept of fantasy and the theological concept of temptation, therefore, is the exploration of this chapter.

"Imagining" and Fantasy

Old Testament psychology perceives the unexpressed drives of man as "imaginings." The Hebrew word for this is *yetzer,* meaning "to form," "to frame," "to purpose." In noun form and in reference to the mind, it means "imagination," "device," or "purpose." Genesis 6:5, speaking of Noah's generation, says that every imagination of the heart of man was only evil continually. In Genesis 8:21, it is assumed that God is in touch with the imaginings of man: "I know the purposes which they are already forming." I agree with Erich Fromm when he says that "in the Jewish view, man is born with the capacity to sin, but he can return, and redeem himself . . ." through the antidote that the Torah provides for his evil inclinations.[1] However, the imagination of man is not just the source of evil, for David prays in 1 Chronicles 29:18, "O Lord, the God of Abraham, Isaac, and Israel, our fathers, keep forever such purposes and thoughts in the hearts of thy people, and direct their thoughts toward thee" (RSV). As Fromm again says, the Hebrew word *yetzer* indicated that "evil (or good) impulses are possible only on the basis of that which is specifically human: imagination . . . only man . . . can be evil or good."[2]

The same basic idea of "imagining" appears in the New Testament. David is quoted in Acts 4:25 (RSV) as asking why "the Gentiles rage, and the peoples imagine vain things." The same word is used to mean "to meditate upon," "to attend to," or "to practice," in 1 Timothy 4:15. Jesus, in Luke 21:14, says, "Settle it therefore in your minds, not to meditate beforehand how to answer" (RSV). Here the imagination runs ahead of a person and fills him with anxiety about his confrontation with adversaries. Later in this chapter we will see how contemporary psychoanalysts talk about "anticipatory anxiety."

These imaginings and meditations are constant in every reference, both in the Old and the New Testaments, in one respect: They are always *in relation to God,* whether good or evil. The capacity of man to form, shape, and frame images or fantasies is a distinctly human capacity dramatized in relation to God. Yet this is the testing, trying, and tempting ground of human character.

From a contemporary psychological point of view, fantasy formation is the subject of extensive study. In psychoanalytic theory, fantasy happens on both a conscious and an unconscious level. On the conscious level, it is daydreaming or freely wandering thought. Fantasy formations are defenses in that they permit a measure of gratification without calling for action or inviting punishment. The adult tends to make a great secret of his daydreaming. The child openly speaks of his.

Unconscious fantasies, however, are much more complex. One of the more common unconscious fantasies is the rescue fantasy. One fantasies himself as being a deliverer or of being delivered, as in the king-slave type fantasy. In most of these fantasies there is a quality of yearning or aspiration. One reaches out to something beyond the self, one tries to attain the infinite. This is particularly true of late adolescence.

In both conscious and unconscious fantasies, satisfaction is gained entirely from a mental activity, estranged from reality. Both are woven with a kind of hopelessness that any fulfillment in reality is in fact possible. A fantasy may be the first phase of a creative or destructive act, but further phases must be performed by a person who is prone to translate and express himself in action and does not remain a dreamer.

One psychoanalyst puts his finger on the relation between fantasy and temptation in his discussion of "the function of anticipation." One anticipates guilt feeling in "forestalling guilt-laden action." "Behind these issues shimmers the deep problem of the common roots of responsibility for moral action and for self-observation." [3] Meditating beforehand may be in the face of real and external threats, but in its most devastating form it is in the face of moral condemnation from one's own internalized values. This is the stuff of which temptation is made.

TEMPTATION

Temptation is a time of testing of both man and God. Many things can be tested at the human level: a sword, a reputation, or a person's convictions. The main thrust of the biblical testing is the trial of man or of God. God tests man to know what is in his heart (Deut. 8:2). God permits both human and divine testing of man's faith. The tests of persecution are those from which the Lord's Prayer asks deliverance. The meaning of temptation that hovers most closely to fantasy formations is that found in James 1:12–15. A person, in this sense, is not tested by God but enticed by his own desires. These desires are the conception but not the birth of sin.

Considerable moral confusion surrounds the pietistic assumption that a fantasy is as bad an act, a temptation the same as sin. The biblical and psychological sources point to the fallacy of this. The wisdom of the practical-minded author of James puts the difference clearly. An example of its fallacy is that Jesus was tempted in the wilderness. In this story (Matt. 4:1–11; Luke 4:1–12) the universal nature of temptation is detailed. There are three common testings of the fantasies of man aimed at bringing them into relation to the Reality of life, to God.

First, Jesus was tempted to "command stones to turn to bread." This would be to respond in action to the fantasy of shortcuts to satisfaction. Jesus was hungry after fasting for forty days. The loneliness of the vigil, the hunger for food, and the pressure of temptation all combined could cause him to feel that he deserved one bit of magic in his own behalf. He had the possibility at hand. Yet his unity with God gave him the sense of reality that bread is earned and baked, not made from stones. Any other direction is cliff-hanging on the edge of sanity.

The basic hungers of a person are fertile sources of fantasy and temptation to take shortcuts to turn fantasies into reality without work or discipline. The instant syndrome of today is a case in point. The business or professional man plans his daily work often on the illusion of instant transportation. This fantasy is fed by airline advertisements that one can be here now and at a distant place in an instant. The preparation of food is being programmed by the instant syndrome—instant coffee, instant dinner, instant ovens. The realm of human intimacy—both sexual and otherwise—is plagued by the fantasy of instant intimacy through distortions of encounter groups, sensitivity training, and so on. All these examples can be efforts to turn hard things into easy things without discipline. The real test of character lies in the ability to wait for long-term satisfactions deferred rather than settle for a short-term gratification of an impulse.

Second, Jesus was tempted by the "authority and glory" of all "the kingdoms of the world in a moment of time." This was an extension of the instant syndrome. In a moment's time he could acquire the prestige of office, rank, and position without the discipline of service, the demonstration of the ability to function, and the kinds of suffering that genuine personal power involves. He was tempted by the trappings of preeminence of position minus the long, hard journey that authentic strength in relation to the world requires.

The status seekers are in the world to be ministered unto, but the suffering servants are in the world to minister. This was the same Jesus who, after he was tempted, tested, and proven, went to his own home village and spoke as the son of a local carpenter, saying: "The Spirit of the Lord is upon me, because he has anointed me to preach good news to the poor. He has sent me to proclaim release to the captives and recovering of sight to the blind, to set at liberty those who are oppressed, to proclaim the acceptable year of the Lord" (Luke 4:18–19, RSV).

Third, Jesus was tempted with the fantasy that he was an exception to the laws of nature and human nature. He was tempted to throw himself down from the pinnacle, on the fantastic belief that he would be unhurt if he did. He saw this as putting God to the test or tempting God. He was—even under the pressure of hunger, social deprivation, and the stress of an unknown future—able to place this pinnacle fantasy in perspective. He refused to consider himself exempt from the laws of nature. As Hebrews puts it, the basis of Jesus' compassion for others was that he was tempted just as they are, yet without sin.

In essence, this is a trilogy of fantasies which are common to mankind. To come to terms with them as one faces the demands of adult life is a time of testing and trial. The alternative of consecration to the God of Reality is to make a Faustian pact with the god of deception and especially self-deception. Such an alternative is an "approach-avoidance" of the sufferings and disciplines required for a clear-headed sense of realism. It permits a person to live in a world of his own, dreaming rather than "being."

Paul Tillich relates temptation to such "dreaming innocence." We are prone to project our essential nature into a "history before history" as a paradise or into the future as a utopia. Both of these are our potentiality but not our actuality. They defy place; *ou topos* means "no place." They defy time; paradise precedes time. By *innocence* Tillich means man's "nonactualized potentiality." If the innocent actualized his fantasy, he would no longer be innocent. Innocence means "lack of actual experience, lack of personal responsibility, and a lack of moral guilt." [4]

In this state of dreaming innocence a person feels free. As a creature that is finite, however, a person feels his freedom to be limited. Not knowing where the limits of freedom are is the source of man's basic anxiety. The anxiety narrows freedom and at the time stimulates the person to defy the limits of freedom. Thus whatever freedom we have is an anxious freedom (*sich ängstigende Freiheit*). These set limits on man's freedom are symbolized in the temptation story in Genesis as the "divine prohibition." As Tillich puts it,

At the moment when man becomes conscious of his freedom, the awareness of his dangerous situation gets hold of him. He experiences a double threat, which is rooted in his finite freedom and expressed in anxiety. Man experiences the anxiety of losing himself by not actualizing himself and his potentialities and the anxiety of losing himself by actualizing himself and his potentialities. He stands between the preservation of his dreaming innocence without experiencing the actuality of being and the loss of his innocence through knowledge, power and guilt. The anxiety of this situation is the state of temptation. Man decides for self-actualization, thus producing the end of dreaming innocence.[5]

Thus temptation is the crucible of conscience and character. The awareness of freedom has its earliest beginnings when a child learns to walk. He begins to know that he can run away and do things on his own. It becomes all the more vivid when he discovers that he can think privately. He can tell people to shut up on the inside of his head, and nobody rebukes him for it. Awareness of freedom becomes more extensive when he goes to school and develops a group of peers outside the home and outside the school. This sense of freedom is raised to a peak of storm and stress when he discovers his sexuality, free of taboos of incest, outside the home. Limitless freedom is intensified when he learns to drive a car and has access to one. Consequently, conscience does not become a *Kampf*, a battle, until late adolescence. Then the battle of conscience—which is in essence the struggle between the fantasy of limitless freedom and responsible freedom—is joined at full scale.

Parents, teachers, and pastors tend to catch the anxiety of freedom which adolescent persons experience. They are likely to communicate a morality of safety and seek to keep the young person in a state of dreaming innocence. Thus, all sorts of restraints, rules, and removals of privacy are used to keep the state of dreaming innocence intact. The young person either capitulates and develops a heavy fantasy life untested by reality, or he rebels and breaks communication with the parents, teachers, and pastors.

A second kind of approach to the young person's major time of testing and/or temptation might be called a morality of neglect. Here the authority persons may assume a kind of maturity that is not there. They simply shrink from the conflict that the storms and stress of young people's lives entail, or they become so preoccupied with their own pursuits they are oblivious to the young person. The end result is similar in either instance. Thus the young person is thrust upon the security and approval of his peer group. If this group is populated with some young persons with good judgment and experience, a good conscience can be formed, nevertheless. At any rate, chance is very high, and risk is uncalculated.

A third, and to be recommended, approach to the heightened awareness of freedom of a young person is what I have chosen to call a morality of calculated risk. Such an approach moves on the assumption that there is no way to keep persons in a paradise of safety or a utopia of dreaming innocence. Temptation is unavoidable in the sense that a human life has to be tested under careful conditions of freedom in the same way a ship has to be given a shakedown cruise, a plane has to have a test-pilot stage, and a car should be test driven. Therefore, a process of collaboration should develop between the young person and the parent, the teacher, or the pastor. The purpose of the collaboration is to calculate the risks involved in translating fantasies into time and space through the use of energy and money. Thus the fantasy formations over which the young person has a fever of concern are taken seriously. They are moved toward reality and responsibility.

The bounds of the habitation or the limits of freedom tend to be set by life itself. The main task of the spiritual guides of young persons is to enable them to identify what these limits are. The tests or trials of any fantasy formation have a specific set of logistics:

Time. How much time will this pattern of hope, if turned to action, take? Where will this time come from and does it conflict with other commitments of time? How important are these other commitments of time? Does something else have to go if this is done? Also, the schedule or routine of hours out at night becomes a ground of negotiation of freedom with adolescents.

Space. Every fantasy has the advantage of not having to occupy space, traverse space, or justify the use of space. This may begin with fights young family members have over a room of their own. It may continue with wanting the use of the living room or a basement for various kinds of parties. It accelerates in the use of cars, the making of trips, and the kind of private space a car provides for sexual freedom, freedom to drink, use drugs, or to race the car. These seem to be rather secular concerns, but they are the symbols of freedom and self-actualization to the young person.

Energy and health. The young person quite often is unaware of the limits of the body; especially is this true of those who have no handicaps, no organic inferiorities, no illnesses, no pain. This makes the main forms of death among young persons to be automobile accidents, suicide, and combat casualties. Yet the subtle factors of stress, drug effects, and fatigue chip away insidiously at the health of young persons. The calculation of these factors into the risks they take should be a part of the "logistical collaboration about times of testing."

Promises and relationships of trust. A fourth factor in the calculation of risk in a time of testing of the character of a person is that of promises they have made and had made to them, and the relationship of trust these promises symbolize. The real testing of the relationship between men and women in sexual responsibility to each other is the testing and trying of promises, unuttered or expressed, that go between partners. The young person learns the risk of being hurt in such promises and the achievement of having kept his promises.

All of this discussion of the trials and errors of adolescents must be tempered by Baron von Hügel's definition of the main temptations of those who aspire to be spiritual directors of others. He spoke, as Douglas Steere says, of being "liberated from the shriveling but widely pervasive temptation . . . of regarding his own religious experience as normative, and of seeking to shape all souls like his own." [6]

One should not think for a moment that, inasmuch as adolescents are focused upon here, temptation and testing is limited to this age span of life. Far from it. The Tempter departs only for a season. Jesus experienced temptation again and again, sometimes in the sentimental appeal of a friend like Peter. So it is with every person. For example, the middle-aged person suffers the temptation of monotonous repetition of decreasingly meaningful tasks. He wrestles with the power of his anger at accumulated injustice more than with the power of his foot on an automobile accelerator. Apparently, the great classic of temptation "to curse God and die" came to Job, a man of mature years. It came through the medium of his wife, the mother of his children. The issue was whether or not Job, because he was a just man, was exempt from suffering.

Nor are fantasies the private possession of the young. The young men shall see visions, and the old men dream dreams. An old man, suffering the temptations of the persecuted, wrote an apocalypse, a day-waking dream. In it, he thought of a New Jerusalem in which there was great companionship with God, the wiping away of every tear from the eyes, the removal of death, grief, and pain. No. There is no temptation but such as is common to man.

NOTES

1. Erich Fromm, *You Shall Be As Gods* (New York: Holt, Rinehart, and Winston, 1966), p. 162.

2. Ibid., p. 161.

3. Leo Spiegel, "Superego and the Function of Anticipation with Comments on Anticipatory Anxiety," *Psychoanalysis: A General Psychology,* ed. R. M. Lowenstein, et. al. (New York: International Universities Press, 1966), p. 334.

4. Paul Tillich, *Systematic Theology,* 2: 33.

5. Ibid., pp. 35–36.

6. Friedrich Baron von Hügel, *Spiritual Counsel and Letters,* ed. Douglas Steere (New York: Harper & Row, 1964), p. 11.

QUESTIONS FOR FURTHER STUDY

1. Do a careful linguistic study of the words *temptation, anxiety,* and *decision.* How are they related to each other? This will be particularly rewarding if you use Greek and/or Hebrew.

2. Write a paper on a comparative study of the Book of Job, Archibald MacLeish's play *J.B.,* and C. G. Jung's *Answer to Job* with the psychology of temptation as your theme.

3. Study closely—and without fear—your own most meaningful fantasies. Even write them down. Are they really fantasies, or are they hopes of yours that were crushed by the discouragement of others and of life itself? Pick out a friend, a counselor, a professor—or all three in one person—and discuss this with him.

4. If you are suffering specific temptations that involve the possibility of incurring heavy moral guilt, ask in what ways you are seeking through these contemplated acts to establish freedom from domination of others, a territory of your own privacy, and a right to learn from your own trials and errors. Make a diary to be seen by no one but you.

13

DECISION MAKING
AND RESPONSIBILITY

To decide involves becoming responsible. The word decide *comes from a* Latin word, *decaeder,* meaning "to cut off." In parliamentary procedure, one way to move toward a decision is to limit debate. A more certain way is to cut off debate. To decide means to bring to a termination such things as a controversy, a struggle within onself, or a debate. To decide means to settle a thing and to determine a direction. The word *decide* comes from the same Latin derivative as do the words *homicide* and *suicide*. Death itself is a termination, an *eschaton*. It is decisive. Decisions involve coming to terms with time. Time is a matter of life and death, which involves not only the simple passage of time, but also the matter of tim*ing,* finding the right moment *in* time. As the writer of Ecclesiastes puts it:

"For everything there is a season, and a time for every matter under
　　heaven:
a time to be born, and a time to die;
a time to plant, and a time to pluck up what is planted;
a time to kill, and a time to heal;
a time to break down, and a time to build up;
a time to weep, and a time to laugh;
a time to mourn, and a time to dance;
a time to cast away stones, and a time to gather stones together;
a time to embrace, and a time to refrain from embracing;
a time to seek, and a time to lose;
a time to keep, and a time to cast away;
a time to rend, and a time to sew;
a time to keep silence, and a time to speak;
a time to love, and a time to hate;
a time for war, and a time for peace" (Eccles. 3:1–8, RSV) .

Therefore, the cut-off points in time are the stuff of which decision is made. Time is the Kantian category of the mind related to decision in much the same way that space is the category of the mind related to nonverbal communication.

THE ABILITY TO DECIDE

The chapter on the expansion of consciousness emphasizes the importance of opening up the awareness of persons. The constricted mind, however, has a dimension of decisiveness about it. The big issue about commitment is that it calls for closure at some point or other. Decision must be made. Therefore, the person in the counterculture, the Consciousness III person, is characterized by a sort of Lotus Eater's decisionlessness. The parents of these persons often wonder if they will ever find a direction in life, make some clear decisions, and stick with them. They even ask about the intrinsic ability on anyone's part to make a decision. This issue is a live one in both psychology and religion.

The various streams of psychological theory place different emphases upon the real ability of persons to decide. Contrary to popular misconceptions, the behavioristic schools of psychology in deed and fact tend to assume, as Skinner says, that "some sort of 'self-determination' is involved . . . in deciding *which* of two courses of action is to be followed." Further, says Skinner, " 'Deciding' . . . is not the execution of the act decided upon but the preliminary behavior responsible for it." In other words, deciding is "premonitory" or "preamble" behavior. One of the best examples of this is the decision of a person to commit suicide. Prior to this premonitory behavior, the person may be depressed, experience frontal headaches, and be joyless by day and sleepless by night. After a decision has been made, there may be a period of waiting for the actual perpetration of the act. At this time, the person may seem suddenly quite serene, happy, and moving about setting his life back into order after a time of immobilization and illness. The experienced clinician will not be fooled by this dramatic, seeming recovery. Instead, double attention is given and even considerable initiative will be taken in alerting relatives and friends close to the person to stay near the person in this critical span of time.

Skinner elaborates on his conception of the ability to decide in a more recent work, *Beyond Freedom and Dignity,* when he relates decision making to the escape from aversive conditioning to a state of being where one feels free, free of the threat of coercion, restriction of one's movement, comfort, and thinking. He says:

Freedom is a possession. A person escapes from or destroys the power of controller in order to feel free, and once he feels free and can do what he desires, no further action (or decision to act, I might add) is recommended and none is described by the literature of freedom, except eternal vigilance lest controls be resumed.[1]

However, Skinner is not far from Freud in his agreement with John Stuart Mill that "liberty consists in doing what one desires."

Skinner further observes about decision making that taking "a relatively irrevocable step" may shift the process of deciding from premonitory behavior into real closure. Thus, the process of deciding may come to an end even before the act is consummated. A common way to do this is "simply to announce our decision." [2]

A suicidal person uses his decision as a cry for help in his announcement of the decision. If the act of suicide is a desperate cry for help, then the announcement of its impending possibility should be taken seriously in all cases. Providing emotional supplies and support at this point will tend to meet the deprivation the person feels. This kind of intervention between the decision and the announcement of the decision, on the one hand, and the act itself poses another set of alternatives for living and hoping.

The public announcement of a decision suggested by Skinner also appears in the more positive decision to become a Christian or to be married. One makes a public confession of his faith in Christ in many communions. This is calculated to commit the person to his own decision and clench it into action. The engagement begins with the announcement of plans to be married. Both of these positive experiences exemplify the relation between decision, public commitment, and behavioral acts.

The existential and/or phenomenological psychologists place decision making and the acceptance of responsibility for one's decision at the heart of their conceptions of human life. Søren Kierkegaard saw the experience of becoming a self as a process of decisive "willing." He says that there are three states of selfhood in terms of the kind of decision a person makes. First, there is the person who is in despair for not having decided to be a self. This recoiling from any decision is a decision in its own right. Not to decide is to decide. In the second place, there is the person who wills or decides to become a self and fails to do so. The decision and the act must be a unit in becoming an authentic self. Then, too, failure to achieve one's goals produces shame in the same way one's sins of the past produce guilt. In the third place, there is the person who decides to be a self and falls into despair over having actually become a self. This is the despair that comes from the burden of responsibility for having actualized one's self. These three forms of despair are related to the decision-making process, and the crucial events attached to either having taken responsibility as a responsible self or not having done so.

The phenomenological approach to psychology would emphasize the value setting of a person's own internal perception of the data and the time limits of decision. The value orientation of one person causes him to make one decision on the basis of similar data and another person to make another decision. The discernment of data is determinative in decision making and not just the data themselves. To one person, one set of facts is valued more highly. To another person, another set of facts will be valued more highly. Also, one's values may cause him to edit out certain facts from consciousness. Thus, these data may be there all the time, but the person does not see them.

Persons like Carl Rogers and Prescott Lecky insist that an empathic exploration of these value systems is a dynamic part of the decision-making process. If a person engages in dialogue with a person of warmth, acceptance, empathy, and understanding, then the perception can be widened to see more data and therefore accept, without being threatened too much, the truth of certain data.

Psychoanalytic theory has a curious blend of thinking about decision making. Considerable weight is given to the way in which parents use taboos, restrictions, and prepackaged prescriptions for behavior to replace the careful development of the child's ability to make his own decision. The superego becomes the automatic response of the adult on the basis of these previous programmings of behavior computed into the habit structure of a child. This ordinarily occurs before the child has learned much about decision making for himself.

The ability to decide between the instinctual desires of the id and the regulatory prohibitions of the superego is the function of the ego. Ego strength is another way of saying that one has the ability to decide and carry out one's decisions.

The transactional analysts have described decision making in terms of the kind of ego state which activated the decision—whether a parent-ego state, an adult-ego state, or a child-ego state. In all three ego states, the total person is responsible. The real decision in a given behavior is the choice as to which of these ego states is to prevail. The ability to decide is there; the quality of ego state in control determines the behavior. One makes a childish decision, an adult decision, or a parent decision.

SOME LIMITS OF DECISION MAKING

Theodore Sorenson, in a small book entitled *Decision Making in the White House,* couples his discussion of decision making with the awesome responsibilities for decision in the Kennedy administration. He uses the valuable concept of "the outer limits of decision making." The act of decision involved the acceptance of responsibility for the limitations under which we as human beings work. I am combining some of his categories of limitation with my own to make the following pattern of the laws and limits of decision making.

The limits of data. The first phase of decision making is that of data collection. This is the computer level of decision making. Many defective decisions are made because easily available data were not known. The decision to get the available information is a sort of preliminary step in the decision-making process. For example, a considerable number of people today still draw conclusions and make decisions on the basis of biblical information. However, the available data of all the teachings of the Scripture about a given issue are not consulted. A defective decision ensues. Furthermore, decisions about entering a religious vocation can be enriched by participating alongside a practicing person in that vocation as a basis of gathering data about that vocation. Hard data carefully gathered tend to provide a realistic basis for a decision.

The epistemologist would immediately raise the question at this point of the ability of a person to know. Pragmatically, the gathering of data depends on how much time one has to collect and process data. More abstractly, this is not all there is to the human limits of data. The age level at which a person seeks to make a decision limits that person by reason of inexperience, the prematurity of the organism for handling abstract ideas, and so on. The senile person's physical and mental equipment are impeded in their usefulness. The mentally deficient person can receive and process data to a lesser extent than other persons. Even with the fullness of one's powers of cognition, the human mind at best has limits of knowing. The Greek philosopher, Gorgias, took these limits to the extreme when he said that we are unable to know anything; if we were able to know anything, we could not transmit it to others; and, if we did transmit it to others, they could not grasp it. Short of this extreme, available time and one's degree of maturity and experience limit data collection for decision making. Beyond this, one enters a disclaimer by saying that mystery shrouds every important decision with the anxiety of the unknown.

The limits of time. The collection of data cannot go on ad infinitum. Available time determines to a great extent how much data can be gathered. Furthermore, once all the available facts are in hand, the deadlines for decision making cannot be ignored with impunity. Procrastination in applying for an available grant is a form of decision making by default. If a deadline set for having one's application in is let pass, then one may be passively deciding not to apply. From this vantage point, one can say that there are two types of decisions: *active decisions,* in which one aggressively gathers data within the limits of time and makes the decision himself; and *passive decisions,* in which one allows the passage of time to make the decision for him.

The limits of prior decisions. Another frame of limitation in the decision-making process is that of prior commitments and decisions. Ordinarily, there are legal restrictions in many such decisions. For example, in this country, one cannot decide to marry one person when one is still married to another person. A person who is a citizen of one country cannot very easily become the citizen of another and remain a citizen of both. In religious decisions within a monotheistic, exclusive faith such as Judaism, Christianity, or Mohammedanism, one cannot form ties with one at the expense of the other. In syncretistic religions, such a multiplicity of loyalties can be. The statement of this principle by Jesus is that a person cannot serve both God and mammon.

The limits of available alternatives. A given decision is limited by the number of available alternatives. The phenomenon of hoping is closely geared to the multiplicity or paucity of options available to a person. A man or woman who is deciding to change jobs is limited by previous decision about training for a given position. Even with available training from the past, the number of positions open sets the pattern of decision making. The task of the effective counselor in bringing hope to a discouraged person is to have the imagination to discover additional alternatives that are realistically available to a person. The anxiety of a person increases as the number of ways through, out, around, beneath, or over a given frustration or deprivation decreases. Sartre described hell as the state of being where there are no exits, no alternatives, no room for decision making. The abandonment of hope, it seems to me, is precipitated by the inability of a person to see enough available alternatives or the realistic lack of such alternatives.

STRESS AND DECISION MAKING

Recent studies of stress have come out of American combat involvement in the Vietnam War. They tell us important things about the relation of stress to decision making. In a highly specific study of the release of hydroxycorticosteroids—a stress-produced substance—into the bloodstream, a medical research team concluded that the "minimizing of introspection" appears "to contribute to the maintenance of a relatively low level of 17-OHCS," the substance just mentioned.

Men who had decisions made for them had a low level of struggle of ideas within their perception. The men were involved in physical activity and mechanistic tasks, which in turn caused a low level of stress. On the other hand, the officers had an assigned role in the group that provided additional stresses without as many ways of handling the stress as compared with enlisted men. Peter G. Bourne says of them,

> Unlike the enlisted men, officers are primarily influenced in their behavior by radio messages coming from the higher command outside the camp. This involves rapid decision making on their part and the tactful handling of commands (to them) made with the weight of a superior rank hampered by the ignorance due to a forty-mile physical separation [on the part of their superiors].[3]

Several conclusions of general importance can be said about these data. First, decision making increases in direct proportion to the amount of responsibility a person accepts. Stress increases accordingly. Second, responsibility involves an assigned role, and decision making involves status anxiety in relation to one's superiors. In addition to making decisions about how to get the work done in a rapid way, the decisions are multiplied as to how also to please one's superiors. Third, the amount of time for making this double set of decisions is extremely short and opportunity for reflection, consultation, and data collection is highly limited in the decision-making process. Fourth, the ignorance of one's superiors by reason of not being in close touch with the enemy or the men doing the fighting puts the officer in the position of teaching his superior what the situation is. The ability of superiors to learn from subordinates calls for decisions many superiors have not yet made, much less acted upon.

This can be applied to the ecclesiastical problems of religious decision making at the corporate level of the churches, denominations, hierarchies, and so on. The person who simply carries out orders of ecclesiastical superiors is more dependent and has fewer decisions to make. The person who carries the responsibility of office in the church has a difficult time balancing the amount of time he spends in actually getting the work done with the amount he spends conferring with committees, board members, and executives of one kind or another. With the increased bureaucracy, the acceptance of responsibility is spiraled from one level of officialdom to another. The simple passage of time makes a decision—positive or negative—for which no one is responsible. When role and office as status are split from functional responsibility in making decisions within the time limits available, then either chaos, insubordination, or tactful manipulation of superiors by subordinates—or all three—become the order of the day in a religious fellowship.

RISK AND CHANCE TAKING IN DECISION MAKING

As I sought data for this chapter, I leaped with enthusiasm to a book edited by Ward Edwards and Amos Tversky entitled *Decision Making*.[4] Much to my surprise, the book is a discussion of statistical possibility and probability in making business decisions involving money and commodities and also a discussion of gambling decisions concerning games of chance. The book also involves airline pilots and paratroopers in the kinds of risks they take. Decision theory has been developed outside psychology and religion by economists and mathematicians. A completely riskless decision calls for complete information, infinite sensitivity, and a completely rational decider. Ordinarily decision making involves a decider who "weakly orders the states into which he can get" and makes decisions in order to maximize or minimize something. The perfect choice is a fantasy, a dream, a substitute for action. All other choices call for risk taking.[5] In these kinds of decisions two variables exist: the attractiveness of a choice and the decider's evaluation of the chances or probabilities in either event.

Quite frankly, the authors of this book lose me in a maze of statistical probabilities although they set out to reduce this complexity. They taught me why I would never make a good gambler at the casino, Las Vegas, or the race tracks. I have a measure of courage but a dearth of both knowledge and confidence in statistical prediction of outcome. However, I am a theologian and a pastoral counselor. My tasks cause me to go back to the formulations of Paul Tillich, one of my teachers, when I heard him contrast a "morality of safety" with a "morality of risk."

Persons tend to want a decision that is risk free. The establishment of moral codes often has this as a hidden assumption. If you do all these things, then everything will turn out perfectly. This is the operation of a morality of safety. Disillusionment arises in parents who have observed all of the right things, followed all the prescribed religious rituals to a fault, and demanded that their children do likewise. Then the reverse of their expected outcome actually happens, particularly in their children. They have followed a morality of safety. Of course, such a morality is an integral part of life, especially in a world where danger is at a height due to a mix of drugs, alcohol, automobiles, planes, and rapid communication.

The calculation of chance and risk in travel, for example, is a day-to-day decision involving risk. A devout man I know had a serious accident in an automobile. A close friend of his was terribly upset in her faith in God. She came to me saying that she had trouble believing in a God who would let this happen. She asked me what I thought of this. I told her that our mutual friend was living in a "morality of risk" and not a "morality of safety" when he drove the car. He *could* have stayed at home that day. He *could* have asked a more experienced driver to have driven because he had just learned to drive. He *could* have walked to his destination. He *could* have caught a bus. All of these would have lowered the probability of an accident. However, he *chose* to drive and in doing so increased the probability of an accident. God puts us in a world that is filled with dangers. He participates with us in the calculation of risk and safety. A paradox is that the way to be perfectly safe is to be completely dead—that is, all danger is past!

We collaborate with God in large and small decisions and decide how much risk to take. The "morality of risk" is made up of a calculation of the amount of risk on the basis of the information we have available. To act upon such a decision requires faith, literally a leap into the unknown. People entering marriage want and deserve all the available knowledge. When this is in hand, even if it includes the avant-garde trial time of living together before marriage, great vistas of the unknown probabilities cannot be known. Risk is involved. Only a covenant of faith and trust can negotiate this. No precise contract will insure a perfect marital decision. Vocational decisions are much the same. Acceptance of the hard fact that a deceased loved one is in deed and fact dead and the future must be faced without him is the same. Faith, then, becomes the main ingredient in risky decision making, generously mixed with what little data we can gather in the time that we have. Minnie Louise Haskins put it well when she said,

> And I said to the man who stood at the gate of the year. "Give me a light; that I may tread safely into the unknown!"
> And he replied. "Go out into the darkness and put your hand into the hand of God. That shall be to you better than light and safer than a known way."

NOTES

1. B. F. Skinner, *Beyond Freedom and Dignity* (New York: A. A. Knopf, 1971), p. 32.
2. ———, *Science and Human Behavior*, pp. 242–43.
3. Peter G. Bourne, *Men, Stress, and Vietnam* (Boston: Little, Brown, 1970), pp. 122–23.
4. Ward Edwards and Amos Tversky, eds., *Decison Making* (Middlesex, Eng.: Penguin Books, 1967).
5. Ibid., pp. 14–15.

QUESTIONS FOR FURTHER STUDY

1. Correlate the material in this chapter on decision making with Reich's discussion of Consciousness I, II, and III.
2. Was Harry Truman more decisive than John F. Kennedy? Than Richard Nixon? Why?
3. Is B. F. Skinner so deterministic that he leaves no room for the person to choose or decide? Document your point of view from Skinner.
4. To what extent does William Glasser attribute to the individual the total power of decision in his *Reality Therapy*?

14

SIN AND FORGIVENESS

The psychological literature on guilt is extensive. More recently the phenomenological and third-force psychologists, such as Abraham Maslow, have stressed the importance of acceptance of persons and the reinforcement of their potentials rather than focusing on their guilts and liabilities. When one places these two emphases of psychology into relationship to a person's responsibility to God and the ultimate concerns of human beings, then the discussion turns to the distinctly religious issues of sin and forgiveness. It seems wise to discuss sin *and* forgiveness at the same time rather than to discuss them separately. This prevents either a morbid discussion of sin or an unrealistic discussion of forgiveness. The basic assumption of this chapter is that the realistic acts of wrongdoing of a person—as the person perceives right and wrong—do produce a sense of guilt. When that guilt is felt to be in relation to God, the guilt is concentrated into a sense of sin. When that person perceives God as having forgiven him, specific results occur in the attitudes and behavior of the person. Sin may be perceived in this discussion on a rotary spectrum of various meanings. These meanings, when met with the experience of forgiveness, result in varying changes of attitude and behavior. However, the varied perceptions of sin and the equally varied results blend into each other in much the same way as do the color bands of a spectrum. We refract both darkness and light for the purpose of enriching the understanding of sin and forgiveness.

SIN AS IDOLATRY: FORGIVENESS AS ENLARGEMENT OF LIFE

Confrontation with God always raises the issue of true and false gods. What kind of God is the one whom we confront? Monotheistic religions such as Mohammedanism, Christianity, and Judaism have consistently portrayed sin as primarily the worship of false gods. Having no other gods before the one God is the primary commandment, violation of which ensues in all lesser sins. The hearthstone gods of the worship of family members, the idols of the marketplace, the orgiastic worship of sex, the deifications of covetousness are all constrictions of the person doing the worshiping, desecrations of persons who are being idolized, and the misuses of things coveted. When these constrictions and desecrations are removed, persons are set free. Things become consecrated to God rather than used as ends in themselves when a person is freed from idolatry. Confession of the sin of idolatry leads to the enlargement of life. J. B. Phillips identified this need in his book, *Your God Is Too Small,* as did William Stringfellow in his essay, "Imposters of God."

The thought of idolatry is an ancient one, but it is significant in both psychological and religious realms today. Furthermore, the theologies of the past have been antiquated, but the conceptions of personality espoused by psychologists and psychiatrists have tended to reenact all of the essentials of the power of idols. Erich Fromm writes a whole book entitled *And Ye Shall Be As Gods* in which he identifies man's need to deify the finite as a source of constriction of freedom and division of man's being. Andras Angyal speaks of the way in which the total sphere of life is divided against itself. This process he calls *bionegativity* in his book, *Neurosis and Treatment,* "a personality constellation in which one or more part-processes disturb the total function of the organism." [1] This concept is reminiscent of Plato's definition of sin as the rising up of a part of the soul against the whole. Gordon Allport identified one characteristic of the mature religious sentiment as being *comprehensiveness.* To fix one's life commitment on a restricted, finite, and temporary object of devotion is to have a noncomprehensive sentiment in one's faith. Paul Tillich, who was the theologian more in touch with modern psychology and psychotherapy than anyone else in this century, gave specific voice to the modern psychological interpretation of faulty religion when he defined idolatry:

> Idolatry is the elevation of a preliminary concern to ultimacy. Something conditioned is taken as unconditional, something partial is boosted to universality, and something essentially finite is given infinite significance (the best example of contemporary idolatry is religious nationalism) .[2]

In later theological searching, one could say that the kind of god that dies is the idol.

In the psychology of religious experience, the collapse of an idol—the defection of members of one's family, one's disillusionment with his denomination, church, or pastor, one's deep-running disenchantment with his government—calls for repenting oneself of the former idolatry of these in order that life may grow, expand, and enlarge. In the normal, healthy process of growth, for a further example, a middle-aged person can idolize his sons and daughters. Parents can deify their children as children to such an extent that they will not permit them to grow up. Neither will they, in the process, face the great crises of growth of the middle and later years. As a result, both parents and grown sons and daughters may become constricted, unhappy, and even sick. This particular point of view in the pathology of religion is the subject of a more extensive study in my own book, *When Religion Gets Sick*.[3]

Repentance of the sin of idolatry, then, means to change one's god from a constricted, narrowed, and dying god to a universal, comprehensive, and eternal God. This calls for a change of mind, a transformation of loyalty, and a release of one's clutch on family, nation, denomination, race, sex, school, teacher, or ideological bias. These gods die, pass away, and perish.

Forgiveness is then experienced as an enlargement of one's deepest sentiments to include other families, other nations, other schools, other teachers, other races, the other sex, other forms of thought. Forgiveness, in the sense of being freed from idolatry, is more than just a sticky, sentimental, and sweet exercise. It is the kind of expansion of one's life such as happened to Peter in his acceptance of Cornelius, a Gentile. Peter was prompted to know that God is no respecter of persons. The end result of such a forgiveness for the worship of a tribal god is the reactivation of the process of growth, the discovery of newness in relation to others, and the enrichment of one's appreciation of others. However, the whole process requires at least a fleeting glimpse of a God greater than one's idol, a clean-cut decision to trust that eternal God, and a rehabituation of one's life away from idolatry.

Sin As the Antithesis of Faith: Forgiveness As Invitation to Pilgrimage

When we lean too heavily on the moral instruction of our early years, we perceive sin moralistically. We are likely to assume that sin is the opposite of goodness, virtue, and respectability. Yet, even Jesus asked: "Why do you call me good? No one is good but God alone" (Mark 10:18, RSV). Yet we try to define sin in terms of the behavior patterns and taboos of changing human conditions. This in itself is a kind of idolatry of our own ideas of right and wrong.

However, the more lasting and dynamic conception of sin is that sin is the antithesis of faith. The Apostle Paul stated it best: "Whatever does not proceed from faith is sin" (Rom. 14:23, RSV). The particular behaviors of life are expressions of one's faith, not the cause of it. Breaking out of an old taboo in response to a larger calling may be an act of faith, that is, launching out into the unknown as a response to the calling of the Eternal.

Lewis Sherrill, in his interpretation of the emergence of a strong, dynamic, and courageous person of faith, sticks closely to the understanding of sin found in the Book of Hebrews. The person of faith moves out and away from the easy securities of a superficial life. He is an explorer, a pioneer, a seeker after a "city not made with hands." The person who shrinks back from this quest is the one who sins. To shrink back into childhood is the adolescent's temptation to sin. The adolescent who acts as if he can have the freedoms of adulthood with all the indulgences ordinarily given a child by its parents is really sinning. In relation to his parents, he cannot eat out of one hand of his parents and eat off the other hand of his parents without being a shrinking person.

A word of clarification is needed here. One student asks, "In the normal development of a person, are we to say that any shrinking back is sin?" The normal development of a person is not a steady, even line of forward growth. As was seen in the discussion of the religious development, such persons as Gesell have emphasized the uneven "spurt and jag" in the growth of a person. Times of spurts of growth are followed by times of consolidation and securing of the gains in growth. Times of adventure in successfully making a transition from one phase of life to another are followed by a time of recuperation, renewal, and serenity in life. The life of pilgrimage is like this. Those who perceive life as a saga, says Lewis Sherrill, tend to want a battle at all times. However, the life of pilgrimage is like the heartbeat—a surge of action followed by a time of renewal and rest to be followed by another surge of action, and so on.

For the person, for a further example, who is facing the very real possibility of death, this demand of faith is acute. To shrink back from this reality is both understood and even encouraged by those around us. Robert Browning described this act of faith in his poem, "Prospice."

> Fear death?—to feel the fog in my throat
> The mist in my face.
> Where he stands, the Arch Fear in a visible form.
> I was ever a fighter, so—one fight more.
> The best and the last!
> I would hate that death bandaged my eyes and forebore,
> And bade me creep past.
> No! let me taste the whole of it, fare like my peers,
> The heroes of old,
> Bear the brunt, in a minute pay glad life's arrears of pain, darkness and cold.
>
> O thou soul of my soul! I shall clasp thee again,
> And with God be at rest.

Both the experience of birth and that of death provide models for facing the anxiety of separation with a sense of courage and adventure. Repentance for the sin of shrinking back implies a commitment to have done with the easy securities of the established certainties. Forgiveness for the lack of faith rewards a person with an invitation to pilgrimage. The life of a person of faith is characterized by a sense of curiosity about what is yet to be revealed and to be experienced. This person is no shrinking violet in the face of the demands for new learning, new disciplines, new ideas, and new growth. He is no Consciousness I person, still living as if the small town and rural realities were the whole of life. He is no Consciousness II person, vesting faith in the shrunken and shrinking obsolescence of his organization, corporate structure, or national pride. He is not even a Consciousness III person acting as if now will always be as is. All three of these forms of consciousness are false securities. They all three have built-in obsolescences. To shrink back into the permanent security of any of them is destructive.

The "eyes of fire and the eyes of faith" of which Roszak speaks call for participation in life as an act and adventure of faith. Yet this calls for constant vigilance and responsiveness to the invitation to pilgrimage.

In a very real way, when any of the three states of consciousness of which Reich speaks becomes a way of life, a sacred or secular religion of nostalgia results. One builds a life style that gets all of its clues from one's habitat. His milieu becomes his security blanket, externally symbolized in Love America or Leave It slogans, a crew cut, and a hawk view of war. Another security blanket is the need to become avant-garde in order to symbolize one's way of life in casual clothing, long hair, and various textures of rock music. All of these things not only provide companionship with others of like mind, they also provide security. In Sullivan's phrase, they are "security operations." If one shrinks from the demands of life and growth until he has no hair, the symbol of hair itself is gone! Such a gearing of life has a way—with the passage of time— of becoming stuck in neutral while life as a fluxing, changing process flows by. Then, his way of life becomes an experiment in nostalgia—a grieving for the way things used to be. As sentimentality, it passes the test. As faith, it is sin, a shrinking existence. Freud spoke of the religion of one's personal past as an illusion. In his context, he was pronouncing the religion of nostalgia as sick. "To put away childish things" calls into being a kind of faith that is felt as God's approval, God's forgiveness.

SIN AS DESTRUCTIVE HABIT: FORGIVENESS AS THE RESTORATION OF STRENGTH

For the average person, sin means destructive habits. In our efforts to define sin as something more than a symptom, we are likely to assume that sin as a destructive habit is unimportant. To the comfortable and the respectable this may be so; not so to the person in the clutch of an addiction to alcohol, to some other drug, to work, to ungovernable temper tantrums. These persons are often laden with guilt. They have such a low image of themselves that they do not consciously dare to ask for God's help. They live in isolation from people around them. Even asking for mercy as a sinner is beyond their sense of power. They consider themselves helpless to do anything about their habit. One of the central features of their condition is that they feel impotent, powerless, incapable of controlling their lives.

Psychologists of religion and pastoral psychologists have been scolded by O. Hobart Mowrer for relying too heavily upon "cheap grace" known as acceptance and upon the psychoanalytic assumption that insight will resolve the habit. The talking cure is not enough, says Mowrer. To the contrary, the behavior itself should be challenged as wrong behavior, as sin in religious terms. To Mowrer this is a crisis in religion and psychiatry.

William Glasser, a psychiatrist himself, formulates a pattern of therapy known as "reality therapy," which is based upon well-articulated assumptions akin to Mowrer's. He is, however, much more specific and less scolding. Glasser rejects the idea of unconscious motivation and the assumption of sickness as a behavior concept. He sees these as teaching a person that he is not responsible for his own actions. Therefore, he is likely to blame his behavior on the past, on other people, and on his status as a sick person. Consequently, he actually rarely does anything about changing his actions because he never accepts responsibility for them as his behavior. Glasser insists upon an ethical rather than a seemingly valueless or neutral approach to behavior. The elements of justice and injustice in one's treatment of himself and others is focal.[4]

Add to Glasser's interpretation ideas taken from transactional analysis as formulated by Eric Berne and others. They point out ways in which persons with defective "scripts," or established programming of their lives, continue in destructive habits because of a sense of impotence or powerlessness they have. One prayer confesses: ". . . there is no health in us," but the transactional analyst would deny that there is *no* health in us. To the contrary, there is a responsible adultness in all of us which, when challenged, can rise with strength. To say that no health exists in a person aids and abets a person's childishness, infantilism, and irresponsibility.[5]

When one comes to terms with, confesses, and rethinks his behavior and makes a decision to change, a reward of forgiveness resides in the decision: He has now thrown off the sense of weakness and begun to feel real strength. The result of feeling genuinely forgiven is freedom from impotence and helplessness. The resolve itself is a source of strength. An outstanding example of this "strengthening with might in the inner person" is found in Ezekiel's encounter with Yahweh, when Yahweh commanded Ezekiel to stand on his feet that he might speak *with* him (Ezek. 1:1). Some specious kinds of forgiveness are often experienced as a further confirmation of one's helplessness. Such forgiveness is not really forgiveness at all if it results in a sort of impotent helplessness. The effective repentance for sin is the one that meets with a forgiveness that enables rather than disables a person to make restitution for wrong he has done. When destructive habits are gradually extinguished, the person who is thus strengthened is able to make restitution except, as Alcoholics Anonymous members put it, where to do so is to cause more harm to those one has offended.

SIN AS SELF-ELEVATION: FORGIVENESS AS RESTORED JOY IN BEING HUMAN

The Greek tragic myths such as Prometheus stealing fire from heaven reflect a common theme of mankind's need to be gods. The story of the tempter in Genesis reflects his promising the man and the woman that they would be as gods, knowing good and evil. Jesus was tempted to have the whole world fall down and worship him. He resisted this attempt to elevate himself or deny his humanity (Luke 4:1–14). Paul and Barnabas were perceived as "the gods having come down in the form of men" by the people of Lystra. They resisted this appeal by saying that they were "men of like passion" with them (Luke 14:8–18).

Succumbing to the need to be gods is the sin of self-elevation. The avoidance of one's own humanity is the "childish feeling of omnipotence." This form of sin is the reverse side of the feeling of impotence in the case of the sin involved in destructive habits. Søren Kierkegaard would say that self-elevated persons are intoxicated on their own possibilities and infinitude, whereas persons caught in a destructive habit are overwhelmed by the necessities of their finiteness.

The person who asks the question, "Am I in God's place?", usually can answer no only after having experienced considerable suffering. Karen Horney identified the need to be as god as a "search for glory." To turn from this way of life calls for a surrender of one's competition with God; a person calls off one-upmanship in compulsive competition with other people. Forgiveness that follows is expressed in a distinctly human fellowship with other human beings. One joins the human race. In Erikson's terms, this becomes a quest for intimacy and fellow-feeling with other persons. To experience the forgiveness of the sin of self-elevation opens one to what other people would try to teach. This is particularly true in marriages where the desire to win, rule, and dominate can be very intense. The hardness of heart is the unwillingness to learn from another, to relinquish the desire always to be right and therefore have one's way. Accepting one's own humanity, frailty, finitude, and partial knowledge is rewarded by the discovery of a new comradeship with other people and a co-laborship with God. This is necessary for interpersonal growth, especially in marriage.

SIN AS STUPIDITY:
FORGIVENESS AS THE GIFT OF WISDOM

The fool is more often condemned in prophetic religion than is the sinner. In Hebrew Wisdom literature, great tributaries of which flow into Christianity, sin is seen as the foolish lack of aim on the part of people who have sense enough to know better. This is not one of the most profound understandings of sin, but it is one so obvious that the plain truth of it is missed. Also, it is probably one of the most neglected meanings of sin.

The psychiatric community deals with this set of attitudes when they speak of the sociopathic personality. Those persons show poor judgment repeatedly and do not seem to learn from experience. Other people, trying to substitute their wisdom for the poor judgment of the person in trouble, often express self-fulfilling prophecies such as, "If you don't watch out, . . . is going to happen to you." It is as if the foolish person moves pell-mell in that direction, bent on his own destruction.

Another characteristic of the sociopathic person is his self-image as an extremely clever person who has been around and has much wisdom about the world. Other persons are stupid to him. Kindness, self-sacrifice, and devotion are signs of weakness to him. The basis of appeal to such a person seems to be twofold—an appeal to his own self-interest and an appeal to his lack of cleverness. The thought of being a sinner does not reach this person, but the thought that he might be a fool is a jarring idea.

When a person admits to having been the fool, an agonizing appraisal can take place. Forgiveness for having been so stupid begins with profiting from experience. Later behavior is preceded by meditation before an unwise thing is done again. The beginning of wisdom is the fear of the Lord; the outworking of wisdom in behavior is profiting from one's own experience. Usually such reflection and use of wisdom grows out of a long-term relationship to a trusted person who will be consistent but frankly honest when an issue requiring judgment is in need of decision. However, to this person who thinks he knows it all and needs no one, forming a durable and trusting relationship is very difficult to accomplish.

SIN AS ALIENATION:
FORGIVENESS AS THE GIFT OF COMMUNITY

Sin as alienation from God and man is the composite and end result meaning of sin. Idolatry alienates one from God and those persons and/or things that are put in God's place. Shrinking back from participating with God and man in the demands of growth in personal and corporate life alienates and estranges a person. Destructive habits preoccupy and hinder one's relationship to self, others, and God. Dividing walls of hostility estrange the self-elevated and ambition-ridden person. The foolish person seems to be asking to be cast out, estranged, and isolated.

Albert Camus speaks of the depths of alienation in a man who seemed a stranger to his own mother at her funeral. He later was convicted on flimsy evidence of having committed murder in cold blood. The basis of his conviction of a death-penalty crime was his lack of concern, alienation, and matter-of-fact callousness witnesses had observed in him at his mother's funeral. He was convicted of premeditated murder because of the seeming inappropriateness of acts everyone saw him commit at his mother's funeral. When the last moments before his execution arrived, he affirmed his sense of being a stranger in the universe as the way things should be. He laid his "heart open to the benign indifference of the universe" and hoped there would be a crowd at his execution who would greet him with howls of execration.[6]

The modern novelist, like Camus, speaks of "the stranger." He glorifies alienation as the natural and optimum state of man. The psychotherapist Andras Angyal says that alienness from a mythical enemy is the central figure of the neurotic world view. The neurotic person is "the utter stranger." As Freud spoke of sexual and hostile inhibitions of Victorian religions, we could today speak of alienation as a universal neurosis. For example, if such a person is part of a group, such as the family, any new member is experienced as an intruding stranger. Sexual responsibility for such a person is difficult because one must go to a stranger for this. The person's own alienation in a strange world is projected upon others, and "they" are seen as outsiders.

The central characteristics of alienation are: first, in psychoanalytic terms, the absence of attachments or object relationships to persons who are significant and emotionally satisfying; second, in existential terms, the absence of feeling and the apparentness of a callousness and hardness of spirit. Both these meanings appear in the Ephesians letter of the New Testament. In Ephesians 2:12, the readers of the original letter are referred to as having been "alienated from the commonwealth of Israel, and strangers to the covenants of promise, having no hope and without God in the world" (RSV). The Gentiles are spoken of in Ephesians 4: 18–19 as being "alienated from the life of God because of the ignorance that is in them, due to their hardness of heart; they have become callous and have given themselves up to licentiousness, greedy to practice every kind of uncleanness" (RSV).

In the first instance, in Christ Jesus "those who were far off have been brought near." They have established a profound, emotionally satisfying, and significant relationship to the person of Jesus Christ. They were being transformed from strangers and sojourners into "fellow citizens with the saints" and into "members of the household of God." This transformation effected not only a union of the alienated person with other persons, but also "created one new man in place of two." The alienation of the person from himself was overcome; a cleft within his being was healed. The experience of strangeness becomes a part of a person, dividing from within his being.

The second meaning of alienation is that of callous detachment. This is the kind of alienation of which Camus's *The Stranger* speaks. Monsieur Meursalt was accused of "great callousness" at his mother's funeral, data used against him to convict him of cold blood murder of an Arab on the beach barely two days after his mother's death. Camus speaks for a considerable portion of the human race today who point to the advantages of being uninvolved, detached, and objective in the realm of feelings and sensitive awareness of the need for relationship and participation with other persons.

Forgiveness, seen from the perspective of sin as estrangement or alienation, is the restoration of a broken relationship. At the distinctly human level, this can be concretely illustrated in the role that anger and conflict play in human relationships. Anger should be differentiated from irritability. Irritability arises from minor frustrations, fatigue, pain, or all three combined. Anger, however, does not arise from the somatic pressures of one's being. Rather, anger is related to specific, realistic injustices. Anger can be defined as a realistic response to a specific injustice. Failure to communicate is more often than not the cause of injustice. If the person knew what lay behind an act perceived as unjust, he would understand. As Lin Yutang said, to understand is to forgive. Reconciliation often takes place where a person says, "Oh! I did not *know* that! Now, I see!"

For these reasons, the best way to deal with anger is quickly. One, as Jesus urged, agrees quickly with his adversary while he is in the way with him. He does not, as Ephesians says, let the sun go down on his anger. To the contrary, one is kind and tender-hearted, forgiving injustices, and doing so because one has experienced forgiveness from God.

However, anger that accumulates from day to day, week to week, and month to month, year to year, and generation to generation becomes hatred. Hate is to anger as fatigue is to tiredness—hate is the accumulation and sedimentation of anger unresolved, unconfessed, and denied over long periods of time. Paul said that we should be mature in all things except anger. In anger we should be as a child. Children deal with their anger quickly and do not harbor grudges in the way adults do. The alienated perceptions of adulthood imply that to be an adult means to be able to carry a grudge.

The grudge view of alienation creates a wall of hostility between a person and other persons and gradually runs a rift in one's own being. The grudge toward parents, siblings, associates, authority persons, and so on can take several directions. The grudge can become a source of apathy, denial, callousness, and unconcern. The classic picture of alienation in the New Testament and in contemporary ethical nihilism and *anomie* are remarkably at one on the description of this kind of alienation, as has been seen. The second direction a grudge can go is toward one's self. Hence, the person becomes depressed, and the philosophical question is that of suicide, that is, is life worth living or not?

The third direction a grudge can take one's alienation is in blaming others—even God—as being totally responsible and oneself as being without any culpability at all. This alienation is a projection type of estrangement. For this person to change is to redistribute and to take his full share of blame. The pharisaic grudge of the elder brother expresses anger that will not be reconciled at any price.

The fourth eventuality of the grudge that alienates is to be overcome by a nonmanipulative incarnation of responsible love. This love is not a power move, but a move toward total understanding without punitiveness. This is the kind of understanding love that casts out fear, relieves anxiety, accepts responsibility, and takes initiative. To exert this initiative is not always met with acceptance, but when it is accepted as true and authentic, reconciliation takes place. Grudges are resolved. Dividing walls of hostility are removed, and the resistance one builds within oneself against positive affections for the hated person are no longer needed. Forgiveness results in the joy of communion.

This model of forgiveness is what Mansell Pattison calls a "reconciliation model of forgiveness in which one learns" to accept oneself when one realizes one is unacceptable "and to seek reconciliation from the estrangement one's behavior has brought." [7] Pattison says that the real issue in the forgiveness of sin is not punishment or reward, but reconciliation of a broken or impaired relationship.

The establishment and/or restoration of fellowship is the core issue in forgiveness when one sees all sin as being bound up in the problem of alienation and estrangement. The basic trust necessary for this can be expressed in terms of faith and covenant with man and God. The basic autonomy called for here is a double movement of initiation of I and Thou toward each other. The necessary competence required is the refusal to play games with oneself and others. The human arenas in which this reconciliation takes place are the arenas of the struggle for leadership, the need for sexual harmony, and the need for a coherent set of beliefs that are clear if not final. The joys that such a reconciliation and forgiveness afford are an even balance between intimacy and privacy, generative creativity in relation to others and personal self-enjoyment, and basic integrity without being a pious Pollyanna.

NOTES

1. Angyal, *Neurosis and Treatment,* p. 58.
2. Tillich, *Systematic Theology,* 1: 13.
3. Wayne Oates, *When Religion Gets Sick* (Philadelphia: Westminster, 1971), pp. 25–47.
4. William Glasser, *Identity and Society* (New York: Harper & Row, 1971).
5. Eric Berne, *Transactional Analysis in Psychotherapy* (New York: Grove Press, 1961).
6. Albert Camus, *The Stranger* (New York: Random House, 1942), p. 54.
7. E. Mansell Pattison, "On Failure to Forgive or to Be Forgiven," *American Journal of Psychotherapy,* 19 (1965): 106.

QUESTIONS FOR FURTHER STUDY

1. Get Young's *Analytical Concordance to the Bible.* Write down the Hebrew and Greek words for "sin" and "forgiveness." In turn, look these words up in a Greek lexicon. Make careful comparisons of meanings.
2. Mary Thelen, in her book, *Man As a Sinner,* hypothesizes that contemporary psychotherapies are secular versions of sin and forgiveness. Compare what has been said in this chapter with Stein's *Contemporary Psychotherapies.*
3. Compare the playboy philosophy of sex with the idea of sin as stupidity.

15

COMMITMENT, ALIENATION,
AND THE COUNTERCULTURE

We concluded the discussion of sin with an emphasis on alienation.
Alienation is the antithesis of commitment and a synonym of uncommitment is alienation. However, before we look at the positive or
negative aspects of commitment, a clear perception of what commitment
means is necessary.

THE MEANING OF COMMITMENT

The general meaning of commitment is to give one's self in trust, put
one's life into the charge or keeping of someone else, to entrust or deliver
one's self up into the hands of another. When one takes this general
meaning and puts it into the context of the Judaeo-Christian understanding of commitment, at least three different meanings appear.

First, to commit one's self means to take one's stand alongside the
living God as over against being a passive recipient of the molding
influences of one's culture. This meaning of commitment is found in
Romans 12:1 in which Paul exhorts his reader to present or take one's
stand alongside God rather than to be shaped, molded, or schematized
according to the present age.

Second, to commit one's self means to give up, surrender, and totally
transfer one's being into the hands of another. In everyday clinical work
one sees this when a person makes a decision to turn himself over to a
doctor for serious surgery. He literally puts himself into this person's
hands, and that person is allowed to take full charge in his life. This
sort of total transfer to a superior power is exemplified in Jesus' quotation
of Psalm 31:5 when he said, "Into thy hands I commit my spirit."

Third, commitment means to dedicate, separate, and set apart for God
either things or persons. A more commonly used word for this is consecra-

tion. This involves rites of separation in which a person is set apart for God. It involves purification in which the person becomes conformable in character to God. It involves reverence in which one treats both persons and things as holy. This is the sense in which the name of God is treated as holy in the first sentence of the Lord's Prayer. We pray "hallowed be thy name." In praying such a prayer one makes the name of God holy and vows to treat or keep the name holy. "To make holy" is an essential part of commitment.

THE CAPACITY FOR COMMITMENT

When one surveys the personal, idiosyncratic histories of individuals, much that has already been said about personality development can be focused on the problem of the basic ability of a person to commit himself. Freud formulated the concept of primary narcissism. By that he meant that a person does not get beyond the point of commitment to himself. He does not form "object relations," emotional attachments to other persons. The ability to commit one's self to persons, human or divine, beyond one's own realm of being is either highly limited or not existent.

John Bowlby, in his study of attachment and loss to which reference has been previously made, gives us a less judgmental and more functional review of how such a narcissism could take place. He relates it to the very early estrangement and separation from one's primary loving persons, particularly one's mother or effective substitutes for one's mother. He says, as will be remembered from the discussion of personality development, that when a very young baby's attachment to either his mother or mother surrogate is broken again and again, each time the child goes through a triple phase of protest, despair, and apathy. Finally the child no longer risks commitment of affection to anyone but becomes absorbed in things, food, and so on.

Andras Angyal deals with the problem of commitment in a negative manner in his discussion of "the pattern of noncommitment." He says that the inability to commit one's self is the outcome "of an abiding confusion as to whether the world is basically friendly or inimical." A lack of commitment arises out of a painful state of uncertainty. The noncommitted person is characterized by a "constant struggle against confusion and for a clear cut, reliable, unshakable attitude toward life, for guideposts and rules to live by." Angyal says that "in some cases this futile, endless battle for clarity, for settling the doubt, leads to total incapacitation." [1]

Angyal points out that this kind of life style begins in the traumatic effects of inconsistent behavior in adults who have the life of the child in their hands. For example, the child will be alternately treated extremely harshly and then in an overindulgent manner. The child may be overindulged by one parent and mistreated by the other. Such treatment produces strongly contrasting images of possible loyalties and commitments for a person. As a result he goes haltingly from one side to the other in trying to make a confident commitment. His capacity for commitment is severely damaged by long-term habituation to such inconsistent behavior in the supposedly responsible adults who have his life in their hands. When such a person does make commitments, they are divided commitments, substituted for wholehearted commitments, which wholeheartedness is precluded by strong ambivalence and emotional confusion. This is the double-mindedness of which the New Testament speaks and says that the double-minded person is unstable in all his ways. From the start the noncommitted person cannot be wholehearted about the things that he feels and believes.

For the double-minded person there are several ways to deal with and dispel the confusion in life. Something must be done to manage the perpetual uncertainty. The first way of dealing with the confusion of a good-bad world for the noncommitted person is to divide it sharply in two. This consists of a compulsive removal of all intermediate grades between good and bad, a division of the world into the good guys and bad guys resulting in a double commitment of overidealizing the good and totally condemning the bad.

A second way of dealing with confusion used by ambivalent, noncommitted persons is to build an ordered system of thought that seemingly reconciles the contradictions of life, explains them in terms of chance, and searches for laws and regularities to reconcile what seems to be mutually exclusive. The compulsive need for symmetry characterizes the basically noncommitted person. Everything must fit perfectly before he commits himself at all. The end result is that no commitment is really ever made.

A third way of dealing with confusion and disorder in the life of the uncommitted person is to find a set of safe rules to live by. Underneath this quest lie deep dependent needs for going by the book, devising ritualistic rules for meeting specific situations, and thereby losing spontaneity. The inability to make decisions and commitments by assessing the dynamics of present situations in the light of already-made commitments is resolved somewhat by learning foolproof rules of behavior, a few slogans that work, and sticking with these.

A fourth way of dealing with confusion used by the fundamentally uncommitted person is what Angyal calls a "desperate dogmatism which arbitrarily overshouts doubt." This person protests too much. He tries too hard. In fearing to be spilled, as Shakespeare says, he is spilled all over. Often religious overzealousness is mistaken for basic commitment when at its roots is an insecure, confused, and defensive person who is not supremely committed to anything except his own survival.

Angyal concludes his perceptive statement of the pattern of noncommitment as a way of life by saying that the noncommitted person uses a method of evasion that

> consists in saying 'yes' and 'no' at the same time. The person undertakes a new course of action, and by doing so says 'yes' to it; but he does not commit himself wholeheartedly, and so, by implication negates it. As this childhood play at adult activities continues, he does not earnestly reach out for the real thing. He may appear to go through the normal developmental stages and outwardly act his age, but his actions and relationships lack reality. He refuses to take responsibility in the sense of identifying himself with his actions and saying unequivocally, 'here I stand.' The person is always eyeing two possibilities, choosing a little of both, but neither completely. In this way he turns his life into a farce and deprives himself of real fulfillment. He usually feels that in avoiding commitments he leads a brave fight for personal freedom, but since he does not use it when he has it, the fight turns out to be a fight for freedom to sit on the fence.[2]

To the contrary, the genuinely committed person does not live life in a yes-but mood. He lives life on a yea-yea or nay-nay basis. Whatsoever is more than these is indeed and in fact evil.

CULTURAL ALIENATION AND COMMITMENT

All that has been said about the capacity for commitment refers to the personal, idiosyncratic aspects of individual commitment. The plea of the Apostle Paul that one take his stand with God is a plea to persons as individuals. However, it is set in the context of the individual's resistance to the shaping power of a cultural era, an age, an epoch, which are all terms for which the New Testament tends to use the phrase *the world*. It is not enough to deal with commitment in terms of an individual's response to God.

Kenneth Keniston uses the word *alienation* as a synonym for uncommitment and as an antonym for commitment. He argues that alienated youth of today, for example, are uncommitted not only because of idiosyncrasies of their individual pasts. They are uncommitted because of the cultural dilemmas of upbringing facing not only their parents but everyone else's parents. They do not commit themselves because of social stresses and because of the historical losses of an entire generation. Their "alienation was not only an idiosyncratic stance toward the world, but a diffuse reaction to a society and to a definition of conventional adulthood that was 'alien to the alienated.' " Keniston insists that one cannot understand commitment in purely personal terms. One must also understand what persons today are being alienated from and the society that is alienating them. His discussion, therefore, is a study of the "social forces of alienation," uncommitment, and so on. In Keniston's studies, he produced several indices to uncommitment or alienation: distrust, pessimism, resentment, anxiety, egocentricity, the sense of being an outsider, the rejection of conventional values, rejection of happiness as a goal, and the feeling of distance from others.[3]

The world from which these young persons are alienated is a world in which scientism, technology, and the corporation dominate human existence. These forces demand conformity, invidiously plan individuals' lives without consulting them, dictate the shape of the ego, and continuously reflect a utopian spirit. This causes people to "huddle ever more defensively in the present." There is an idolatry of technology, affluence, and little vision of the good life beyond the present period of prosperity.

Theodore Roszak takes Keniston's indictment of the technocratic and bureaucratic revolution one step further. He says that we in the Western world have developed what he calls a "psychology of single vision." This was begun by Christianity and its interpretation of commitment as singularity of devotion and wholeness of heart. This was carried over into the scientific revolution, which in turn took over this broadest ideal of singularity of commitment and wholeheartedness. The scientific revolution evolved into a technological society which is wholeheartedly devoted to the building of an artificial environment. This building of an artificial environment "may be best understood as an ever-deepening condition of idolatry." This idolatry is "a condition of our powers of perception and intellection which has only an indirect, and far from obvious, relationship to moral behavior." Leading exemplary, conventional, moral lives, the leadership has produced what Roszak calls "the *only* idolatrous culture in the history of mankind."

Therefore, the alienation of the counterculture is not an uncommitment as much as it is a deep, passive commitment to keep one's self from the idolatry of a scientific and technological culture that continues to build an artificial environment of concrete, steel, pollution, affluence, success, and remote control of human lives and destinies. Yet no creative alternative appears. Going counter to this culture of idolatry is interpreted as uncommitment by those who are caught up in the idolatry itself. These persons are committed, but they are committed to an idolatrous culture:

> The life's energy of generations can be expended *developing* the thing, covering it over with concrete and plastic and sprawling supercities, finding faster ways to travel over and across its surface, consuming its substance and inventing substitutes for its depleted elements. In this busy way the time may be passed, and we shall get used to the idolatrous life.[4]

However, those who oppose and resist this form of life are interpreted by many as being alienated or uncommitted. The truth of the matter is that they are committed to being uncommitted to an idolatrous culture.

However, as was pointed out previously, Roszak enters empathetically into the situation of the young person whose commitment to uncommittedness lashes out in first one direction and then another. He lashes out first at the Vietnam War, then against a chemical company as a symbol of the military and industrial complex, then against opponents of open housing, then against pollution and the rape of nature, and so on. Yet, Roszak says that these commitments seem to have a short-term duration to them and do not go deep enough nor extend long enough to produce a prevailing way of life for either the young people as individuals or the culture as a whole. He expresses concern for the young persons who are committed to being uncommitted to an idolatrous culture in that they have not found a moral equivalent for war, a creative alternative for scientific technology, or a durable and comprehensive sentiment that will characterize and identify a disciplined way of life.[5]

As such an alternative Roszak insists that the most careful utopia will not challenge the imagination of people because they will always find loopholes. People are too busy with the job at hand to take such a utopia seriously. He suggests that a Socratic method of working deeply into the awareness of young people is needed. They should be confronted with such questions as: "What are you, and what do you want to become? What prevents you from becoming this other, better you? Why does change make you afraid? What are your true needs? *What are you in the world to do?* Are you in charge of your life, and if not, who is?" Gradually, the whole person must be brought forth to answer.[6] He insists that these are not simply personal piety questions but they are "at once personal and political questions that point to what it means to be involved in the psychological dimensions of politics." He asks that "methods be developed for challenging people to set their own priorities, to confront them with the fears, hatreds, and hangups that betray those priorities." Then he comes back to the point of the personal and religious experience and says that "the field of play is the individual soul." He uses the pragmatic test and says,

> Nothing counts more heavily against the technocracy than a successful diversion, for there is no underestimating the influence of an authentically happy disaffiliate in a society of affluent self-content. Every drop-out who drops into a freer, more joyous, more self-determining style of life—a style of life that *works*—breaks the paralyzing official consensus.[7]

Underneath Roszak's assumptions seems to lie the basic belief that persons as totalities are the criterion of value in a technological culture, the basis for rebellion, and the raison d'être for commitment to oppose the system. From this sense of personal value comes the power of decision to commit one's self to a way of life that is comprehensive, nonidolatrous, and free of the bondage that idolatry to technological values has produced. Along with this belief there is an assumption of the freedom of the individual person to decide and the necessity to bring about the end of the wasteland of the idolatry of scientism and technology on a person-to-person basis. The major contribution that Roszak seems to be making is to give a distinctly religious interpretation to the call to be strangers and pilgrims in an idolatrous world whereas one is at the same time committed to the building of a "city not made with hands" that affirms the creation rather than destroys it.

This puts the so-called uncommittedness and alienation of contemporary youth into a larger context with a more positive appreciation. Quite candidly, one could say that the seeming lack of ambition of many young persons may be, though not necessarily, rooted in their thoroughgoing commitment to a different set of values from simply getting and spending and laying waste to one's natural powers. One could say that some, though not all, of the sexual casualness of young persons is related to their awareness of the hypocrisy of their elders in the sexual realm. They are ignoring the teachings—verbal, of their elders—and adhering to the teachings—behavioral, of their elders! After all, Peyton Place was written when the present generation of late adolescents and young adults were still in the playpen. They did not think of that! One could say that the preoccupation of the youth culture with drugs is related to the hypochondriacal use of drugs by their elders. The major difference is that they use nonlegal drugs and their elders use legal ones. However, it is easy to come up with half-truths such as these without at the same time challenging the commitment of young people to their verbal ideals. Do they talk a good line, as did their elders, condemning their elders' talk? Yet, do they not copy in behavior the worst elements of the behavior of the members of the Establishment? Do they do any better than the Gentiles do?

There are evidences of a new asceticism, a new mysticism, and a new insistence upon teaching experiences as the determiners of the directions of personal commitment. It seems to be that the creative impulses of emerging young adults today call for a commitment that leaves out the inconsistency of a previous generation and produces a wholeheartedness and singleness of vision. This wholeheartedness and singleness of vision would be focused upon a simplified way of life freed of the trappings of affluence, technocracy, and status seeking. This wholeheartedness and singleness of vision would further be focused upon a mystical consecration to the contemplation of the Eternal rather than the temporary and the transient. Finally, this wholeheartedness and singleness of vision would be focused upon the infinite value of persons as persons to whom one is to be related rather than as things whom one is to use for one's own purposes.

HINDRANCES TO WHOLEHEARTED COMMITMENT

We started this chapter with a definition of commitment in terms of taking one's stand alongside the Eternal, giving one's life up to a larger devotion than to one's self, and consecrating and hallowing life and persons. However, there are basic hindrances either at the personal or the political level to this kind of commitment. These blockages must be removed at increasingly profound levels of human decision.

A LOW SENSE OF PERSONAL WORTH

One of the most pervasive hindrances to valid personal commitment is a low sense of personal worth. One does not commit that which he does not value. The young drug addict who is hooked on heroin may have started out with the low evaluations of himself by other people, such as parents, teachers, judges, probation officers, and so on. The real disaster occurs, however, when that young person begins to believe these things himself. He begins to see himself as a "nego." As an I or a nego, he is nothing in his own eyes. He is to himself "nobody's nothing"; he does not see himself as being valuable to anybody for anything. He has come to objectify himself as a thing which in itself is of no worth. The contradistinction to this self-percept is that of valuing one's being too highly to use it as a thing or as a worthless thing. The Judeao-Christian wisdom on this is that we are made in the image of God, we are persons for whom Christ died. Even though we are strangers and pilgrims in an idolatrous world, we are members of the commonwealth of those who care. Out of this caring relationship comes a feeling of ability and a feeling of singlehearted devotion—valuing ourselves as we are valued by God and those to whom we are profoundly related.

DETACHMENT FROM PEOPLE

The opposite of attachment and affection is detachment and loss. Freud and, later, Bowlby, identified the early roots of detachment and loss. Angyal identified the developmental process of inconsistency of treatment that aided and abetted the growth of detachment and the lack of commitment of persons. On the basis of these early experiences, it is easy indeed for a person to assume that all people are like the persons who have abandoned him and are as untrustworthy and fickle as the people who treated him inconsistently. Wendell Johnson and others in the general semantics movement have pointed out that this "allness" lumping of people into emotional categories is one of the pathologies of thought that hinder us from making clear decisions and clear commitments about the people around us. In fact, these pathologies may cause us to test and con otherwise trustworthy and dependable people into reproducing the behavior of our parents, former teachers, and so on. A person may be set on proving that *all* people are liars and that *none* of them are consistent to *any* degree at all under *any* circumstances at *any* time, at *any* place. Therefore, he may remain uncommitted to anyone but himself on the basis of frailties and weaknesses of other people. The end result of this is that he can "shut himself within himself and let the devil pipe his own."

Somehow or other we must risk being hurt again. We must reach out toward a "love that knows no barrier." Experientially, the human potential movement of Maslow, Schutz, Clinebell, and others is establishing reliable experiments in trust and openness that are aimed at encouraging people with such hindrances to make decisive commitments to attach and relate themselves more durably to other people. This restoration of basic trust is, as Erikson has said, a return to becoming as a little child who learns from others how to translate basic trust into religious faith. Freud, earlier than he, specified the dynamics of identification whereby a person learns to trust and love another person in such depth and over a long enough period of time that he begins to take on the same likeness of the other person. This cannot be with some applied spray job of religious clichés. To the contrary it is lived out day by day, week by week, month by month, and year by year in viable, specific human relationships. This particular ingredient seems to be missing in the bureaucracy of the churches, the schools, and the labor forces of our country. Wherever it thrives, there is the yeasty possibility of the fermentation of profound personal and religious commitment.

Probably the most vital source of such durable relationships for the development of commitment is in the careful study of the living biographies of people who have now become a part of history. Not the least among these are the religious persons such as the person of Jesus and the persons of other people who did live a life of commitment. The roll call of faith in the eleventh chapter of Hebrews culminates with the affirmation that we are encompassed about by such a great cloud of people who laid down their lives for what they believed and for those in whom they believed. The person of Jesus is pointed to as the pioneer of these persons of faith. During the formative era of my own decisive commitments in life, for example, I found my own trust in life was stimulated by studying for myself the four Gospels as they describe the actions and teachings of Jesus Christ. I further supplemented this with the study of the specific biographies of John Knox, John Henry Newman, Walter Rauschenbusch, and others. These persons became demanding and challenging models for commitment. Furthermore, the lives of suffering people are a stimulus to commitment as well. The letters of Thomas Wolfe, Freud's interpretation of dreams, and the biographies of persons like Dostoevski provide something more than just a Pollyanna view of commitment.

The blockages to forming deep relations to persons also can be dealt with dynamically by writing one's own spiritual autobiography and getting back into touch with one's own heritage. Many persons today are uncommitted because they are basically marginal persons. By this I mean that they have amputated their own heritage and are seeking to live as if they had neither father nor mother. As a result the deep-running sources of positive value from their past lives are cut off at the same time they defend themselves from the damages and difficulties of their past. Sometimes this is too great a cost to pay, and a person can discover a real wealth of strength and commitment by reevaluating his own spiritual autobiography. This can be written down, members of small groups can discuss life stories with each other, and, with effective leadership, springs of creative commitment can be opened up from one's own past.

DISENCHANTMENT WITH CAUSES

The focus of a healthy commitment quite often is pinpointed on a cause of some kind or another. However, one of the disasters of the last two decades in the lives of young persons particularly has been the collapse of causes and the subsequent disenchantment of young persons with the cause. Collapse of many young people's ideals in their opposition to the Vietnam War has made many of them reluctant to commit themselves to any cause again. Protest-despair-apathy—these were the three phases Bowlby mentioned. They are an almost exact epitome of the reaction of young persons to the great tragedies of campus protests. The disenchantment of persons with causes quite often makes them very reluctant to attach themselves to subsequent causes.

One shaft of light may be helpful here. One reason for disenchantment lies in the short-term nature of the cause. When one compares the historical commitment of many Quakers to the opposition of war in any form with the relatively short-term passions of more recent demonstrations against war, he sees the difference. These people have added to their social enthusiasm the indefatigable patience of the centuries. Likewise, many of the causes to which people give themselves are self-limited in time anyway. They do not have the long-term potential that opposition to war has. Underneath short-term commitments is the faddish need for the spotlight of public attention. When the spotlight is gone, the commitment is gone.

Therefore, some discipline of disenchantment is needed. If one lives under the illusion that poverty is going to be banished in one four-year administration of the federal government, then he has committed himself to disenchantment. To the contrary, the life-long commitment of a Pappenheim to the liberation of exploited women in central Europe during the late 1800s and early 1900s was characterized by its lack of faddism and its long-term durability.[8]

The very nature of authentic commitment, it seems to me, is the acceptance of the discipline of disillusionment. In this discipline one commits himself to a cause. At the same time he commits himself to doing away with the illusions he himself has about his cause. He becomes more and more realistic with the passage of time.

This, it seems to me, is the antidote for Roszak's anxiety about the short-term character of the commitments of contemporary youth. To commit one's self means to give one's self up to a higher power than one's self, to take one's stand with a set of beliefs and a cause. It means being set apart and made holy by the transforming vision of greatness which one has chosen to be habitual. For that vision of greatness to be habitual it must live in time. It must take root in space. It must be concerned with history. It must be concerned more with making history. Such commitment is a transforming experience, and human life is both generated and regenerated through the experience of commitment.

EDUCATION IN COMMITMENT

Commitment is a learned response. The gap between the overcommitted and the noncommitted is a failure of transmission of the educative process at the point of healthy commitment. The issue seems to be who can learn from whom? Margaret Mead says that there are different cultures in terms of the foci of commitment. For example, there are the *prefigurative* cultures in which children learn primarily from their forebears in deep identification with and commitment to their elders. There are *cofigurative* cultures in which both children and adults learn from their peers and are committed to them. Then there are *postfigurative* cultures in which adults learn also from their children.[9] It may well be that we are making the transition from being predominantly a prefigurative culture to being a culture which learns primarily from its peers. The movement may be rapidly coming to the point of a more postfigurative culture in which we as older adults will find our richest meaning and deepest fulfillment in learning from our children and other persons considerably younger than we are.

Mead puts it vividly when she says, "Even very recently, the elders could say, 'You know, I have been young and *you* have never been old.' But today's young people can reply, 'You have never been young in the world I am young in, and you never can be.'"[10] Adults have two alternatives in a situation like this. They can, as Mead in the same context says, fear that the young are being turned into strangers before their very eyes and that they are to be feared "like the advance guard of an invading army." Better, they can look upon young persons as scouts into unknown territories, adventurers and adventuresses who are discovering things of which the adult has never heard. Yet, they can be debriefed by the adult with an open mind who both learns from the youth and shares with him his reactions as a student, literally. The locus of commitment is not to one's own generation but to the learning process itself. Thus, the young person, in Erikson's categories, can sharpen his identity on the whetstone of his relationship to older persons, and the older person can come to old age with dignity and without disgust.

All that has been said here points to a fresh reappraisal of the teachings of Jesus. These teachings fingered the relationship dimensions of commitment. He came to the point that he no longer called his disciples anything but friend and in which he enjoined upon them to call no man father. The relationship was one of constant invitation to come and learn. He entertained these disciples as they returned from healing and casting out demons with the same excitement that he enjoyed showing them that diseases of people were subject to him. Although all power was given to him in heaven and earth, he easily shared it with them and held them responsible for their use of it. Today the major crisis of personality is that of the learning process. Is the learning process being subverted into a meritocracy whereby credentials-seeking people are finding new ways of lording it over others and creating rank for themselves? Or is it one in which we are genuinely disciples of each other and the teacher can learn from the student as well as the student from the teacher? Is it one where parent learns from son or daughter as well as the reverse of this? Learning as reciprocity is a kind of commitment that has no end.

NOTES

1. Angyal, *Neurosis and Treatment*, p. 157.
2. Ibid., pp. 187–89.
3. Kenneth Keniston, *The Uncommitted: Alienated Youth in American Society* (New York: Harcourt, Brace and World, 1965), pp. 1–25.
4. Roszak, *Where the Wasteland Ends*, p. 136.
5. Ibid., pp. 107–41.
6. Ibid., p. 435.
7. Ibid., pp. 434–35.
8. Lucy Freeman, *The Story of Anna O.* (New York: Walker and Co., 1972).
9. Margaret Mead, *Culture and Commitment* (New York: American Museum of Natural History, 1970), p. 1.
10. Ibid., p. 43.

QUESTIONS FOR FURTHER STUDY

1. Relate the section of "education for commitment" to reading Jerome Bruner's *The Process of Education*.

2. Is the root cause of so-called failure of communication between parents and late adolescent persons that of the inability of either to learn from the other?

3. Search out an effective group leader in your department of psychology, your department of sociology, or your department of religion, and get as many as seven other people who will join with this leader in the exploration of each of your personal autobiographies.

4. Answer Roszak's questions on pages 8–9 for yourself.

16

LOYALTY AND CONSCIENCE

Commitment—that is, to take one's stand, to give oneself up to a larger devotion, to consecrate oneself to a person or persons who themselves embody that way of life—involves a relationship of trust, confidence, and mutual self-giving. This relationship becomes a guiding pattern in decision making and moral choice. This whole matrix of relationships involves the psychology of loyalty, moral integrity, and conscience.

Moral integrity is built upon something, a rationale for one's actions. That rationale is a psychologically and religiously significant part of the life of human beings. That rationale from which moral integrity is built is the stuff of which conscience is made. Conscience is the sum total of one's loyalties and one's patterns of moral decision making. No psychological study of religion is complete without an exploration, therefore, of the relationship between loyalty and conscience. These provide the structure and patterning of morality.

PATTERNS OF MORALITY

From an ethical and social behavior point of view, there are at least four different patterns of morality: the forensic pattern, the prudential pattern, the situational pattern, and the covenantal pattern.

THE FORENSIC PATTERN

I have deliberately chosen the word *forensic* to describe the patterning of human behavior and conscience by concretely stated laws. The reason for the choice of this word is to avoid some of the somewhat unfair negative connotations of a word such as the legalistic view of morality and conscience. The great forensic systems of religious behavior such as can be found in Judaism and Catholicism are by no means purely negative, compulsive, and unenlightened in their structuring of human conscience and behavior.

To the contrary, one finds in the statement of the law such enlightened comments as follow: "You shall not hate your brother in your heart, but you shall reason with your neighbor, lest you bear sin because of him. You shall not take vengeance or bear any grudge against the sons of your own people, but you shall love your neighbor as yourself: I am the Lord" (Lev. 19:17–18, RSV). Furthermore, the law is looked upon by the psalmist in the Old Testament as a source of delight, as the basis of meditation both day and night, and as a deep rootage of the devout human existence (Ps. 1). When one is empowered by learning the righteous ordinances of God, he is enabled to praise God with an upright heart (Ps. 119:7). These ordinances are sweet to the taste, provide understanding, and are a lamp to the feet and a light to the path (Ps. 119:103–105). The psalmist expresses profound affection for the law by saying that he loves the law, it is meditation all the day, it makes him wiser than his enemies, and it provides him with understanding that a teacher cannot provide (Ps. 119:97–99). Furthermore, there is a certain situational tailoring that goes on in the application of the law of Moses. For example, the commandment concerning adultery comes down with a harsh penalty of death for the man who commits adultery with the wife of another man because of the fact that this man's property rights in relation to his wife have been violated, and because the progeny of the man who is married to the woman has been thrown into jeopardy by another man having invaded her sexuality. However, the same act in relation to a slave girl is looked upon with forgiveness and payment can be made for it by the priests when a guilt offering is made (Lev. 19:20–22).

More than this, the law of the Jews was focused upon the person of Moses who had hazarded destruction by the Egyptians in order to lead the people of Israel out of the slave pits of Egypt. This is built into a deepening of the motivation of persons toward the keeping of the commandments. The Deuteronomic version of the law of the Sabbath, for instance, cites the deliverance of the people of Israel from the slave pits of Egypt as the cause for their observance of the Sabbath. To observe the Sabbath was to declare not only their freedom but that of their maidservants and manservants and strangers within their gates from the clutches of slavery.

In the New Testament the law is looked upon as a tutor to prepare people for the coming of a more grace-filled life in Christ. Jesus did not come to destroy the law but to fulfill it. Therefore, as long as the freedom of man will need some structure to give it form, the forensic patterning of morality will continue to have force. Even the situational approach to morality is built upon specific cases. As one reads both Jewish and

Catholic forensic statements of morality, he will discover that these laws were originally devised in many instances on the basis of specific situations in which decisions were made in terms of time and circumstance. Situationally decided, ethical actions today are no exception. As soon as these decisions are made situationally, the decision takes on precedental value and sets the pattern for later decisions. These in turn can become traditions, and with the passage of time traditions can become more powerful than written law.

THE PRUDENTIAL PATTERN OF MORAL BEHAVIOR

The treasure house of human wisdom has been systematized into patterns of ethical behavior based upon the identification of persons with the wise man and wise woman of the earth. The Jewish faith builds this into its ethical patterning of behavior through the Wisdom literature. Anywhere one reads in the Book of Proverbs, he finds the prudential design for human conscience. Even a slave who deals wisely will rule over a son who acts shamefully:

Wisdom builds her house,
but folly with her own hands tears it down. . . .
The talk of a fool is a rod for his back,
    but the lips of the wise will preserve him. . . .
The simple believes everything,
    but the prudent looks where he is going.
A wise man is cautious and turns away from evil,
    but a fool throws off restraint and is careless (Prov. 14:1, 3, 15, 16, RSV).

The prudential frame of reference for the formation of conscience assumes a kind of loyalty to the real or symbolic wise old man. The average person of today carries about with him wise sayings that he remembers from people with whom he has been associated in the past. He not only remembers these sayings but passes them on to other people around him. They in turn become a kind of structure and fabric for the ordering of his life. Yet, they regularly are saturated with a relational quality. These proverbs and wise sayings have been passed on to him by other people whom he reveres, trusts, and accepts as wise persons.

THE SITUATIONAL CASE-HISTORY PATTERNING OF ETHICAL BAHAVIOR

In his book *Situation Ethics: The New Morality*, Joseph A. Fletcher rejects the idolatry of codes by the legalists and the hedonism and self-seeking of the antinomian. He espouses the situation ethic. He says, "the situationist enters every decision-making situation fully armed with the ethical maxims of his community and its heritage, and he treats them

with respect as illuminators of his problems. Just the same he is prepared in any situation to compromise them or set them aside *in the
situation* if love seems better served by doing so." [1]

The decision to compromise or certify a given ethical norm is made
"by accepting reason as the instrument of all judgment," and "by accepting revelation as the source of the norms while rejecting all revealed
norms or laws but one command—to love God and your neighbor." [2]

This point of view is based upon the assumption of the use of case-
history method in making an ethical appraisal of a given situation. The
factual data of the long-term, contributing, and precipitating factors in
a moral crisis are necessary for full-orbed and reflective moral judgment.

Furthermore, the situationist's method assumes the developmental
process in human life. The use of reason, for example, in assessing a
given ethical situation implies the use of intelligence. Intelligence itself
is conditioned by age factor. The age factor symbolizes growth and
development. A given type of behavior varies in its meaning from one
level of age to another. For example, even legal jurisprudence and prudential ethics distinguish moral responsibility on an age basis. Some
offenders are called juvenile delinquents and others are adult offenders.
Even within the church and in theology the nature of sin is assessed in
terms of the accountability of a person at an age of responsibility. An act
of a five-year-old child, for example, is ethically different when it is
performed by a fifteen-year-old adolescent. In turn, the fifteen-year-old's
behavior is ethically different from the same act performed by a thirty-
five-year-old adult. If the same behavior persists as a habit without
change in a person over a period of forty years from the time he is
four or five, this is ethically different from the same act being performed only three times—once at five, once at fifteen, and once at thirty-
five—without continual repetition in between.

A student in hearing this kind of comment raised issue and made
the charge, "You are confusing psychology and ethics." My point is that
the psychology of personality development and the careful assessment of
a given person's life history is *both* a psychological and ethical process
and no neat distinction can be made between the two. To insist upon too
clean a distinction between psychology and ethics is to live life in too
highly compartmentalized an existence, and the compartments themselves become meaningless abstractions.

However, no clear view of the situational approach to conscience formation and morality is possible without a close psychological assessment
of the meaning of a *situation.* Probably the best formulation of the
meaning of a situation in morality is found in the first edition of
Gardner Murphy's book entitled *Personality: A Bio-Social Approach to
Origins and Structure,* published in 1947. Murphy entitles one of his
chapters "Situationism." Situationism means that "human beings re-

spond as situations require them to respond; and that whatever their biological diversities, they will, if capable of learning, take on the attributes which the situation calls for." [3] However, in the particular individual personality, Murphy contended that "life depends, to a large degree, on relatively irreversible *commitments,* and each commitment constitutes a field." Murphy continues, ". . . field determination goes deep; and once a commitment has been made, there is usually no possibility of going back to the unformed stage." [4] A situation, then, is formed when a new commitment is made. The field of forces thus established by a commitment introduces a new element in the matter of ethical decision making: commitments. This points toward a covenantal approach to the formation of conscience.

COVENANTS AND CONSCIENCE

Murphy's penetrating insight into the nature of a situation as beginning with the formation of a commitment goes more directly to the heart of the relationship between loyalty and morality than the rationalism of Fletcher. When one makes a commitment, he makes it with his whole being, not just through a rational process. He tends to build his sense of self-worth and moral integrity on the basis of the way he has made, kept, or broken his promises or covenants. He tends to perceive his relationships to other people as being faithful or faithless in terms of the way he has managed his covenants with them. Even if he perceives himself cleverly as having conned or manipulated other people into believing that what he said was true, he even then sees himself as the clever one who can promise people anything, get them to do what he wants them to do, and not take his promises seriously. The North Star in the universe of conscience seems to be the fact that man is a promise-making, promise-keeping, and promise-breaking organism.

This perception of the psychology of loyalty and conscience can be perceived from two frames of reference, philosophical and psychological.

A philosophical point of view. Probably one of the clearest philosophical statements has been made by Josiah Royce. He says that loyalty is "the willing and practical and thoroughgoing devotion of a person to a cause." This cause is "never something wholly impersonal but concerns other men and loyalty is always social." He says that there seems to be "the union of the personal and the seemingly super individual" about loyalty. Lovers are loyal not only to one another as separate individuals but to their love, to their union, which is something more than either of them or even than both of them viewed as distinct individuals. One cannot be loyal to a merely impersonal abstraction, nor can he be loyal simply to a bundled-together collection of various separate persons viewed merely as a collection. "Where there is an object of loyalty, there is, then, a union of various selves into one life." In other words, there is a covenanted community to which one is loyal.

More than this, loyalty rises above simply a specific community and focuses on the whole human race. Royce says that "all those duties which we have learned to recognize as the fundamental duties of the civilized man, the duties that every man owes to every man, are to be rightly interpreted as special instances of loyalty to loyalty." One might call this loyalty that consists of basic integrity in keeping one's covenants for their own sake, as well as loyalty to the largest good of the whole human race. This bespeaks of Kant's categorical imperative in which he says that the ethical life should be lived in such a way that one would be willing for his thoughts and actions to be taken as a universal standard of conduct for all mankind.

Royce goes further and relates loyalty to conscience. He sets aside conventional morality as a conglomeration or maze of precepts which regularly come into conflict with each other. These moralities do not provide a method of direction through the maze of precepts nor a principle that unifies the moral life and enables us to resolve the conflicts between various precepts. For example, one needs some kind of principle to resolve the conflict between the expectation that he be just and at the same time be kind; that he be generous and at the same time that he stand up for his rights; that he live for others but at the same time be careful of his own dignity; that he love all mankind but that he have honor and resent insults; that he take no thought for the morrow but that he be careful to have a good program of insurance; that he forget himself but at the same time love his neighbor as himself; that he be moderate in all things but that he not be a fanatic in goodness. Some principle of arbitration or resolution must be developed lest one be caught in an inconsistency of conscience.

Royce insists that these paradoxes are soluble in terms of loyalty. If one perceives himself as a loyal person and being loyal to his own loyalty, this is an adequate expression of what is usually spoken of as "the dictates of conscience." It can become a test for what is right and wrong in doubtful moral situations. Thus, conscience is not just a rational process, but also involves the mysteriousness of ethical demands. The intuitive certainty that one has when he has to say that he does not know why he considers a thing right, but that he is sure of his conscience in the matter is grounded in his loyalty to his covenants. What is actually happening is that his loyalty to himself and others as a loyal person tells him what to do in doubtful cases. Thus conscience becomes a total emotional possession of ours which enables us to make finite, correct, or mistaken judgments on moral questions as they arise. It consists of one's answer to the question Who am I? in terms of the major loyalties of his plan of life. This is the moral expression of a person Royce defines as "a human life lived according to a plan." He defines the self as a life in so far as it is unified by a comprehensive purpose. The composite loyalties of an individual furnish these purposes and make of us "a conscious and unified moral person." In summary, Royce defines conscience in this way: "To have a conscience, then, is to have a cause, to unify your life by means of an ideal determined by this cause, and to compare the ideal and the life. . . . your conscience is simply that ideal of life which constitutes your moral personality." [5]

On the basis of this definition of conscience, Royce says that there are two characteristics of loyal conduct which are inseparable: decisiveness and fidelity to decisions made. This philosophical discussion culminates at the point of these two characteristics. In order to probe more deeply the nature of loyalty and conscience, the psychological data concerning decisiveness and fidelity are needed at this point.

A psychological approach to loyalty and conscience. Inevitably loyalty and conscience involve the development of the moral judgment of persons. From a psychological point of view, one could say that an effective ethical and moral perspective such as Royce ascribes to conscience implies the capacity to make judgments that are sound and durably dependable.

The first psychologist one turns to is Jean Piaget who did a detailed empirical study of the development of the moral judgment of the growing person. He began by investigating children's attitudes and behavior when they played a game of marbles. The focus of concern was the child's conformity to the rules of the game. In the earlier stages of development, the child uses the marbles as free-play materials with no awareness of any social rules. He develops his own personal and private rituals of play which have little or nothing to do with anyone but himself and usually involve conformity to his own muscular or psychomotor needs. Piaget calls these "motor rules." In stage two, which involves the child at the ages of about three to five, the rules of the child's elders become something that the child imitates. However, he incorporates these rules into his own idiosyncratic, socially isolated world, and they fit his needs rather than he conforming to them. It is not until the years of seven and eight that the child develops a socialized way of playing the game in accordance with mutually agreed upon rules. In other words, ethical interaction seems to become most vivid when children are in the second to the third grade. Even then though, the grasp of rules is still vague and approximate in what may be called stage three. Stage four of the development of an awareness and appreciation of the rules comes to its full flower in the years from eleven to twelve when the rules are understood, obeyed to the letter, worked into a code, and seem to challenge the fascination of the child.

Another set of perspectives presented by Jean Piaget concerns the development of a child's ideas and attitudes concerning telling the truth or telling lies. At first, the child thinks of a lie as simply naughty words similar to profanity or vulgarity. Later the idea of untrue statements is held without any intention to deceive. Only finally do untruths become connected with the intention to deceive. In the second place, younger children think of a lie in terms of the distance it varies from the truth with no regard to the intent of the person doing the talking. They evaluate guilt as they get a little older in terms of the motives and intentions involved. In the third place, younger children judge the big lie which does not really deceive anyone as worse than the lie which succeeds in deceiving someone. To the contrary, older children think of the lie which succeeds in being deceitful in intent as being worse. In the fourth place, an unintentional falsehood that does a lot of damage is judged worse by a younger child than a deliberate lie which does not do any damage. Older children tend to reverse this sequence. In the fifth place, younger children are inclined to say that a lie is measured as bad in terms of the way one is punished for it, whereas older children think of it as bad in its own right whether one is punished or not. In the sixth place, younger children believe that it is worse to tell a lie to an adult than it is to a child their own peer. Older children see either as equally blameworthy.

Throughout Piaget's specific studies such as the two just mentioned, he develops what could be called a working hypothesis for the growth of the moral judgment of a person. At least two different moralities emerge in childhood among the children of the culture from which Piaget drew his subjects. The earlier morality is what he calls *a morality of constraint*. This morality is formed in the covenantal relationship between the child as an inferior and the adult as a superior. Whatever the adult says is turned into a moral absolute by the child. These givens are taken as constraints, are unquestioned and sacred. The child is literalistic, perceives things in terms of acts and not in terms of motives, and weighs things in terms of the overt consequences alone. Justice is reducible to what the parent commands.

However, in the second place, as a child grows older the morality of constraint should normally be replaced by *a morality of cooperation*. Here moral judgments are built on the basis of the interaction of the individual with his peers and are reciprocal, mutual, and distinctly social two-way sets of moral values rather than being parallel or unilateral or one-way moral values. Motives take a larger place than simply the acts themselves. Justice is set into a social context and perceived in terms of equality and equity.

Piaget concentrated his thinking upon the development of a moral suasion in childhood. However, Erik Erikson concentrated on adolescence. When a person moves past puberty into adolescence, he begins a quest for an ideology which provides an inner consistency, coherence, and durability to one's values. As has been seen before in the chapter on personality and religious experience, Erikson says that fidelity is the central virtue of adolescence. He defines fidelity as "the *ability to sustain loyalties freely pledged in spite of the inevitable contradictions of the value systems.*" [6] In describing this quality of loyalty which is the prevailing atmosphere of the mature conscience of a young person, Erikson says that "youth needs, above all, confirming adults and affirming peers." [7] It takes adult persons to provide content for the loyalties of youth and to be worthy objects of their fidelity. It takes the consensus of peers to cause these loyalties to become behavioral realities.

In both Piaget and Erikson, one discovers that the maturation of conscience into a rational morality requires a context of dependable and trusted relationships both in authority positions and in peer-group positions. These attachments, devotions, and loyalties are to persons, as Royce much earlier said. The covenantal community provides the inspiration and direction for the sustenance of a well-nourished and clearly directed morality. The system of loyalty is the basis of conscience, and the pattern of covenants is the design of morality.

THE VICISSITUDES AND TRIUMPHS OF LOYALTY AND CONSCIENCE

The developmental views of the growth of conscience and loyalty are attended by specific descriptions of negative, untoward events, or vicissitudes that occur in the stages along life's way. These happenings cause people to falter and fail in their loyalty to those to whom they have consecrated themselves. Each of these vicissitudes presents a challenge, however, to the more-or-less adult personality. They can be dealt with courageously. A few of these vicissitudes and possible triumphs are as follows:

THE IMPACT OF GRIEF AND LOSS

In the earliest years of life, attachments are formed to mother, father, and/or effective substitutes for parents. If anything happens to one of these important persons such as loss by death, divorce, or desertion, it tends to be characteristic of small children to accept responsibility for the happening. They may feel that they were the cause of the death, the divorce, or the desertion. In their fantasy lives, therefore, they may become overcommitted to the deceased, divorced, or defected parent and develop a heavy fantasy life of imaginary loyalty to this person. This fantasy formation becomes the stuff of which their conscience is made. Thus, an unrealistic conscience develops based on a fantasy-loyalty.

Even later in life, in young adulthood, this same kind of fantasy-loyalty can become the governing principle of the moral decisions of a person. For example, a man or a woman may lose a lover to whom he had given his unqualified loyalty. The person may have been killed in an accident, in military combat, or may have died of natural causes. The person may have rejected him as was the case of Anton Boisen as he describes his life in his autobiography *Out of the Depths*. A similar example is that of Kierkegaard in his lifelong devotion to Regina Olsen, whom he never married yet held in his fantasies all his life.

The opposite side of this kind of overcommitment to a fantasy formation of loyalty is that of the loyal defender of the parent or parent substitute who was left alone by the death, divorce, or desertion of the other parent alongside the growing child. The child may develop a forced set of loyalties, for example, in the defense of the one who was deserted, left, or equally bereaved. A young boy, for example, can grow up perceiving himself as the loyal defender of all women if his mother was divorced or deserted by his father. This loyal-defender role may be unrealistic, overlook the fallacies and foibles of women, and tend to pedestalize all women. This can lead to unrealistic forays of defense for women who are basically indefensible. Yet it can provide motive power for much that is classified as a caring ministry.

Of course, such a person—in all of the instances mentioned above—is living in a world of illusion. It is inevitable that life in reality will present this person with some disillusioning experiences. The triumph of life comes in the reformation of loyalty and conscience through voluntarily giving up such illusions and fantasies as have been entertained. Likewise, the acceptance of too much responsibility for the behavior of others can be faced realistically and refocused. Quite often this can be done through effective pastoral counseling or psychotherapy in which the person discovers the elements of idolatry and childish feelings of omnipotence involved in the acceptance of more responsibility than one human being can carry. Such a breakthrough results in the triumph of fresh growth, the hopeful discovery of more and more realistic loyalties, and the transformation of disillusionment into a mellowed spirit of wisdom.

THE CRISIS OF BETRAYAL

A child may grow from infancy to adolescence giving his loyalty undividedly to parents who confer ethical ideals upon him. When he discovers that these persons in one way or another are not what they pretended to be, then he feels betrayed. This is one of the most repeated vicissitudes of loyalty and conscience. An example of this is the person who is an adopted son or daughter. He is not told this by his parents but is regularly caused to believe that he is the blood relative of the adoptive parents. Then the child discovers at the age of twelve, fifteen, or seventeen, for example, that he is adopted. Quite often this occurs by the inadvertent appearance of a distant relative who tells "the straight story." The child checks the story out with his parents, and the great revelation of the truth takes place. This creates a rift in the credibility of the previously trusted objects of loyalty, the parents. The child's confidence is shaken. His fidelity is loosened. Massive ambivalence is introduced into his sense of what is right and what is wrong, what is true and what is false.

Another example of this experience of betrayal is the adolescent who has an idealized image of the perfection of his mother and father's love for each other. He lives in the aura of this perfection and perceives it with an overidealized loyalty and devotion. This becomes his own ego ideal for his personal relationship to a member of the opposite sex in a possible later marriage. Then he discovers that one or the other parent is being unfaithful in marriage and/or that both parents are basically suspicious and distrustful of each other and contemplating divorce. The divorce may or may not happen. This discovery is emotionally reacted to as if it were betrayal. The young person's own moral behavior may change dramatically. He may begin to act out and to do socially unacceptable things. The behavior has a double-minded kind of motivation. On one side, the behavior is a striking out with anger at the parents. On the other side, the behavior is a burst of rebellion and imaginary freedom in which the young person seems to say, "If it's all right for them to do this, anything is all right for me to do."

This crisis of confidence in the face of real or imagined betrayal can be turned into a triumph of loyalty and conscience. The young person can also have supplemental relationships of confidence and trust in father and mother surrogates outside the family. An effective teacher, professor, pastor, or therapist may become a consistent and reliable stabilizer of the confidence and trust of the young person. Such a surrogate can become a bridge over the troubled waters between that state of overidealization of parents and the state of realistic acceptance of them as human beings who make mistakes, can be misguided in their good intentions, and have overpronounced needs to appear perfect in their son's or daughter's eyes. A great part of developing a mature sense of loyalty and conscience is the acceptance of one's parents as fallible human beings for which there are no historical replacements. One cannot send one's parents back to the factory and get new ones! One cannot trade them in on newer models. One has to go through the agony and the possible ecstasy of repairing the damage, rebuilding the old habitations, and doing so on a more realistic foundation. Here the whole process of forgiveness is at stake. One rejects either the alternative of projecting onto parents all of the blame or that of introjecting into oneself all of the blame. Instead, realistic forgiveness and reappraisal of life as it is offer a clearer path to a mature sense of moral direction in life.

THE INCONSISTENT LOYALTY AND CONSCIENCE

The loyalty figures in the home, in the school, and in the government quite often are inconsistent in their leadership of the growing person. They may alternate between harshness and overindulgence, between sincerity and deception, between reliability and undependability. One parent, for example, may have a protective, sentimental, and overindulgent relationship to a growing son or daughter while the other parent has a harsh, overexposing, and denying relationship to the son or daughter. The attempt of a growing person to be loyal to both parents, to different types of teachers, and to different demands of the federal government seem to be impossible to perform. Therefore, the conscience loyalties of such a young person are *withheld*. He is not invested in either side of the inconsistency! Both sides of the inconsistencies are perceived as stupid, foolish, and unreliable. As a result, the loyalty-conscience development of such an individual is turned inward upon himself or herself. His own narcissistic satisfaction is the primary devotion which guides him. The trail toward a mature, functioning set of loyalties that ensues in high aspirations and noble endeavors for such a person as we are describing here is a long, long winding trail fraught with many dangers. Impulsive behavior, reckless activity, and disregard of others may produce irreversible consequences.

A genuine triumph can be developed for such a person if a consistent environment of responsible, coherent authority people can be established outside the being of such a person. To establish trust, to develop loyalty, and to grow a conscience when a person is past eighteen or nineteen years of age is a grueling but not impossible task. The behavioral-modification therapists have taught us a very great deal about how to develop such a consistent milieu in which teenage delinquents and offenders can grow a conscience. William Glasser, in his emphasis on reality therapy, has done much to devise patterns of treatment that do not permit a person to use the cop out of blaming his plight on other people or relying on the faults of others as justification for irresponsibility.

THE VICISSITUDE OF BOREDOM

Much deviant behavior is not ill-intentioned as much as it is a search for diversity and escape from boredom. As a person comes to ethical closure in his personal, occupational, sexual, and religious commitments, he is faced with the ever-narrowing demands of the loyalties he has chosen, the covenants he has made, and the responsibilities that they produce. Fidelity becomes polarized at this point. Covenants can become stuffy if they are not ventilated, aerated, and enriched. Those to whom we are loyal may refuse to possess us and encourage us to qualitatively different kinds of devotions to a variety of enriching relationships to other people. Erikson rightly says, "Fidelity without a sense of diversity can become an obsession and a bore; diversity without a sense of fidelity, an empty relativism." [8] For example, vocational commitment to a religious task can become a stuffy, monotonous, and boring process unless one has an avocational competence. It is not by chance that the Jews expected their growing young people to know the law and to have a trade. The active minister who has additional skills such as cabinet making, farming, or artistic design has a tangible diversity in his life that makes him more effective as a religious leader. One can take this too far and become a dilettante who dabbles in everything and has no central focus to his vocational commitment. Thus he arrives at the empty relativism of which Erikson speaks.

Similarly the loyalty-conscience formation of a person in marriage may become stuffy, narrow, and unventilated. The great crisis in the maturation of the psychosocial dimensions of the sexual life comes when a couple has to face the presence of more than one member of the opposite sex in each of their lives as husband and wife. A realistic sorting out of the qualitative devotions to these additional persons is necessary for the maturation of a responsible marital loyalty. One morality of safety is that of isolating oneself from all members of the opposite sex in any connection whatsoever, if indeed this is possible. This is a constricted loyalty that allows no diversity and pushes the conscience-loyalty pattern of a person into an atmosphere of boredom. The other hazard is that of becoming so shallow and indiscriminate in extramarital liaisons with the opposite sex that one arrives at an empty moral relativism. Intimacy can take place without possessiveness. Loyalty does have room for diversity. Yet both call for clear-headed communication in the maturation of the covenant of marriage.

Against the backdrop of all that has been said in this chapter, one student observed, "Covenants with ourselves seem to be more basic to our morality than do any others." This covenant, even the atheist raised without mother and father, can have. This seems to be the spirit of Shakespeare when he said,

> And these few precepts in thy memory
> Look thou character. Give thy thoughts no tongue,
> Nor any unproportion'd thought his act.
> Be thou familiar, but by no means vulgar;
> The friends thou hast, and their adoption tried,
> Grapple them to thy soul with hoops of steel;
> But do not dull thy palm with entertainment

Of each unhatch'd, unfledg'd comrade. Beware
Of entrance to a quarrel; but being in,
Bear that the opposed may beware of thee.
Give every man thy ear, but few thy voice;
Take each man's censure, but reserve thy judgment.
Costly thy habits as thy purse can buy,
But not express'd in fancy; rich, not gaudy;
For the apparel often proclaims the man,

. . . .

Neither borrower nor lender be;
For the loan oft loses both itself and friend,
And borrowing dulls the edge of husbandry,
This above all: to thine own self be true,
And it must follow, as night the day,
Thou canst not be false to any man.[9]

However, this is qualified by what we have found in contemporary psychology: Many persons view their "selves" as of little worth. They live with low self-images. To be true to this is to be true to the untrue. Even persons who "think more highly of themselves than they ought to think" are often betraying a deep inner lack of personal worth. The self that is of genuine value is the self to which to be loyal and true.

In conclusion, the hypothesis of this chapter has been that the psychology of ethics is best understood in terms of the loyal formation of covenants, the loyal keeping of covenants, and the continuing maturation of covenants. Thus, a covenantal ethic can be perceived both psychologically and religiously when proximate loyalties are brought under the continuing enlargement of the ultimate loyalty to God.

NOTES

1. Joseph A. Fletcher, *Situation Ethics: The New Morality* (Philadelphia: Westminster, 1966), p. 26.
2. Ibid.
3. Murphy, *Personality,* pp. 867–68.
4. Ibid.
5. Josiah Royce, *The Philosophy of Loyalty* (New York: Macmillan, 1930), pp. 17–175, esp. 175.
6. Erik Erikson, *Insight and Responsibility* (New York: W. W. Norton, 1964), p. 125.
7. Ibid.
8. Erik Erikson, *Identity: Youth and Crisis* (New York: W. W. Norton, 1968), p. 245.
9. Shakespeare *Hamlet,* act 1, sc. 3, 1. 58–80.

QUESTIONS FOR FURTHER STUDY

1. Paul Lehman's book, *Contextual Ethics,* was not discussed in this chapter. In what ways are the points of view of Lehman and this author comparable and different?

2. Hugh Hefner's playboy philosophy is widely read among students. Compare and contrast his point of view with that of Josiah Royce and that of Joseph Fletcher.

3. In your study of physics, do you find any relationship between Murphy's situationism and nuclear philosophy?

4. With the discussion of the vicissitudes and triumphs of conscience and loyalty, write a brief autobiography of your own ethical development.

17

ECSTASY AND THE NONRATIONAL

The human being perceives himself as being rational when he is at his best. Aristotle spoke of the nutritive, the sensitive, and the rational soul. One feeds, absorbs, and excretes: This he has in common with plants and animals as a nutritive being. One sees, hears, touches, tastes, and smells: This he has in common with animals. One perceives, interprets, deliberates, decides, evaluates, and philosophizes: This he has in common with other rational beings. So goes Aristotelian thinking. As has been seen before, Aquinas saw the essentially human dimension of life as the rational aspect of the human being. This has set the prevailing mode for religious experience for centuries.

Yet, the nonrational has for some time tended to be identified with the specifically religious dimension of human experience and has been a minority presence in the religious community.

WHAT IS ECSTASY?

Two authors have dealt definitively with what might be called "an anatomy of ecstasy." One of them is a less well-known and more recent author, Marghanita Laski, and the other is a more well-known and often-quoted person, Rudolf Otto. The former is a more empirical writer, and the latter is a more philosophical thinker. A careful review of these studies will give a vivid portrait of what ecstasy is. One does not define ecstasy; he describes it.

Marghanita Laski did an empirical study of ecstasy from three angles of vision. First, she questioned fifty-three persons with the same focused interview. The fifty-three persons consisted of twenty-six males, twenty-seven females, including a boy of ten, a girl of fourteen, and a girl of sixteen. They came from a broad spectrum of kinds of work: three civil servants, three secretaries, two publishers, two economists, two BBC producers, two cameramen, a medical student, a mathematician, an engineer, a geographer, an actor, a composer, a musicologist, a sculptor, a potter, a music teacher, a commercial artist, a literary agent, a salesman, an administrator, a lecturer, a floor manager, a cosmetician, a trades union official. No unskilled laborers, mentally ill persons, or unemployed persons seem to have been interviewed. It seems that most of the persons came from the middle classes. Laski regrets also that no persons engaged in commerce were included.

Laski, in the second place, took autobiographical accounts of ecstasies and poetic descriptions of ecstasies from literature that was not necessarily religious in content or meaning. Her literary sources were William Wordsworth, Alfred Lord Tennyson, Richard Jeffries, Margiad Jeffries, Robert Nichols, Friedrich Nietzsche, Arthur Koestler, Virginia Woolf, Karl Joel, Bernard Berenson, H. Warner Allen, Carlo Levi, George Gissing, Charlotte Brontë, George Eliot, George Meredith, D. H. Lawrence, E. M. Forster, Jacquetta Hawkes, C. E. Montague, Emily Brontë, Ovid, Richard Church, C. P. Snow, Marcel Proust, Frederick Woods, and an anonymous drug user.

In the third place, Laski consulted distinctly religious texts for descriptions of religious ecstasy. She quotes Heinrich Suso, St. Catherine of Sienna, an anonymous clergyman, Plotinus, Angela of Foligno, George Fox, St. Teresa of Avila, Hugh of St. Victor, David Brainerd, St. Alphonsus Rodriguez, St. Ignatius Loyola, Jacob Boehme, Joseph Salmon, St. Augustine, Louis of Blois, St. Francis of Sales, and other anonymous persons.

From these three sources of data Laski draws some valuable conclusions about the nature of ecstasy. First, she decided that there are two major kinds of ecstasy: "One manner, which I have called withdrawal . . . involves a more or less gradual loss of normal perceptions . . . can be deliberately induced or involuntarily achieved. . . ." The second kind of ecstasy, says Laski, "I have called intensity experience. . . . Intensity experiences . . . cannot be voluntarily experienced and are typically rare." These experiences of intensity Laski divided into three kinds, although they blend into each other: (a) adamic ecstasies, which return a person to the simplicities of life, produce a sense of purification and renewal of the self; life and the world are transformed, and a person feels lovingkindness to all, (b) knowledge-contact ecstasies, such as one has upon a great new discovery communicated from someone or somewhere else, (c) union ecstasies, which are characterized by feelings of union with someone or something else.[1]

These experiences, of whatever kind, are triggered by specific events that have high value and reverence to the person who enters an ecstasy. The triggers Laski found are: natural scenery, such as fine weather, being

near the sea, and so on; sexual love involving the total person; child-
birth, especially the sight of the first child; exercise and movement, such
as swimming or flying; religion, such as being in vespers in a foreign
cathedral; art, especially religious art; scientific knowledge, such as
solving a difficult mathematical problem; poetic knowledge; creative
work, such as suddenly being able to express something in permanent
form; recollection and introspection, such as calling up vivid images from
the past; beauty and the encounter of the beautiful, and so on.[2]

In describing the kinds of feelings they experienced in ecstasy, the three
sources of data revealed *feelings of loss and feelings of gain.* They felt
that they lost the feelings of difference, of time, of place, of limitation, of
worldliness, of desire, of sorrow, of sin, of self, of ability to use words
or images, and of sensory awareness. The feelings of gain were the gain
of a feeling of unity, of timelessness and eternity, of an ideal and heavenly
place, of release, of a new life, of satisfaction, of joy of salvation and
perfection, of glory, of contact, of mystical knowledge, of new knowledge, of knowledge by identification, of ineffability.[3]

Along with these feelings of loss and gain were what might be called
psychosomatic effects or quasi-physical feelings. There were feelings of
movement in an upward motion; there were feelings of insideness and
outsideness; there were light-heat feelings; there were darkness experiences; there were feelings of enlargement and improvement; the sensation of pain was described; there was a feeling of liquidity, such as
bubbling, being filled, and so on; quietness, peace, and calm took the
place of noise and stress.[4]

Significantly, Laski discovered somewhat serendipitously that there
are counterecstatic agents which she calls antitriggers and experiences
which are the obverse of ecstasy which she calls experiences of desolation.
First among the antitriggers is the presence of other people. Most people
are alone when they experience ecstasy, and more of them expressed the
need to be alone. The spirit of commercialism is an antitrigger. Man-
made activity such as floating litter counteracts ecstasy. The exercise of
reason and the use of reasonable language is an antitrigger to ecstasy.
Ugliness, brutality, and war are antiecstasy triggers.

The opposite of ecstasy, Laski says, is desolation. Desolation is characterized by uncoordinated diversity, such as "an inextricable jumble";
feelings of time and death, such as "the shadow of death"; feelings of
restriction, such as "the prison of hell"; feelings of grief, such as anguish,
sorrow, hopelessness; feelings of sin, such as imperfection and disfigure-
ment or deformity; feelings of the horrors of this world, such as "the
pains and torments of this wretched life"; feelings of loneliness, such as
abandonment, being cast out, and so on; feelings of ignorance, such as
"not being able to get my mind to work"; feelings of "downness," such
as being fallen, ruined, and so on; feelings of emptiness and loss, such as

"a profound emptiness"; feelings of dryness, such as spiritual aridity; feelings of turmoil and anguish, such as a terrible apprehension or pain and grief.

These experiences of desolation Laski found to be triggered by such things as dirt and squalor, bad weather, falling, drowning, being crushed, the experience of war, of coldness and darkness, and dirgelike music. It seems that life is either quickened and enlivened by near-ecstatic triggers or deadened and depressed by near-desolation triggers.[5]

The work of Rudolf Otto on the nature of ecstatic experience is much more philosophical in nature. Nevertheless, it corroborates the fine detail of Marghanita Laski.

Otto's work is an "inquiry into the non-rational factor in the idea of the divine and its relation to the rational." He insists that orthodoxy is in some measure the mother of rationalism, a sort of preoccupation with doctrine and the framing of dogma. The nonrational dimension of religious experience Otto names the sense of the "numinous," which is "a sense of personal insufficiency and impotence, a consciousness of being determined by circumstances and environment." [6] This Otto gives the name of "creature consciousness" or "creative feeling" to the sense of the holy. This feeling immediately and primarily refers "to an object outside the self" which submerges and overwhelms the creature.[7]

A further dimension of the numinous, nonrational expression of religion Otto calls the *mysterium-tremendum*, which is filled with the experience of *awefulness*, the fear of God. One shudders or feels horror and uncanniness. The element of overpoweringness joins with awefulness in the experience of majesty. Added to the "aweful majesty" is the element of energy or urgency in which one senses a "force that knows no stint nor stay," but is "active, compelling and alive." [8]

The *mysterium* in the idea of the holy, according to Otto, rests in the comprehensibility of God. God is "wholly other" and thoroughly beyond the creature. This is expressed in the feeling of nothingness, void, and emptiness found in Buddhism. Therefore, the Eternal holds a lasting fascination and is uniquely attractive. A person "feels a something that captivates and transports him with a strange ravishment, rising often to the pitch of dizzy intoxication . . . ," says Otto.[9] This comes as near to describing ecstasy as one can get.

Taking Otto's clue to the meaning of ecstasy, one can develop a wide-ranged approach to the experience of ecstasy in the Old Testament. For example, a "great dread and darkness" fell upon Abraham in his sleep. The Lord communed with him during his deep sleep, predicting slavery, judgment, and oppression for his descendants (Gen. 15:12–13). Jacob, at the River Jabbok, wrestled with God. Jacob said that he saw "God face to face, but that his life had been preserved" (Gen. 32:30). With the burden of the memory of having killed an Egyptian, Moses was deeply disturbed by his encounter with Yahweh who called him to go to Egypt again to deliver his people. He hid his face because he was afraid to look upon God (Exod. 3:2, 4:24). Deuteronomy speaks of Moses as a man "whom the Lord knew face to face" and speaks approvingly of "all the mighty power and all the great and terrible deeds which Moses wrought in the sight of all Israel" (Deut. 34:10, 12, rsv). The sense of creatureliness, the awe-inspiring power of God, and the overpowering majesty of God appear vividly in these accounts of face-to-face encounters of Abraham, Jacob, and Moses. In the broadest sense, we could speak of them as ecstatic and nonrational experiences which nevertheless prompted decisions and actions of man. In fact, they took precedence over prudential behavior; in doing so they shifted the course of history.

As one comes to the New Testament, the word, *ekstasis*, is used. The word takes on much more specific meaning than in the Old Testament. In the New Testament ecstasy literally means "standing outside of oneself." If commitment means taking one's stand with God, ecstasy means standing apart or outside the usual self of everyday life. In ancient Greek and Hebrew literature the word *ekstasis* had two meanings: first, in Aristotle, the word means "a displacement." One's self is displaced from its routine expressions, roles, environment. For example, in Ezekiel 26:16, princes are spoken of as stepping down from their thrones, getting out of their roles and their embroidered garments. Instead, they "clothe themselves with trembling." In 2 Chronicles, wholehearted obedience to Yahweh results in being given "rest round about," both personally and politically. This "rest round about" or serenity was so out of the ordinary that the term *ekstasis* is used to name it. An individual and a nation is, apparently, moved up out of one orbit of existence into another.

A second meaning of *ekstasis* is that a person passes out of his usual self-control. This shift of control can be either a *trance* or the feeling of *amazement*. Trance experiences are like those of Peter in Acts 10:10, which he explains after the fact in Acts 11:5. Similarly, Paul describes his experience in the Temple in Jerusalem after his "debriefing" from his Damascus road conversion. In a trance he received guidance from God to get quickly out of Jerusalem because the Christians would not accept his testimony that he had indeed been changed by God.

The experience of amazement came upon the family and friend of Jairus at the healing of his twelve-year-old daughter (Luke 8:41 ff.). Similarly, the ecstasy of amazement fell upon those who saw Jesus heal the man brought to him—the paralyzed man (Luke 5:26). Also, when Peter brought health to the man lame from birth at the Gate Beautiful, the people who saw the man "were filled with wonder and amazement" (Acts 3:10). These references exhaust those in the New Testament where the word *ecstasy* is used literally. They refer to the kind of flash of insight that comes to a person in a time of radical change in lifetime prejudices, as in the case of Peter admitting to himself that a Gentile could become a Christ-believer. Or, they come when a life is in total threat and an immediate decision must be made, as in the case of Paul in Jerusalem. They may come when one is overwhelmed by observing firsthand the radical restoration of a person to health and hope after severe illness, handicap, or hopelessness.

GLOSSOLALIA, ECSTATICISM, AND THE NONRATIONAL

The New Testament experience of the nonrational and ecstaticism is not exhausted by the study of its use of the word *ekstasis*. A recurrent form of ecstatic experience is spoken of in the New Testament as "speaking with tongues." Mark 16:9–20 is a later addition to the older manuscripts, but it includes reference to many experiences that are ecstatic and nonrational in content: baptismal regeneration, exorcism of demons, speaking in tongues, snake handling, poison immunity, and the healing of the sick. Acts 2 records the story of the coming of the Holy Spirit who in turn overcame the barriers that different intelligible languages presented for the union of all mankind, beginning with the Jews. Practically all of the interpreters of the Scripture hold that this reference is to understandable languages, not to unintelligible sounds. The coming of the Holy Spirit produced an ecstasy that lifted men and women above the barriers of many different languages. The energy of the experience enabled them to understand at a more than rational level. This defied differences of language.

In the first letter of Paul to the Corinthians "speaking with tongues" meant something very different. I agree with my colleague, Frank Stagg, when he says that "they were motor phenomena brought on under the excitement of religious experience. They could result from a genuine encounter with God. On the other hand, 'tongues' could be an effect highly desired, expected, sought, and displayed for one's own enhancement. The utterance was unintelligible." [10] This group of Corinthians were a problem-ridden community, and the experience of glossolalia was a divisive, conflict-producing event. Stagg again says that Corinth was "immature, unstable, and unhealthy, not a model church! It was there that glossolalia was most prized." [11]

Today a cyclical upsurge of glossolalia occurs periodically in this country among religious and not-so-religious people alike. Piaget makes a helpful distinction in understanding the psychology of glossolalia although he makes no direct reference to the phenomenon. He identifies two types of speech in children: *collective monologue,* in which the child makes sounds that are intelligible to him but to no one else; and

socialized speech, in which the child speaks in language that is understood by others. It seems to me that glossolalia is often a first stage in
the experience of the numinous by a person in his religious pilgrimage.
In my own clinical observations I have identified four different expressions of this infant-cry expression of religious ecstasy.

First, I have noted the programmed glossolalic. This is the person who
has grown up in a tradition in which glossolalia has been handed down
from one generation to another as a faith-ritual of the initiated group.
Paul Morentz, a psychiatrist, interviewed sixty glossolalics in churches
where speaking with tongues is considered deviant behavior. He found
several motifs of behavior: hostility to authority, the wish to compensate
for feelings of inadequacy, the wish to rationalize feelings of isolation,
the wish to dominate, strong feelings of dependency and suggestibility,
and a wish for certainty. However, he points out that these variations do
not occur in such a pronounced way among Pentecostal churches where
it is a part of expected religious ritual.[12] Therefore, I would agree and
say that as ritual glossolalia is not necessarily a sign of deviance or of
ecstasy in the strict sense of both words.

Second, I have observed that glossolalia appears normatively in highly
intellectual and sophisticated persons who have severely denied any
religious feelings at all. When these persons have entered a profound
religious awakening, they quite spontaneously utter deeply emotional
neologisms or new sounds. These sounds are tactually and auditorially
meaningful to them in their phenomenal field whereas they are not
meaningful to other persons. This is particularly true today when there
is such a heavy taboo upon speaking about religious feelings; these
sophisticates never develop a meaningful language identifying the feelings of ecstasy.

Third, I have observed that glossolalia appears among emotionally
shy and inadequate persons. It expresses the need for intimacy, a need
that is difficult to put into words. Members of main-line denominations
often discover the close-knit intimacy of a group of glossolalics. They
find in the experience a way of expressing the tenderness and yearning
of their spirits that comes through glossolalia that does not come any
other way. This seems to be the testimony of Sherrill in his book, *They
Speak with Other Tongues.*[13]

Fourth, I have found that speaking with tongues is on occasion an
aftermath, though not a cause, of a severe psychotic break with reality.
As Pattison says, it occurs as one among many expressions of regressive
behavior. I interpret it as a desperate appeal for help in most instances.
Even here, I do not see glossolalia as a necessary symptom of mental
illness any more than I see the preoccupation of a paranoid patient with
the FBI, the local police, or the Internal Revenue agents as a sign that

these agencies are in and of themselves sick if someone is worrying about them. As Pattison says, "The phenomenon of glossolalia *per se* cannot be interpreted except in terms of the socio-cultural context." [14]

Yet it must be noted that many of the enthusiasts for glossolalia have indeed broken through to the nonrational and ecstatic levels of religious experience. For persons who are prone to equate the sane with the rational, to analyze and verbalize everything they accept, these experiences are often considered invalid, crazy, or offbeat. Yet these accusations themselves can be as defensive and denying as one finds among the persons who speak with tongues. The final test of either the validity or the sanity of glossolalia is the fruits of the behavior. As John Kildahl says, "I prefer to define religious experience by its fruits, rather than how it is induced. Excellent and sufficient behavioral criteria for religion are offered by the Old Testament prophet Micah: to do justice, to love kindness, and to walk humbly with God. In the New Testament, the Letter of James urges that true religion consists of helping those in need." [15]

THE RESURGENCE OF THE NONRATIONAL IN THE COUNTERCULTURE

It is not by chance, it seems, that the ecstatic experiences of glossolalia have characterized some of the noninstitutional expressions of religion in the counterculture. The central, valid hallmark of the glossolalic movement, in my opinion, is the deep-running hunger for intimacy it represents. This intimacy is itself an ecstatic need. There seems to be a double movement within the counterculture: both toward and away from intimacy. Theodore Roszak says that the life of Reason, spelled with a capital *R,* has "all too obviously failed to bring us the agenda of civilized improvements the Voltaires and the Condorcets once foresaw." [16] He says that the irrational continues to intrude itself into life in the form of "sensuous contact, fantasy, spontaneity, and concern for the person." [17] Therefore, Roszak calls for a return to the charismatic and even shamanistic leader who "stands apart from his people—not in a position of institutional authority, but in a position of talented uniqueness." This leader's "uncanny influence over us does not lie in any office he holds but in his own manifest skill." He increases this skill by devoting himself "to a life of severe discipline and solitude. He fasts, he prays, he meditates; he isolates himself in order that he may watch out for such signs as the presences make visible for his education. Above all, he becomes adept at cultivating those exotic states of awareness in which a submerged aspect of his personality seems to free itself from his surface consciousness to rove among the hidden powers of the universe." [18] These are "trance-inducing . . . practices." In short, Roszak is asking for a leadership of persons who are disciplined in the ecstatic and nonrational dimension of human life and behavior.

However, much of the counterculture, says David French, gives lip service to an ecstatic kind of intimacy that ensues in responsible community, but they are not in fact committed to the disciplines required of them. He contrasts an experience in an American commune with the life of an Ethiopian village. In the latter, he says, the villagers were characterized by a straightforwardness in all of their relationships. "They could be so direct, in fact, that they would become almost nonverbal, communicating by a kind of telepathy. And the same sense of involvement extended outward, to their families, their extended families, and tribal environments. In other dimensions, it went even beyond that: an almost mystical sense of spiritual fullness seemed to entwine them with generations dead and yet unborn." [19] Yet, French says, the American commune was a facade of intimacy. "Alone behind their walls of words, people preserved distances between each other by ceaselessly talking. It had become compulsive." [20]

The seeming difficulty in the counterculture lies in the absence of the kind of leader that Roszak describes. The search for this leader has been the poignant story of the movement. Various people from Leary to Ginsberg and Watts and others have seemed to reach out toward this kind of ecstatic leadership. Yet they have not made it in terms of creating the shamanistic power of the ecstatic sort that Roszak describes. The leadership of Martin Luther King among the black people came very near to being what is needed, but he was killed. The demonic aspects of the nonrational took over, and he was destroyed. Without this leadership, without authentic intimacy, and without a new meaning of creative work, David French says that the "counter culture is dying. . . . Eaten away from within by its Establishment heritage, the movement has lost its energy, is left with nowhere to go." [21]

Yet, the drug culture remains, and this leads to another aspect of ecstasy, the nonrational, namely, "chemical ecstasy," as Walter Clark calls it.

DRUGS AND ECSTATIC EXPERIENCE OF THE NONRATIONAL

The drug culture of the 1960s and early 1970s is definitely a part of the contemporary surge of secular ecstasy. Also, they use music and dancing to produce this kind of ecstasy. The prophets or *nabi* described in 1 Samuel 10:5–13 and 19:18–24 as well as 2 Samuel 6:13–17 escalated themselves into an ecstatic frenzy through music and dancing. Even David the king leaped and danced before the Lord. It was he who vowed to the daughter of Saul that he would continue to "make merry before the Lord." Furthermore, some kind of herb effect may have been used to produce ecstasy, bring the prophets together, and inspire confidence in them by Elisha in 2 Kings 4:38–41. A pottage was prepared for the sons of the prophets. "One of them went out into the field to gather herbs, and found a wild vine and gathered from it his lap full of wild gourds, and came and cut them up into the pot of pottage, not knowing what they were" (2 Kings 4:39, RSV). Elisha sensed the fear of the sons of the prophets of eating that which they did not know. He threw meal into the pot, and they could eat it without fear at his word. Here was a group of ecstatics who had a leader with all the charismatic power of which Roszak spoke earlier.

Similar fears of psychedelic drugs prevail in the minds of people today. Walter Clark says that the drug movement of today is definitely a part of the

> generalized movement [which] focuses on the cultivation of the inner life in response to the hunger for the expression of the non-rational aspects of the psyche. . . . Its religious expression . . . is mysticism, prophecy, speaking in tongues and other forms of religious ecstasy. . . . But someone who has long been fed on the husks of religious dogma, and who hungers for a more vital encounter with God, or Ultimate Reality, or the Ground of Being, or whatever he may call the source of the movement which he intuitively feels will stir the deepest chords within himself, cannot be satisfied with [social] activism . . . because his drug-induced religious experience vitalizes his religious life and demonstrates the error of those who think that only the logical and rational aspects of religion are valid.[22]

Clark is convinced that no one can speak with authority about drug-induced ecstasy who has not used the drugs himself, as Clark himself has used them.

The oldest communal expression of the use of drugs in producing religious ecstasy now in existence is probably the Native American Church, a group of Indian Christians who use peyote in their sacred rituals. The community has a specific Christian commitment; it requires family responsibility, hard work, abstinence from alcohol, and love of one another of its followers. It might be added that the Native American Church sprang up from the soil of the earth without being aided and abetted by the mass media, without the sophistication of university communities, and always has been within the set and setting of Christian values. Clark contrasts the Native American Church by deploring the stance of the larger conventional churches about the use of drugs such as psilocybin, LSD, and so on to induce religious ecstasy. He says that for this reason "any religious use of the drugs will have to be carried on in cults, outside traditional institutions. This is a pity, for it deprives the churches of a powerful influx of ecstatic energy—the very element of which they are in shortest supply."[23]

Clark, however, with all his enthusiasm for chemical ecstasy, is aware that the resistance of the traditional churches to the use of drug-induced ecstasy is a subhead resistance to their opposition to any kind of ecstatic experience within the church. "Every ecstatic movement . . . had its critics who were the contemporary defenders of the faith. The church has created schism rather than tolerate the vitalizing energies of the Waldensians, the Hussites, the Lutherans, the Anabaptists or the Wesleyans." [24] This is a deep-running commitment to the rational and fear of the spontaneous and nonrational. I do not agree with Clark in his insistence upon the use of psychedelic drugs. I think psychedelic drug ecstasy calls for the supervision of persons who know far more about biochemistry than even the average medical doctor today knows. However, I do agree with Clark that ecstaticism of any kind is usually tabooed by the people in control of the churches. This is indeed tragic, and schism can be prevented. However, this calls for openness on the part of the ecstatic as well as the person who has not had such experiences. Yet hard experience indicates that the arrogance, the closedness of mind, and the power to create schism seem to be as prevalent among the contemporary ecstatics as it is among their more rational and common-sense, nonecstatic counterparts. Ecstaticism loses its way when pride of experience replaces sensitivity to the anxiety and fears of the uninitiated. Established religious leaders lose their way when they move to excommunicate the ecstatic.

ECSTASY, THE APOLOGY FOR WONDER, AND THE POWER OF MAKING MERRY

David insisted on "making merry before the Lord" and in the process apparently experienced much ecstasy. He was not without criticism, either. Michal, the daughter of Saul, David's predecessor as king, criticized him severely. He was not in the tradition of a king's role. He was not behaving in the prescribed manner. Here, without the use of drugs, the experience of worship prompted merriment, happiness, joy, ecstasy. This theme departs from the somberness of Western religious rituals. Michal represents the mood of the many; David's behavior represents the loose and relaxed spontaneity of a few today.

Among these few is Sam Keen with his emphasis upon the less-structured, more-spontaneous, less-planned, and more-serendipitous expressions of the spiritual life. He calls it an apology for wonder. Wonder is begun with the element of *surprise*. Wonder "breaks into consciousness with a dramatic suddenness that produces amazement." This feeling is followed by *puzzlement* when fresh questions about existence are asked. One has mixed or *ambivalent feelings* about the surprises that puzzle. Keen says, "The heart of the experience of wonder [is] an *awful-promising surprise*." Such a spontaneous experience is the foundation of a value structure of life in which we prize, accept, and affirm things and persons with no utilitarian objective in mind. Only the imagery of apocalypse and revelation really get at the meaning of wonder. "To wonder is to die to the self, to cease to impose categories, and to surrender the self to the object. Such a risk is taken only because there is the promise of the resurrection of meaning." [25]

Underneath these subjective dimensions of wonder, rest the supporting foundations. These are the more objective aspects. First, *contingency* undergirds wonder. An event, object, or occasion of wonder comes without any rational explanation or easy relationship to things already known. The eye has not seen nor the ear heard such a thing before. It stands apart. Mystery is the stuff of which wonder is made. This is not mystery in the sense of ignorance. Rather, it is the experience of the more we know a person, an environment, a thing, the more mysterious they become. The revelation of God overwhelms us with wonder because we sense his hiddenness and mystery. This mystery is not ignorance but the feeling of the tether of our minds. Second, mystery is pervaded by *presence,* in that the object of wonder ceases to be just an object and becomes a reality that has reached out, *presented* itself, and we are grasped by it. The It ceases to be an It and becomes a Thou.

Such an experience of wonder is not received by man-the-maker and man-the-worker but man-the-admirer, the responding person. The receiving of the gifts of life, the appropriation of that which costs nothing, the experience of grace itself are stimuli of wonder. They cause one to catch his breath, to expel his breath in a shout, to revert from words to movements of the body, to make merry before God. Consequently, ecstasy involves the total being of a person in music, movement, nature, and intimacy with other people. The whole ecstatic frequency is missed by the work-oriented, production-demanding life of man-the-maker who fabricates, invents, draws lines, sets boundaries, and establishes rational categories. To the contrary, the life of ecstasy "is accomplished joy, enthusiasm, a sense of being a part of a moving reality that is greater than oneself. . . . The self escapes isolation and death by identification. . . . Ecstatic identification may take many forms. The most universally sought after and convenient path is love. . . . Perhaps the most powerful medium of ecstasy has been mystical identification with God (alias Spirit, The All, The One, Ground of Being, etc.) ".[26]

The antithesis between these two frequencies of the religious life— the ecstatic and the rational—has been the source of tension and creativity schism and intimacy in the religious community. Aristotle said that the rational man is just what he is and nothing else. Yet, the same Aristotle said that when the mind is set free from its present conditions it appears as just what it is and nothing more. Ecstasy, in the finest expressions of its fruits in human behavior, has been the awe-inspiring wonder that sets people's minds free from their present conditions. This brings the vital balance of the "golden mean." The integrity of the individual and communal religious life calls for the vital balance between the spontaneity of ecstasy and the rational structures of life.

NOTES

1. Marghanita Laski, *Ecstasy* (Bloomington, Ind.: Indiana University Press, 1967), pp. 369–70.
2. Ibid., pp. 26–27.
3. Ibid., pp. 30–31.
4. Ibid., pp. 32–33.
5. Ibid., pp. 160–212.
6. Rudolf Otto, *The Idea of the Holy* (New York: Oxford University Press, 1958), p. 9.
7. Ibid., p. 10.
8. Ibid., p. 23.
9. Ibid., p. 31.
10. Frank Stagg, E. Glenn Hinson, and Wayne E. Oates, *Glossolalia* (New York: Abingdon, 1968), p. 38.
11. Ibid., p. 39.
12. Mansell Pattison, M.D., "Behavioral Science Research on the Nature of Glossolalia," *Journal of the American Scientific Affiliation* (September 1968), p. 76.
13. Lewis Sherrill, *They Speak with Other Tongues* (Westwood, N.J.: Fleming Revell, 1965).
14. Pattison, "Behavioral Science Research on the Nature of Gossolalia," p. 76.
15. John Kildahl, *The Psychology of Speaking in Tongues* (New York: Harper & Row, 1972), p. 65.
16. Roszak, *The Making of the Counter Culture*, pp. 145–46.
17. Ibid., p. 227.
18. Ibid., pp. 246–47.
19. David French, "After the Fall: What This Country Needs Is a Good Counter-Counter Culture," *New York Times Magazine* (3 October 1971), p. 21.
20. Ibid., p. 28.
21. Ibid., p. 21.
22. Walter Clark, *Chemical Ecstasy* (New York: Sheed and Ward, 1969), p. 65.
23. Ibid., pp. 163–64.
24. Ibid., p. 164.
25. Sam Keen, *Apology for Wonder* (New York: Harper & Row, 1970), pp. 27–31.
26. Keen, *To a Dancing God*, pp. 77–78.

QUESTIONS FOR FURTHER STUDY

1. If you are a lover of English literature or American literature, choose one author such as Blake, Wordsworth, Whitman, or Wolfe, and give a brief report to the class on their expressions of ecstasy.

2. Get the criticism of "enthusiasm" by John Locke and present it to the class. (What is the etymology of the word *enthusiasm?*)

3. Interview some persons you know who speak in tongues or go to a meeting of a group of such persons. Use the phenomenological approach to understanding their frame of reference. Write a summary of your findings.

4. What part does *play* have in authentic religious experience? Robert Neale in his book, *In Praise of Play*, says that this has been a neglected dimension of the religious life. Do you agree?

5. Does work addiction short-circuit the experience of ecstasy? Compare what I have said in this chapter with my work, *Confessions of a Workaholic*.

18

RELIGION AND PSYCHOPATHOLOGY

The preceding pages of this book have at many points raised the issue of the relationship of the different kinds of experiences of religion, on the one hand, and psychopathology, on the other hand. The fine lines between creative, religious experience and mental illness are very difficult to locate, primarily because they are moving lines. The accusation of abnormality is hurled at persons whom we do not like, who are different from us, and who depart from the norms set down by us. The constant charge of madness seems to hang over the religious quest for a variety of reasons. The data and issues on this subject must be faced in any adequate text on the psychology of religion.

The accusation of madness was made concerning Jesus during his earthly ministry. He went back to his hometown. The crowds came to see him in such great numbers that they could not eat. His friends heard about the commotion and went out to seize him, for they said, "He is beside himself" (Mark 3:19b–27). The word used here is *exeste,* "to be mad" or "to be beside oneself." The scribes from Jerusalem felt that he was possessed by the prince of demons, Beelzebub. A similar accusation was made of the Apostle Paul by Festus who said, "Paul, you are mad; your great learning is turning you mad." The word used here is *mainē* and *manian,* the word from which we get our word *mania* (Acts 26:24–29). Jesus refused to accept this charge, and so did the Apostle Paul. History has vindicated their witness, but the question of the relationship between religious experience and mental illness has continued.

BIBLICAL DEMONISM AND MENTAL ILLNESS

The charge that Jesus was controlled by demons prompts the question of the relation of demonology to mental disorder. This has in the 1970s become an issue at every level of sophistication. As Edward Langton, in discussing the teachings of the New Testament concerning demonology, says, "the different 'psychic states' or 'splits of personality' or 'frag mentary selves', as they are variously called can assume the guise of different personalities, and act as the individual they are supposed to be, in the most lifelike manner." [1] Langton assumes that one of the main factors, although not the only one, accounting for demon possession as portrayed in the Gospels is the existence of pathological "psychic states which can assume the appearance of individuality." [2]

Professor S. Vernon McCasland studied the Gospels in the light of the contemporary Hellenistic civilization in which the New Testament was written. He drew upon the forms of thought in the situation existent in New Testament times. He says that ". . . physicians in our time call disorganizations of the mind neurosis or psychosis; the ancients called the same phenomenon demon possession. . . . the modern vocabulary refers to compulsions arising from the *id* or from *complexes* or from the *super-ego* which are so strong that the normal self, the *ego*, is unable to retain its rational sovereignty. Disorganization sets in and personality loses its integration." [3]

Leslie D. Weatherhead has pointed out that Jesus makes no reference to devils (though the conversations around him were full of reference to them) apart from the context of disease and the possible exception of the storm on the lake. [4] Nevertheless, Jesus did insist repeatedly that no man could serve two masters; and purity of heart, the priority of the vision of God, oneness of devotion, were all related to the maintenance of the integrity of the total person.

The history of demonology, witchcraft, and exorcism, however, has been carefully studied by Gregory Zilboorg in relation to the way in which a restless surrender of both the church and medicine to doctrines of demonology made of medical psychology "a part of codified demon-ology, and the treatment of the mentally ill became for the most part a problem of legal procedure. The darkest ages of psychiatry set in." He also points out in another connection that the vast fear of demons contributed to what he calls "epidemics of insanity produced by moral contagion." [5]

The two Dominican Inquisitors, Henry Kramer and James Sprenger, wrote their legal handbook [6] for the diagnosis and punishment of persons who were possessed of witches, demons, and evil spirits. The fact that many elaborately detailed discussions of what today would be considered psychiatric disorders appear in the work of these men is ample evidence to validate Zilboorg's statement.

Scientific observers have been quick to evaluate the profound psy-chological dimensions of the religio-legal conceptions of demonology. A process of reinterpretation of these phenomena was initiated by Sigmund Freud. In a paper written in 1923 Freud says:

> . . . despite the somatic ideology of the era of "exact" science, the demono-
> logical theory of these dark ages has in the long run justified itself. . . . What
> in those days were thought to be evil spirits to us are base and evil wishes,
> the derivatives of impulses which have been rejected and repressed. In one
> respect only do we not subscribe to the explanation of these phenomena
> current in mediaeval times; we have abandoned the projection of them into
> the outer world, attributing their origin instead to the inner life of the patient
> to whom they manifest themselves.[7]

Freud goes on to interpret the possession of the soul of the demoniacally possessed patient, of whom he had a record from 1669, in terms of his basic presupposition that the "Devil" was "chosen as a substitute for a father figure." He assumes that God and the Devil "were originally one and the same, a single figure which was later split in the two bearing opposed characteristics." [8] He also says that, "If the benevolent and righteous God is a father substitute, it is not to be wondered at that the hostile attitude, which leads to hate, fear and accusations against him, comes to expression in the figure of satan. The father is thus the individual prototype of God and the Devil." [9] Freud rightly challenges the naïve projection of evil and base wishes (which have been rejected and repressed) upon the outer world, which is certainly obvious in acutely disturbed, mentally ill people. Particularly is this true of the paranoid schizophrenic who externalizes the conscience and reads it back into himself as persecution. However, the more we seek to plumb the illimitable depths of the self, the more we ask the question about Freud's neat distinction between the inner and outer worlds. Is that which is objectively real only that which is on the outside of our geographically definable self? Is, as Gardner Murphy queried, our skin the dividing line between that which is subjective and that which is objective? Obviously, Augustine was much closer to the truth when he affirmed the reality of a Self other than the self within the self.

Carl G. Jung challenges the solipsism of Freud at this point. He says:

> . . . no, the unconscious is everything but a capsulated, personal system; it is
> the wide world, and objectivity as open as the world. I am the object, even
> the subject of the object, in a complete reversal of my ordinary consciousness,
> where I am always a subject that has an object. There I find myself in the
> closest entanglement with the world, so much a part of it that I oft forget
> all too easily who I really am. 'Lost in oneself' is a good phrase to describe
> this state. But this self is the world if only a consciousness could see it. That
> is why we must know who we are.[10]

Jung epitomized this objectivity within the self in his concept of "archetypes" which he says derives from Augustine and is a term which may be used as "an explanatory paraphrase of the Platonic eidos." [11] Jung gave a place of separateness and independence to complex organizations of the personality which exist apart from consciousness and have a life of their own.

As Jung says:

> . . . whatever else may be taking place within the obscure recesses of the psyche—and there are notoriously many opinions as to this matter—one thing is certain: it is first and foremost the so called complexes (emotionally toned contents having a certain amount of autonomy) which play an important part there. The expression "autonomous complex" has often met with opposition, although, as it seems to me unjustifiably. The active contents of the unconscious do behave in a way I cannot describe better than by the word "autonomous." The . . . complexes . . . come and go as they please. . . . They have been split off from consciousness and lead a separate existence in the unconscious, being at all times ready to hinder or reinforce the conscious intensions.[12]

In fact, Jung points out that the archetype of the anima, for instance, takes us into the realm of the gods and is itself endowed with a numinous quality. The anima is just one of the many archetypes of the unconscious; it is chaotic life urge; it confronts us in our most personal life "as our most personal and bitter misunderstanding" with demonic character. "When, for instance, a highly honored scholar in his seventies deserts his family and marries a twenty year old, red haired actress, then we know that the gods have claimed another victim. It is thus that demonic supremacy shows itself to us. (In the middle ages it would have been much easier to do away with the young woman as a witch.)" [13]

Jung translates his concept of evil symbolically into a discussion of the Trinity. He says that "the Christian Godhead is One in Three Persons. The fourth person in the heavenly drama is unquestionably the devil." He posits a quaternity rather than a trinity in the Godhead. Jung goes on to interpret this in terms of ethics:

> . . . according to moral valuation he (the Devil) is man's sin; therefore, it is a function belonging to him and hence masculine. The femininity in the Godhead is kept a secret and to say that the Holy Ghost is Sofia counts as a heresy. . . . The fourth function is contaminated with the unconscious in its train. Then we come to a settlement with the unconscious and must attempt to bring about a synthesis with the opposites. But first of all that breaks out the violent conflicts that would beset any reasonable man when it became evident that he must swallow the absurd superstitions.[14]

In the light of these concepts Carl G. Jung emphasizes the importance of our doctrine of original sin and the inveterate way in which man reformulates and restates this doctrine when his rationalism has made him too proud to accept it intellectually.

However, from a distinctly theological point of view, we must be wary of the gnostic connotations of the preceding doctrine. Jung does not come to grips with the ontological problem, and in his remythologization of the unconscious, he imputes a kind of reality to the devil as he does to God. He does not bring them under the criticism of the categories of created and uncreated beings nor does he make note of the essentially counterfeit kind of apparent reality, barred from a higher source, and vaunting themselves as being "on an equality with God." Victor White presents it in this way:

> . . . finally, it must be made clear that we do not of course contend that "devils" and "complexes" are altogether synonymous and interchangeable terms. When the theologian says that somebody is afflicted by the devil, he is describing his situation in relation to God. When the psychologist says he is suffering from an unassimilated autonomous complex, he is describing an inherent, functional disorder. He speaks a different language; each describes an observed occurrence from a different point of view, or as the scholastics would say, in a different *ratio formalis qua.* Our contention is that the meanings of the two sets of terms (the theological and the psychopathological) are, however, not mutually exclusive; and we would offer for expert consideration the suggestion that, while the meanings are different, each term may be, and commonly is, referable to the selfsame phenomenon or occurrence.[15]

Another important set of clinical observations was published much earlier by Morton Prince in his book, *The Dissociation of a Personality*.[16] He made a biographical study in abnormal psychology of a certain "Miss Christine L. Beauchamp" in whom several different and distinct personalities developed. Her personality would change from time to time, often from hour to hour. With each change her character would become transformed and her memories altered. Prince says:

> . . . in addition to the real, original or normal self, the self that was born and which she was intended by nature to be, she may be any one of three different persons. I say three different, because, although making use of the same body, each, nevertheless, has a distinctly different character; a difference manifested by different trains of thought, by different views, beliefs, ideals, and temperament, and by different acquisitions, tastes, habits, experiences, and memories. Each varies in these respects from the other two and from the original Miss Beauchamp. Two of these personalities have no knowledge of each other or of the third, excepting such information as may be obtained by inference or second hand, so that in the memory of each of these two there are blanks which correspond to the times when the others are in the flesh. All of a sudden one or the other wakes to find herself, she knows not where, and ignorant of what she has said or done a moment before. Only one of three has knowledge of the lives of the others, and this one presents such a bizarre character, so far removed from the others in individuality, that the transformation from one of the other personalities to herself is one of the most striking and dramatic features of the case. The personalities come and go in kaleidoscopic succession, many changes often being made in the course of

twenty-four hours. And it so happens that Miss Beauchamp, if I may use the name to designate several distinct people, at one moment says and does and plans and arranges something to which a short time before she most strongly objected, indulges tastes which a moment before would have been abhorrent to her ideals, and undoes or destroys what she has just laboriously planned and arranged.[17]

Prince says that a correct term for designating such a personality is the "disintegrated personality." He uses this term because each "secondary personality is a part only of a normal whole self." [18] Prince observed this person over a period of seven years from 1898 to 1904 inclusive.

Prince concludes that the mental cohesion of a person "necessarily yields to the disintegrating effects of the strains of life." After having recorded carefully over five hundred pages of clinical material concerning this one conglomerate personality, he felt that the circumstances of her life were such that it was impossible for her to have the freedom from care, anxiety, and responsibility as well as the mental and physical strains attached to these that a unified person should have. Through an extended process of therapy, Miss Beauchamp would appear again as herself. She could talk freely about herself as two of the three "other selves," B I and B IV. But she never was able to integrate her life, her doings, as "Sally," except indirectly.

Spencer L. Rogers, an anthropologist, gives additional data about demonic possession when he records the story of an eighteen-year-old boy in the Banks Islands. His report is very similar to the instance found in Mark 5:2–9.

> . . . he (the boy) complained of a headache. He went to sleep and awakened in a state called "possessed." He was extraordinarily strong, about eight men most of whom were powerful fellows, endeavoring vainly to hold him. In the intervals of these violent paroxysms he spoke, certainly in a voice quite unlike his own. A compatriot, staring into his eyes said to him, "What is your name?" "We are many," replied the possessed boy. "Is it so and so in you?" to which the possessed replied "yes" or "no" till it was ascertained who were in him (various dead relatives, some of whom were known to the writers).[19]

In the same context Rogers also calls attention to the fact that "occasionally a distinction is made" between types of spirits responsible for possession. He says that the peoples of Southern India ". . . recognize two classes of potentially possessing spirits which may cause insanity. One type of demon is the spirit of an ancestor who has been slighted through failure to show him the proper ceremonial respect. The other type of demon takes in a large class of local supernatural beings. A competent exorcist is able to drive out either type and thus cure madness." [20] The spirit of a departed and dead loved one—or hated one—or both—certainly is introjected in the experience of bereavement. Even in more technological cultures one sees a severely bereaved person taking on the mannerisms, the voice, and even following the habits of a dead member of his family. Likewise, the residual results of the long years of identification with a person now dead tend to come forth, in the stress of grief.

One has only to read Shakespeare's *Hamlet* to see the possessing and demonic power of departed spirits upon the lives of those who remain. These insights are extremely relevant to the dynamics of bereavement, and the research of Lindemann and others on grief accentuate the psychological relevance of the primitive beliefs on demonic spirits. (A survey of this material is to be found in chapter 3 of my own book, *Anxiety and Christian Experience*.) [21]

However, we do not have to go to primitive society for insight into the fragmented personality. The multiplicity of selves is starkly apparent in the following autobiographical report of Thomas Wolfe.

> . . . in Paris I couldn't sleep at all—I walked the streets from night to morning and was in the worse shape I have ever been in my life. All the pent up strain and tension of the last few months seemed to explode and I will confess to you that there were times there when I really was horribly afraid I was going mad —all the unity and control of personality seemed to have escaped from me—it was as if I were on the back of some immense rackety engine which was running wild and over which I had no more control than a fly. I came home to my hotel one night—or rather at daybreak one morning—tried to get off to sleep—and had the horrible experience of seeming to disintegrate into at least six people—I was in bed and suddenly it seemed these other shapes of myself were moving out of me—all around me—one of them touched me by the arm—another was talking in my ear—others walking around the room—and suddenly I would come to with a terrific jerk and all of them would rush back into me again. I can swear to you I was not asleep—it was one of the strangest and most horrible experiences I have ever had. There were about three days of which I could give no clear accounting—and loss of memory of that sort is to me one of the worse things that can happen. [22]

Although such inner turmoil as Wolfe describes is agonizing to him, it also points to the creative power of such suffering. Just because a portion of the self may be considered as other than the self does not necessarily mean that it is evil. In fact, it may even mean that the creative, redemptive, and wholesome necessities of life in a given individual are being denied, thwarted, and ruled out of existence. For example, Socrates interpreted the *daimonion* as the guiding voice of his life to which he listened! The creative writing of Thomas Wolfe may even have been burgeoned out of the suffering which he described. In fact, he thought that it was.

SOME RELIGIOUS IMPLICATIONS OF THE PSYCHOLOGY OF DEMONISM

The foregoing discussion has revealed extensive overlapping in the discussion of biblical, historical, and contemporary beliefs in demons, on the one hand, and the scientific statements concerning mental illness on the other hand. Some basic clarifications are needed here. This is an overlapping, but we find confusion *ad infinitum* when the overlapping is taken to be an exact equation of identity. For instance, periodically popular interpretations of the story of the Gadarene demoniac appear in sermons, both spoken and written. Jesus is likened to "the world's greatest psychiatrist"; the treatment he gives to the demoniac is likened to shock therapy, the prefrontal lobotomy, tranquillizing drugs, or whatever happens to be the current discovery in the treatment of mental illness. Such absurdities miss the depth dimensions both of contemporary psychiatry and of the message inherent in the situation-that-was at the time of Jesus' encounter with the demoniac.

On the other hand, one gets the impression that similar absurdities appear when attempts are made to equate contemporary diagnostic categories of mental illness with the few threads of information about the actual disorders of persons in the biblical stories. In both these instances the overlapping nature of the prescientific and scientific descriptions of similar phenomena is turned into an exact equation. Such an exact equation is misleading. One does better to think of demonology as an intuitive and ontological approach to human suffering. Psychotherapeutic approaches are more empirical and observational in nature. The interpretation of behavior as madness and as demon possession both occur in Mark 3:19–27. One cannot say that one is ancient and the other is modern. Rather, the biblical world was not unlike our own: both the interpretation of emotional disturbance as illness and the interpretation of emotional disturbance as demon possession exist side by side both in the New Testament world and today's world. The resurgence of demonology in the early 1970s is proof positive of this hypothesis.

MORE RECENT PERSPECTIVES OF PSYCHOPATHOLOGY AND RELIGION

Valuable understanding of the relationship of religion and mental illness can be gained through the eyes of several explorers of the issues who have more recently done their work.

Søren Kierkegaard (1813–55), who himself suffered much emotional distress, perceived himself at various intervals as a Christian psychologist. He thought of emotional disorder under the concept of despair, which he called "the sickness unto death." "To despair over oneself, in despair to will to be rid of oneself, is the formula for all despair." He saw despair as being self-rejection due to imbalances in at least three great polarities in the human self.

First, despair arises out of an imbalance between the self's awareness of finitude and infinitude. One can become so intoxicated with infinitude that his finiteness or limitations beset him with despair. "The God-relationship infinitizes; but this may so carry a man away that it becomes inebriation; it may seem to a man as though it were unendurable to exist before God—for the reason that a man cannot return to himself, cannot become himself. Such a fantastic religious individual would say (to characterize him by putting into his mouth these lines), 'That a sparrow can live is comprehensible; it does not know anything about existing before God. But to know that one exists before God—and then not to go crazy or be brought to naught!' " (These quoted words are actually autobiographical words from Kierkegaard's journal.) It is as if the person who infinitizes is thrown into despair because he confronts genuine and ultimate infinity in God. Or, the verse can be a source of despair. To be overwhelmed with finitude and lack much if any sense of infinity is "to be desperately narrow minded and mean-spirited." This person's despair arises out of being blended into the nothingness of finitude—"not by evaporation in the infinite, but by being entirely finitized, by having become, instead of a self, a number, just one man more, one more repetition of this everlasting *Einerlei* (sameness). . . . such a man forgets . . . what his name is (in the divine understanding of it), does not dare to believe in himself, finds it too venturesome a thing to be himself, far easier and safer to be like the others, to become an imitation, a number, a cipher in the crowd. . . . This form of despair is hardly ever noticed in the world. Such a man, precisely by losing his self in this way, has gained perfectibility in adjusting himself to business, yea, in making a success in the world. . . . So far from being in despair, he is (considered to be) just what a man ought to be." [23]

Second, Kierkegaard views despair of the spirit of self in terms of the polarity between possibility and necessity. Both possibility and necessity, on balance, are ingredients of healthy selfhood before God. When possibility outstrips necessity, it falls into the despair of possibility. The self lacks reality, and "one says of a man that he has become unreal." In fact, though, "it is really necessity the man lacks." By necessity, Kierkegaard means "the power to obey, to submit to the necessary in oneself, to what may be called one's limit." In ignoring obedience, submission, and limits, one may live in a wishful, yearning world or a melancholy fantastic world, resulting in either unrealistic hopes or unrealistic dread.

The other side of this polarity is that a person may be in despair over necessity and is defeated by the fell clutch of circumstance around him. He sees no hope, possibility, or fresh alternative. He will even curse anyone who attempts to show him a ray of hope in the face of his situation. Salvation for him is impossible. He cannot believe, he says. This is reminiscent of the mentally ill person who is obsessed with the feeling that he has committed the unpardonable sin and that there is no possibility of redemption for him. This is one of the most common kinds of pathological religious expressions. This person is a fatalist—he has neither a self of his own nor God. "His god is necessity." He is unable to pray. "So to pray is to breathe, and possibility is for the self what oxygen is for breathing. But for possibility alone or necessity alone to supply the conditions for the breathing of prayer is no more possible than it is for a man to breathe oxygen or nitrogen alone. For in order to pray there must be a God, there must be a self plus possibility, or a self and possibility in the pregnant sense; for God *is* that all things are possible, and all things are possible is God; and only the man whose being has been so shaken that he became spirit by understanding that all things are possible, only he has dealing with God. . . . If God's will is only the necessary, man is essentially as speechless as the brutes." [24]

The third polarity Kierkegaard poses is the polarity between *consciousness* and *unconsciousness*. The more conscious a person becomes, the more threatening his despair. Kierkegaard says that the devil is complete consciousness, and his despair is in absolute defiance. Over against this maximum despair is the sort of innocence that does not even know that there is such a thing as despair. Yet, in the latter instance, a person is also unaware of himself as a spirit, a true self. He is essentially spiritless. One, therefore, is caught in the despair of not willing to be a self, being afraid of consciousness. This is the despair of inadequacy or of weakness. Or, there is the despair of defiance in willing despairingly to be oneself, to be a conscious self in an isolated, self-sufficient manner.

These three polarities—off balance—are the source of pathological expressions of religion, according to Kierkegaard. On balance, they are the source of health. He says, "Health consists essentially in being able to resolve contradictions. So it is bodily or physically: a draft is indifferently cold and warm; disparate qualities undialectically combined; but a healthy body resolves this contradiction and does not notice the draft. So it is with faith." [25]

Another foray into the relation between psychopathology and religion was set into motion by David Friedrich Strauss who undertook in 1835 to establish that Jesus was a morbid personality. This was taken up by H. J. Holtzmann and Adolf Julicher about 1907. In 1905 de Loosten, Hirsch in 1912, and Binet-Sanglé—all medical doctors—sought to establish that Jesus was mentally ill, had hallucinations, and in Hirsch's interpretation, was suffering from paranoia. Albert Schweitzer, in his doctoral dissertation, *The Psychiatric Study of Jesus,* in 1913 sought to refute these assertions on medical grounds. He concluded that experiences of auditory and visual revelations do not necessarily appear only in mentally ill persons, but also in well persons. In response to these men and to

Emil Rasmussen, who held similar views, Schweitzer concludes, "The medical value of a comparative study of the kind he undertakes is to be rated as exactly zero." [26] Winfred Overholser, at that time president of the American Psychiatric Association, in her introduction to the present edition of Schweitzer's book, says that Binet-Sanglé and others take the writings about Jesus out of their context and to do so is psychiatrically unsound. [27]

Anton Boisen, in 1936, commenting on the work of the above psychiatrists and that of Schweitzer, says that the significant thing about Jesus was not the presence or absence of what to us would be labeled as pathological. Rather, the important thing was that in all his struggles of the soul he emerged triumphant. Boisen, who spent his life working as a chaplain with the mentally ill and who suffered three psychotic episodes himself, says, ". . . in Jesus [there was] poise and serenity and beauty of character. There was a fine adaptation to the world of things as they are. There was the calm and courageous acceptance of a heavy burden of responsibility. There was a mind attuned to that which is timeless. And the explanation is to be found in accordance with the best attested of all his sayings." [28] Jesus and followers of his, like George Fox and John Bunyan, "had given up their lives and found them again, fairer and more filled with power than they had been before, whereas most of our hospital patients would be those who sought to save their lives and had lost them." [29]

Boisen's study of one hundred seventy-eight cases revealed that one hundred thirty cases gave evidence of what he calls concealment reactions, which are in Boisen's categories malignant reactions. These reactions included externalization of conscience (one hundred thirteen cases), fictitious self-importance (ten cases), incapacitation of function (twenty-nine cases). However, in nineteen cases there were evidences of self-blame, a sign which Boisen interprets as indicative of a good prognosis and possible recovery. Other reactions were drifting reactions and panic reactions. Concerning panic reactions, Boisen contended that the sufferers "experienced one of those profound regressions which represents a journey to the lower regions, that grim wilderness of the lost which we are seeking to explore." [30] Those acute disturbances which are accompanied with ideas of death, of cosmic catastrophe, and cosmic identification Boisen regarded as "attempts to break up the sets and attitudes which stand in the way of normal growth and functioning and to make possible a reorganization." [31] They may change a malignant formation into a benign one. Religious concern is generally present, and a study of religious experience at its best is necessary to evaluate properly the meaning of these states of consciousness. This Boisen did in his copious works. He did so by studying successful explorers such as Bunyan, Fox, and others. Then he made comparisons of these persons with patients he had known. Interpreting Boisen faithfully as one of his students, I would say that he steadfastly refused to interpret as "sick" some kinds of experiences that are usually interpreted as mental illnesses. To him, these were the more serious kinds of religious experience, working like an acute fever in the person to heal him of a wrong way of life.

More recently, certain psychiatrists have devoted specific attention to psychopathology and religion. James Knight, writing his book, *A Psychiatrist Looks at Religion*, deals with highly specific case data in detail. He provides reliable clues for the way in which mental illness may come garbed in the form of religious symptomatology. Yet, he says, "It is never the religious expression as such that leads to the diagnosis of mental illness, but an assessment of the total situation within which that expression arises."[32] The great value of the book is his use of specific case material on such problems as suicide, the fear of attending church, the care of the dying, false pregnancy in a male, and so on.

Another helpful approach to the relation of religion to mental illness has been devised by Edgar Draper. In a double-blind research study, he demonstrated conclusively that the religious ideation of patients is diagnostically useful and reliable. In fact, the patient will in some instances respond to a direct handling of his religious concerns and progress toward wholeness of life more rapidly than if dealt with in purely psychiatric or psychoanalytic categories. Draper assumes the expertise of a psychiatrist and/or a disciplined pastoral counselor in such treatment.[33]

Mansell Pattison is another psychiatrist who, in addition to editing a helpful volume entitled *Clinical Psychiatry and Religion*,[34] has done serious work, as has already been noted in this volume, on specific subjects such as glossolalia. Probably one of the most helpful papers he has written is on forgiveness and unforgiveness. He identifies pathological religious phenomena with a punitive model of forgiveness and healthy expressions of religious faith with a reconciliation model of forgiveness.[35] In another article, he says that "belief systems, whether they be religious or otherwise, then are both necessary and influential in personality development."

My own conclusions about the relation of psychopathology and religion have been recorded in two books: *Religious Factors in Mental Illness*[36] and *When Religion Gets Sick*.[37] In conclusion of this chapter, I summarize my own observations about psychopathology and religion.

First, religion participates as a causative factor in mental illness when punitive forms of religion are used as a means of controlling a child in his earliest years. Usually this kind of religion may more accurately be classified as superstitions which are used to inflict anger on a small child.

Second, religion participates in emotional disorder when it is a religion of nostalgia that ties a person to the past, particularly in the experience of bereavement and loss. Spencer Rogers's observations about primitive persons being possessed by the spirit of the dead is easily observed in the religious ruminations of the mentally ill. Therefore, the pastoral care and counseling, the emotional therapy of the bereaved, is a vital part of both preventing and treating the mentally ill. In essence, religion becomes sick when a person worships the dead. This happens in sophisticated as well as primitive persons.

Third, religion becomes sick when it is the vehicle of maintaining a constricted territory for a growing person. The need for one's own place in life is a matter of life and breath. To be denied it in the name of religion adds insult to injury in the wounding of the mental stability of a person.

Fourth, religion becomes sick when in the name of religion a person is encouraged to avoid the developmental tasks of life and to refuse to make the great transitions from one stage of life to another. Acute episodes such as those Boisen mentioned occur at these times. The prognosis is very good with this "transitional mental disorder," as the *Diagnostic and Statistical Manual of Mental Disorders* calls them, granted that adequate and prompt therapy is available.

Fifth, religion participates malignantly in mental disorders when a person persistently shifts blame to others, refuses to forgive others, to accept their humanity, and organizes his life around a permanent sense of unforgivingness.

Finally, much that is called religion in the life of mentally ill patients is a last-straw concern of the person before he collapses emotionally and is only peripheral to his life history. Ordinarily this is more superstition and magic than it is religion.

NOTES

1. Edward Langton, *Essentials of Demonology: A Study of Jewish and Christian Dogma, Its Origin and Development* (London: Eppleworth Press, 1945), p. 145.
2. Ibid.
3. S. Vernon McCasland, *By the Finger of God: Demon Possession and Exorcism in Early Christianity in the Light of Modern Views of Mental Illness* (New York: Macmillan, 1951), p. 26. Used by permission.
4. Leslie D. Weatherhead, *Psychology, Religion and Healing* (London: Hodder and Stoughton, 1951), p. 99.
5. Gregory Zilboorg, *A History of Medical Psychology* (New York: W. W. Norton & Co., 1941), pp. 142–43.
6. Henry Kramer and James Sprenger, *Malleus Maleficarum* (London: Pushkin Press, 1948).
7. Sigmund Freud, "A Neurosis of Demoniacal Possession in the 17th Cen-

tury," *Collected Papers,* trans. Joanne Riviere (London: Hogarth Press, 1949) 4: 436 ff.

  8. Ibid., p. 450.

  9. Ibid., p. 451.

  10. C. G. Jung, *The Integration of Personality,* ed. Stanley Del (New York: Farrar and Rinehart, 1939), p. 70. Used by permission of Routledge & Kegan Paul, Ltd., copyright 1948.

  11. Ibid., p. 53.

  12. C. G. Jung, *Modern Man in Search of a Soul* (New York: Harcourt, Brace & Co., 1933), p. 91. Used by permission.

  13. ————, *The Integration of Personality,* p. 80.

  14. Ibid., pp. 156–57.

  15. Victor White, *God and the Unconscious* (London: Harvill Press, 1952), p. 189. Used by permission.

  16. Morton Prince, *The Dissociation of a Personality* (New York: Longmans, Green & Co., 1913). Used by permission.

  17. Ibid.

  18. Ibid., p. 3.

  19. Spencer L. Rogers, "Early Psychotherapy," *Ciba Symposia,* vol. 9, nos. 1, 2 (April–May 1947), pp. 604–5.

  20. Ibid.

  21. Wayne E. Oates, *Anxiety and Christian Experience* (Waco, Texas: Word Books, 1972).

  22. Elizabeth Nowell, ed., *The Letters of Thomas Wolfe* (New York: Charles Scribner's Sons, 1956), p. 438. Used by permission.

  23. Søren Kierkegaard, *The Sickness unto Death* (Princeton, N.J.: Princeton University Press, 1941), pp. 44–51.

  24. Ibid., p. 63.

  25. Ibid., p. 61.

  26. Albert Schweitzer, *A Psychiatric Study of Jesus* (Boston: Beacon Press, 1958).

  27. Ibid., p. 14.

  28. Boisen, *Exploration of the Inner World,* pp. 137–38.

  29. Ibid.

  30. Ibid., p. 39.

  31. Ibid., p. 56.

  32. James Knight, *A Psychiatrist Looks at Religion* (New York: Abingdon, 1964), p. 98.

  33. Edgar Draper, George E. Meyer, Zene Parzen, and Gene Samuelson, "On the Diagnostic Value of Religious Ideation," *Archives of General Psychiatry* (September 1965) 13: 202–7. See also Edgar Draper, *Psychiatry and Pastoral Care* (Philadelphia: Fortress Press, 1965).

  34. Pattison, *Clinical Psychiatry and Religion.*

  35. ————, "On the Failure to Forgive or to Be Forgiven," *American Journal of Psychotherapy* (1965) 19: 106.

  36. Wayne E. Oates, *Religious Factors in Mental Illness* (Association Press, 1955).

  37. ————, *When Religion Gets Sick* (Philadelphia: Westminster Press, 1971).

QUESTIONS FOR FURTHER STUDY

1. To what extent is affiliation with a church related to mental illness? Do different faith groups have different ratios of mental disorder among their communicants?

2. To what extent is the problem of social justice for the poor a concern that is related to mental illness? Read Reissman, Cohen, and Pearl, *Mental Health of the Poor,* and ask what connection there is between ethical standards of middle-class churches and synagogues and the more secular standards of what mental health is.

3. Read Milton Rokeach's book, *Three Christs of Ypsilanti,* concerning persons who thought themselves to be Christ. Compare this with what Anton Boisen said about Jesus.

4. Are you afraid people will think you a bit crazy if you express aloud your deepest religious feelings?

19

TOWARD A PSYCHOLOGY
OF FAITH

One persistent question ties the foregoing chapters into something of a unity: What are some of the psychological dimensions of faith? The attempt to deal responsibly with this question both correlates and summarizes much that is in the preceding pages. At the same time it gives an overall perspective, hopefully, to the meaning of faith in the life of individuals and communities.

Faith involves relationships between beings. These relationships are ultimately personal. In Hebrew, the most important terms for faith mean "firmness" or "stability" of the trust that one places in another. In New Testament Greek, the relationship of faith is focused upon God. One believes in God as one who is self-revealing and has basic good will toward those who worship him. To some extent the word is used to mean "to trust," "to have confidence in," and "to experience trustworthiness."

With this rather basic understanding of what we mean by the word *faith,* several conclusions as to a psychology of faith can be identified in the review of some of the basic assumptions that run through the preceding chapters.

"RELIGION" VERSUS FAITH

As was noted earlier, Harry Emerson Fosdick said that what some psychologists have called religion, Jesus called sin. Definitions of religion reveal that Jesus was in the great tradition of the eighth-century prophets when he set himself against the empty forms of religion and asked for a dynamic, personal faith. He put the weightier matters of love and justice far above the minutiae of religious institutionalism. We discussed the burst-through of mystical experience. Profound and life-changing conversions, we said, are ordinarily not programmed. The experience of ecstasy and wonder has a way of shaking not only the foundations of a life lived apart from God, but also the foundations of the smugly religious person. It is a threat to both. In all of these the life of faith is a life that breaks the old wineskins. New vessels are necessary to contain it, if indeed it can be contained. Therefore, we can conclude that this book is not necessarily an apology for institutional religion. Neither has it always said what the programmers of religious behavior would want said. To the contrary, valuable as these efforts are in a sociology of the religious life, a psychology of religion is primarily concerned with the deep personal and interpersonal experiences of faith.

RELIGIOUS NOSTALGIA VERSUS THE LEAP OF FAITH

The developmental approach to the spiritual life has been central in this book. Each transition in the developmental pilgrimage of a person or a group—ordinarily both in relation to each other under God—calls for a "leap of faith" as Kierkegaard called it. The life of faith calls for the courage to leap into the unknown. Such a decision is made in the serene assurance that all available knowledge is too little. Yet, the life ahead is decisively affirmed. Paul Tournier, in his book, *A Place for You,* depicts this leap of faith. He says that we live in a rhythm of life between quitting one place in life and seeking for another. He uses the analogy of a trapeze artist swinging on one bar to the utmost distance that it will take him. Then he leaps and reaches hopefully for another bar. The breathless suspense of the "mid-air placelessness" is the anxiety of faith. One's breath and that of all who observe is held until the transition has been safely made. This act of faith is no isolated "loner exercise" performed in an empty tent. To the contrary, the person is equipped with the heritage of a long history of men and women of faith. He is surrounded by a community of faith to whom this leap of faith is both inspiring and meaningful. This transition could never have been made if the person had not had the courage to take the leap. It probably would never have been made without the encouragement of a community of faith. They are a life-support system.

The biblical hero of faith, Abraham, portrays this in his power of decision: "By faith Abraham obeyed when he was called to go out to a place which he was to receive for an inheritance; and he went out, not knowing where he was to go. . . . For he looked forward to the city which has foundations, whose builder and maker is God" (Heb. 11:8, 10). The exact opposite of this is the person who shrinks back from such a demand. Instead he ruminates anxiously on the memories of the past and the security of the visible, the tangible, and the certain. In the great developmental transitions of life from birth to death, one faces this choice. To hang back, to let the demands of new growth go past and pile up, may be possible for the religious person, but not for the person of faith. The kind of religion that ensues is a religion of nostalgia, that is, homesickness for the way things were. The whole of developmental psychology is relevant to this choice of a life of faith and the rejection of a religion of nostalgia.

FAITH AS AMBIGUITY TOLERANCE

However, to exercise a faith that leaps is to face the ambiguities mentioned in the last chapter by Kierkegaard. The contradictions between infinitude and finitude, possibility and necessity, consciousness and unconsciousness, pose all kinds of ambiguities for a person to learn to tolerate. The life of faith in this sense, as Seward Hiltner has often said, is affirmation of existence in the presence of ambiguity. One could call this ambiguity tolerance. Life, for example, is always presenting a person with specific kinds of separation. Those to whom he has cleaved must be left, and they leave as well. Josiah Royce gave a detailed portrait of such fidelity in the discussion of loyalty and conscience. Yet one faces the possibility of being loyal to a fault, of demanding that one's community of loyalty always stay the same, static and unchanged. As Hiltner says, "There seem to be two guidelines about trust that emerge from the study of those awful experiences (Nazi concentration camps). One is that trust should always be, in some proportion, corollary with trustworthiness (or its absence) of others. Hence, it is impossible to have trust without having also discriminating mistrust of the untrustworthy. The other is that trust, while it may be had alone up to a point, tends to be brittle without adequate group support." [1]

An atmospheric difference abides between the faith that embraces ambiguity and the religion that is built on easy either-or naïvetés. A childlike pietism and religious naïveté surrounds those who feel that the life of faith will always and in every instance bring happiness, comfort, freedom from suffering. A hard-nosed realism of a Job who refused to see his suffering as a sign of great sin on his part pervades a faith that accepts ambiguity. A Job-like faith assumes that suffering is borne best and faith is sustained most resiliently in the midst of a company of committed friends. Such a faith has room for pain. Pain makes for thought. Thought generates wisdom. Wisdom makes pain bearable.

MAGIC AND FAITH

The life of faith ceases to be faith and becomes a clever deal with a capricious God when used as a childlike state of managing, bargaining with, and playing magic with God. The life of faith is correspondent with the life of love in relation to God. The love of God is experienced unconditionally. Faith in God is expressed unconditionally. The life of magic places conditions upon one's faith. It is the life, not of faith, but of protasis. In grammar, a protasis is a conditional phrase or clause which precedes a given commitment or statement. We say: *"If* you will do this, *then* I will do thus and so." In prayer, we may say: "If you will heal me, then I will do what yóu ask, O God." To the contrary, a life of faith is more like the life apodosis. Job said, "Though he slay me, yet will I trust him." The Hebrew men said to Nebuchadnezzar when he threatened them with the fiery furnace, "If it be so, our God whom we serve is able to deliver us from the burning fiery furnace; and he will deliver us out of your hand, O king. But if not, be it known unto you, O king, that we will not serve your gods or worship the golden image which you have set up" (Dan. 3:17–18, rsv). Similarly, the perils of life, death, principalities, powers, nor any creature can separate a person of faith from the love of God (Rom. 8:38). Death itself is dead. Beyond this condition, no condition in life is of any avail. As Hiltner again says, "If there is trust, one does not have to push God into fine print."[2] If indeed God is our friend-in-trust, we do not—symbolically speaking—have to keep a carbon copy of our agreements with him in order to check up on him.

FAITH AS "HELPED UNBELIEF"

One of the recurrent themes of the preceding chapters has been that religious faith is basic trust translated through the parent or parent substitutes into an individual's confidence in their trustworthiness. If this is shattered by repeated abandonment, defection, and loss, then the person's capacity to form attachments, make commitments, and exercise fidelity is rendered impotent. He lives a life of unbelief in the sense that he cannot really believe that anyone cares for him enough to be trustworthy.

At the outset, we adopted a phenomenological perspective of psychology. This is a self-emptying attempt to gain entry into the confidence and trust of another by the removal of threat, suspicion, fear, and doubt —by the establishment of a faith relationship, in other words.

Yet, to seemingly increasing numbers of alienated and uncommitted persons, this kind of effort seems unreal, too good to be true. The charge of phoniness, the deliberate and not-so-deliberate testing for reality, and the declaration of helplessness in really believing are monotonous themes in serious discussions of faith in God or man. To a large degree, this describes the condition of human beings as human beings. One can have had loving parents who stood by through thick and thin and—with all their efforts to be effective parents—never forsook or fooled their sons and daughters. Even then the maturation of faith in God remains helplessly unformed.

The meaning of faith in the face of this kind of studied or learned helplessness is that it is a "helped unbelief." Running deep beneath the powerlessness and impotence is a repetitive game that seeks the pay-off of dominating the attention of ostensibly powerful people. The main help of unbelief is the investment of confidence and trust in a person that he can stand on his own two feet before God and will do so if the religious community consistently expects it of him. However, there is the rub. Some sentimental soul is always at hand who needs to help more than this unbeliever needs help. He becomes a sucker for the repetitive game. Consequently, the person, when confronted by one member of the community about being on his own before God, flees to another person who will not expect this of him. Ian Maclaren early identified this person as the "sermon-taster." Today we see him in the chronic counsel-seeker who may have as many as five or six religious counselors at once.

More positively, however, faith seen from the vantage point of the helped unbeliever can be described as the "lonely stand before God." Kierkegaard called it existing as a self before God. Martin Buber called it the "single one" in the Presence of the Eternal. The community of faith can be a tutor to Tournier's trapeze-artist imagery of the person of faith. The community can resonate with and participate vicariously with the person as he makes the leap of faith. In the final analysis, that one person takes the leap. To change the figure of speech, no one can take my stand before God for me. In this sense, each person bears his own burden of the faith relationship. The reward is that each person has his own place in the love of God.

The point of view expressed here suggests the most specific criticism of the phenomenological approach to human relationships. Not even the Lord Jesus Christ was easily received by some people in his earthly ministry. He came unto his own and his own received him not. The Jewish philosopher, Martin Buber, in dialogue with Carl Rogers, says that the human situation itself poses a dilemma:

> But of course, there are limits, and I may be allowed to tell you certainly in your experience as a therapist, as a healing person or helping to healing, you must experience it again and again—the limits to simple humanity. To simple humanity meaning being I and my partner, so to speak, alike to one another, on the same plane. I see you mean being on the same plane, but you cannot. There is not only you, your mode of thinking, your mode of doing, there is also a certain situation—we are so and so—which may sometimes be tragic, even more terrible than what we call tragic. You cannot change this. Humanity, human will, human understanding, are not everything. There is some reality confronting us. We cannot forget it for a moment.[3]

FAITH AS AN ACT OF SURRENDER

The discussion of conversion pointed to the viability of conversion as being most likely in the act of total surrender. This kind of conversion has the deepest consequences, as has been demonstrated clinically in studies of converted alcoholics, drug addicts, and work addicts. This act of faith that enables a person to give up a destructive way of life has several dimensions.

First, such faith involves a surrender of one's childish sense of omnipotence, that is, an acute sense of total responsibility for everything other people do. One sees it in clinicians of every kind—doctors, ministers, social workers, psychologists, and so on—who feel themselves a failure unless they can be everything and totally succeed with persons in their care. One sees it in parents who accept total responsibility for the thoughts, values, and acts of their children. Faith as an act of surrender in such situations can be expressed in the account of a World War II soldier who volunteered for combat without his father's explicit approval. Upon sailing for Europe, his father said to him, "Son, your mother and I have done all for you we can. You're on your own now. You have made your bed and you will just have to lie in it." Then nearly thirty years later he says, "I thought he was angry, then. But being a father now, I can see he was telling me that he cared but that there were limits beyond which he could not go in doing so." He exercised an act of surrender, or a life of faith, in order to survive the pain, the anxiety, and the helplessness of seeing his son in war.

Yet, surrender is not a once-for-all giving up of one's need to be totally responsible and all-powerful. It is a daily, twenty-four-hour-at-a-time exercise of faith. It must be done again and again, not as a work of merit but as a means of spiritual survival as a finite self in one's own right before God. Without this faith, all sorts of substitutes—drugs, alcohol, work—become the insulation of terror, the inducers of sleep.

Second, such an act of faith as surrender has a psychosomatic dimension. When one feels that he must be omnipotent and totally responsible, the physiology of the body is subjected to unnecessary stress. The anger one feels in his impotence mobilizes his body to fight or run. The ceaseless activity he engages in to distract his attention from his loss of control of other people and fortuitous events—such as war, for example—increases the amount of fatigue from day to day. Therefore, the already-existing disorders of the body become more aggravated. If there is pain, there will be more pain. The stress itself will cause the flare-up of symptoms that otherwise would have remained dormant. If the symptoms bring any secondary gains of sympathy, community, or family support, a person may be prone to adopt the illness as a way of life. The alarm stage of stress becomes the protest stage of the person's inner child of the past; the resistance stage of stress becomes the despair stage of the child state; the exhaustion stage of stress becomes the apathy stage of the child state.

This hitting bottom, as the Alcoholics Anonymous call it, can be a prelude to faith in that it tends to be a prerequisite for the act of surrender. As such giving-up and giving-in is an act of faith that aims at the person accepting his own humanity and ceasing and desisting from defying the limits of his body.

Faith As the Discipline of Fantasy and Affirmation of Reality

Manifestly, to think of oneself as being without limits is a fantasy. To have faith calls for a discipline of this and other fantasies. Faith consists of an affirmation of reality and a renunciation of fantasy. Both faith and sin have their seedbed in fantasy. Fantasy defies the limits of life; a sense of reality defines the bounds of one's habitation. Fantasy, furthermore, is the stuff of which a religion of nostalgia is made. One acts as if the ongoing demands of a growing life are not there. He continues to function on an obsolete perception of his relationships, roles in life, and understanding of God.

An example of this is the person who despises anything that suggests religious or spiritual commitment. He does so on the basis of childhood experiences with parental religion and the church. He builds his stereotypes of all religious living out of the stuff of his childhood memories. Without factual examination of adult faith experiences, he lives a life of distrust and uncommitment on the basis of the fantasy formation surrounding real or imagined injustices brought from childhood. In fact, the person who comes to the claiming of faith as an adult without such experiences in childhood is fortunate in being free of these pockets of fantasy from his past.

Another example of the exercise of faith as a challenge of fantasy is often seen in the theological student who has an unrealistic and fantasy-idea as to what being a minister will be like. He has never seen the reality of the actual performance demands of the ministry. Therefore, he may have no faith in himself or God that assures him of a reasonably adequate performance as a minister. Or, he may have such an over-idealized set of fantasies about the ministry that the realities of being a minister either shock him or cause him never to try to do what the ministry both requires and has to offer. The increase of his faith comes to pass as he is given opportunity actually to function as a minister and at the same time to have an experienced minister to coach him. This is in itself an exercise of faith in God, in those to whom he ministers and in the person who coaches him.

A more acute example of faith as a renunciation of fantasy in behalf of reality is seen in the struggle of faith in a bereaved person. To accept the death of a loved person as really so is to renounce the fantasy that he is not really dead. The human mind is replete with devices of denial of death. It was Tennyson, in his *In Memoriam* written concerning the death of a close friend, who said, "We have but faith, we cannot know. For knowledge is of things we see. Yet we trust that it comes from thee, O God, let it grow from more to more."

However, a disclaimer needs to be entered here. Fantasy is not, in spite of the negative evidence to the contrary, totally unrelated to the life of faith. Some fantasies are far out of field from what we experience as reality, but reality is openended and awaits creation. Fantasy lies a bit beyond these open ends of reality. Even the delusional behavior and thought of acutely psychotic persons occasionally has a hook in reality. For example, in July 1945 I interviewed a psychotic patient who was terrified because he thought atoms were splitting in the air and to breathe such air would kill or maim a person. The next month, atom bombs were dropped on Hiroshima and Nagasaki! This does not prove anything. However, we can say that inventions, art, and even systems of thought have their beginning in the fantasy of persons. Faith, in their instance, meant believing in their fantasy's relation to reality to such extent that they both worked and demonstrated that their fantasy could be translated into reality. The crazy ideas of one generation can be an intriguing list of science fiction for the next, the scientific exploration of the next, and the everyday occurrence of the next. However, these fantasies are disciplined, the objects of remarkable commitment, and the result of sustained faith of the person who believed in them.

FAITH AS THE EXPANSION OF ONE'S WORLD

The experience of faith can be the act of making oneself vulnerable, laying one's self open to the stranger, to the person who is different from us, to God between whom and us exists an "eternal qualitative difference." Such an act of faith is necessary for gaining increasing access to the larger family of mankind. God is encountered as one who is no respecter of the slight difference between persons. Someone has said that there is very little difference between human beings, but what little there is means a very great deal to us. Faith in God, freed of its provincialism, opens the shutters of one's soul to all manner of mankind. It means taking into oneself a candid picture of others as they are for their own sakes.

This is the beginning of the faith-community. Colston and Johnson speak as Christians and say:

We believe that the changing world view draws vitality and energy from hope generated by Christian faith. Faith which sees man's possibilities in a dying and rising Lord who cannot be restrained by systems or defeated even by death is the essential core of a liberating and facilitating community. Such a community embodies that faith and gives it concrete expression through its own incarnation.[4]

This expression affirms the role of faith in the adult experience of healthy religion. A certain poverty of spirit hungers for a wider participation than the sameness of those who are like us. The encounter of any other person calls for a crisis of faith—to believe in them or not to believe in them. If indeed God is no respecter of persons, then the insistence upon similarity of everything in the other person in order to make us secure is the opposite of faith. God as the wholly other is a claim of faith that provokes fear and trembling. We are filled with *Anfechtung*—a sense of holy dread. To worship such a God fills one with awe and reverence. Such a God is a consuming fire. He burns away our petty tyrannies arising from the claim to being different from other people.

FAITH AS ABANDON

In the context of our discussion of ecstasy, we can dramatize the meaning of faith as the release and deliverance known as total abandon. One becomes free of artificial constraints. He comes down out of the confines of artificial roles in life. He stands outside of the unnatural pretenses of official prerogatives as well as expectations. For example, a professor does not stand on the protocol of position. A student does not retreat into the subtle maneuvering for position as a student. In such an event, the encounter of God can possibly ensue in what has been called the ecstasy in education.

The prophet, Ezekiel, speaks of princes stepping down from their thrones, removing their robes and stripping off their embroidered garments. Instead they clothe themselves with trembling (Ezek. 26:16). Such abandon is an act of faith and is a prelude or trigger of ecstasy. The disengagement from the trappings of status, position, and office cannot be an irresponsible act that avoids the faithful functions required of one. However, preoccupation with the trappings of office—external symbols, public space, and the vanities of office—actually hinder creative function. The dignitary who stands on his protocol is likely to be a faithless administrator at the personal level. This is much of the stuff that makes a credibility gap. If one is secure enough in his position, has a steadfast faith in God and in those whom he serves, then he can with abandon give himself to his ministry. Role preoccupation short-circuits faith with anxiety of position. It is a deterrent to the authentic life.

In marriage, faith in one's partner's judgment and fidelity is expressed in the abandon of intimate sexual union. Abandon is an evidence of trust and faith in a man-woman relationship. The preoccupation of persons in and out of marriage with love of a man and woman for each other regularly obscures the issue of trust and faith. It is much more productive to ask, "Do you *trust* your lover?" than to ask, "Do you *love* your lover?" The perfection of love is the casting out of fear and distrust. Anger in a love relationship may simply mean that a couple are at last beginning to be open and honest with each other. It can be the beginning —but certainly not the fruition—of faith and trust. We have to trust someone deeply to tell him how we really feel. Suspicion and distrust— a lack of faith in each other—prompt a withdrawal of selves, a death of intimacy, and a maximum of deception. Faith as abandon is, it seems to me, a specific human necessity in marriage. The covenant of trust calls for this kind of letting oneself go.

A considerable amount of literature, counselee conversation, and mass media interpretation today pushes the idea of trial living together as a couple so that a couple will know that in marriage they will be fitted for each other. This kind of covenant overlooks the harsh reality that marriages are tested more in the years after children are born than before they come. When children become adolescents, when they have to go to war, when illness comes, the real tests of a marriage come. Knowing in this sense is a fantasy. The effects of the separations that work and war pose for a couple make of marriage something far different from the playboy and playgirl aura that attends much premarital knowledge a couple has of each other. Without an investment of faith, the element of abandon is present, and a man-woman relationship is still filled with considerable distrust, distance, and even suspicion. Neither premarital experimentation nor a wedding ceremony can necessarily turn faith into knowledge of each other. The basic question of trustworthiness has to be settled in either event. For faith there is no substitute.

However, with openness of trust and security of a caring commitment within, marriage is both initiated and maintained through faith in each other. A sense of abandon in self-giving is rare to find but a beauty to see in the husband-wife relationship. This must have been something of the thought of the writer of 1 Peter who admonished husbands to dwell considerately with their wives, to treat them tenderly as the vessels of the next generation, and to consider them as joint heirs of the grace of life. Thus their prayers would not be hindered. One's faith relationship to God in prayer is at stake.

FAITH AS FIDELITY TO A PERSON

Erikson is right when he says that basic trust is developed in the context of a realistic mistrust of the untrustworthy at the earliest stages of life. He says that fidelity with diversity is the central ethical value of adolescence. Also, Laski said that one type of intensity ecstaticism is identification ecstasy in relation to a person. Bowlby pointed out that the inability to commit oneself wholeheartedly is the result of repeated loss of important persons in whom one invests confidence and forms an attachment. Angyal said that the pattern of noncommitment has one of its taproots in the trauma of having been treated inconsistently. This can be said by way of summary.

When one puts this all together and asks about the meaning of faith, a final conclusion can be drawn. The deep need of estranged, alienated, and wandering persons today is for a demonstrated relationship of fidelity and trust rooted in reality with persons. The formation of a mature conscience happens in the crises of fidelity in the adolescent years. A demonstrated relationship of trust demands consistent persons for the identification of the growing person. Such persons provide a space station of dependable, trustworthy identification for the adolescent. One lone, consistent person may be the focus-impact relationship through whom young persons are enabled to get their lives all together. A supporting community of faith that is trustworthy may provide power and substance to enable the person to believe that this can happen in more than one instance. The organism of the group makes it a faith community. In this kind of identification with person and group the word of Law, Wisdom, Love, Grace, and/or Trust is made flesh. Without it people sit in darkness and await a great light.

NOTES

1. Hiltner, *Theological Dynamics*, p. 69.
2. Ibid., p. 157.
3. Buber, *The Knowledge of Man*, p. 172.
4. Paul E. Johnson, *Personality and the Christian Faith* (New York: Abingdon, 1972), p. 231.

QUESTIONS FOR FURTHER STUDY

1. If you are interested in Paul Tillich's theology, get his book *The Dynamics of Faith* and study further on the meaning of faith in relation to courage and ambiguity.

2. Get the confessions of faith of your own religious group, such as the Thirty-nine Articles of the Episcopal church (found in the Book of Common Prayer) and such as the Philadelphia Confession of Baptists. Try to identify the psychological assumptions about human nature implicit in these statements.

3. Get your fellow class members to write their own personal statement of the meaning of faith in one paragraph. Read them carefully, classify them, and report them to the class.

SUBJECT INDEX

SUBJECT INDEX